HANGING CHARLEY FLINN

THE SHORT AND VIOLENT LIFE OF THE BOLDEST CRIMINAL IN FRONTIER CALIFORNIA

MATTHEW BERNSTEIN

UNIVERSITY OF NEW MEXICO PRESS
ALBUQUERQUE

HANGING
CHARLEY
FLINN

ISBN 978-0-8263-6504-0 (paper)
ISBN 978-0-8263-6505-7 (electronic)
Library of Congress Control Number: 2023934402

Founded in 1889, the University of New Mexico
sits on the traditional homelands of the Pueblo
of Sandia. The original peoples of New Mexico—
Pueblo, Navajo, and Apache—since time immemorial
have deep connections to the land and have made
significant contributions to the broader community
statewide. We honor the land itself and those
who remain stewards of this land throughout the
generations and also acknowledge our committed
relationship to Indigenous peoples. We gratefully
recognize our history.

Elements of this book were previously published in
"The Shadow," *Wild West* 30, no.6 (April 2020) and
appear here in a much revised and expanded form.

Cover illustration adapted from photograph by
Chris Stewart, courtesy of the Huntington Research
Library.
Designed by Isaac Morris
Composed in Madrone, Octin, Vendetta

Dedicated to
Ron and Mary-Jane Bernstein

Contents

Map of Mortimer's Whereabouts, 1858–1873

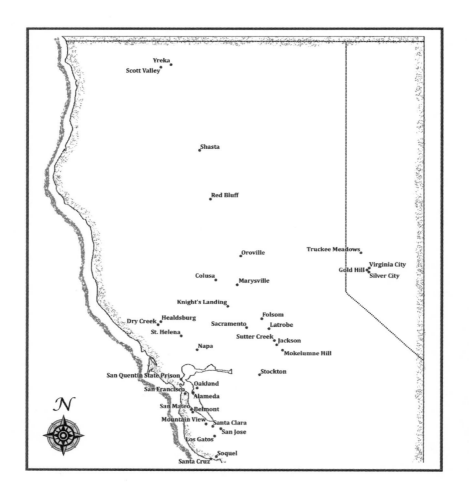

Map 1. Map of Mortimer's Whereabouts, 1858–1873, by Matthew Bernstein and Chris Stewart.

Skeleton Key Map of San Francisco, 1870

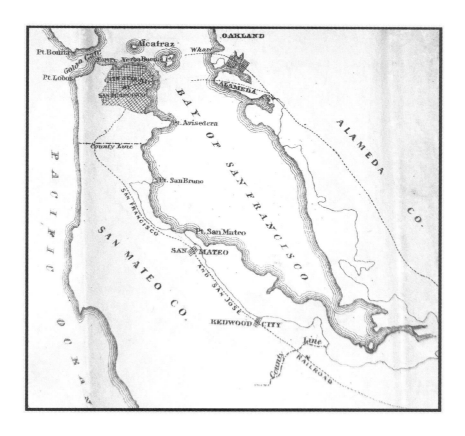

Map 2. Skeleton Key Map of San Francisco, 1870. Courtesy of the Huntington Research Library, photographed by Chris Stewart.

Map of Sacramento, 1873

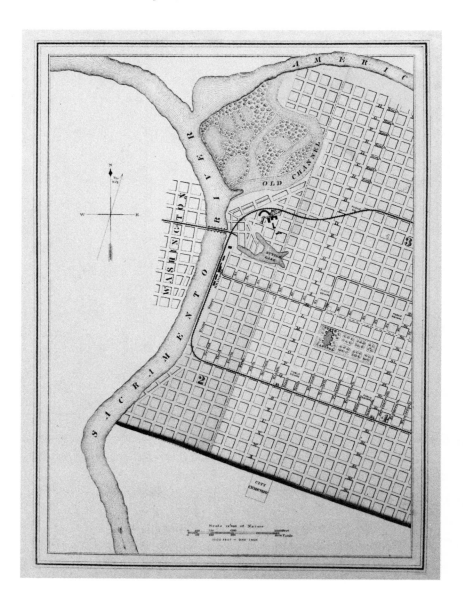

Map 3. Map of Sacramento, 1873. Courtesy of the Huntington Research Library, photographed by Chris Stewart.

Acknowledgments

The wild life of Charles Mortimer could not have been written without the rich histories provided by hundreds of authors.

Some of these contributors were lawmen active in Old San Francisco and Sacramento, such as Captain Isaiah W. Lees, Detective Ben Bohen, and Officer Abraham Houghtailing, whose words were jotted down in interviews. Others were newspapermen, among them Mark Twain, who tracked Mortimer's movements and covered his exploits. Two men in particular—E. B. Willis, a special Sacramento County deputy and the editor of the *Sacramento Record*, and Thomas S. Duke, San Francisco's captain of police decades after Mortimer's reign of terror and the author of *Celebrated Criminal Cases of America*—were both lawmen and writers.

As always, the Huntington Research Library offered immeasurable help. Before the library temporarily shuttered due to the Covid-19 pandemic, I photographed half of the Huntington's copy of the Mortimer memoir. So that I could view the missing pages, the former policeman and veteran Western historian John Boessenecker graciously let me peruse his personal copy of the memoir. My gratitude to Gregory Lalire and David Lauterborn of *Wild West* magazine for putting me into contact with Mr. Boessenecker. Furthermore, Boessenecker's exceptional histories on lawmen and outlaws also helped provide a rich backdrop, as did the consequential works of California historian William B. Secrest. Western historian Erik Wright also provided valuable feedback.

A special thank you to Anne Decroubez who shared with me information on a distant relative of hers who had the misfortune of crossing paths with Mortimer. Sacramento Cemetery Manager Lori Bauder provided invaluable assistance, as did Thom Lewis of the West Sacramento Historical Society. The diaries of Alfred Doten made available by librarian Donnelyn Curtis of the University of Nevada, Reno, and the microfilm provided by the librarians at the University of Nevada, Las Vegas, brought Mortimer's actions in Nevada into focus. Criminal genealogist Gwen Kubberness's terrific research solved several mysteries. So, too, did Holly Hoods's article for the *Russian River Recorder*, fleshing out Carrie Mortimer's backstory. The enthusiasm of Michael Millman of the University of New Mexico Press was also greatly appreciated.

Finally, my personal team of giants—Gregory Urbach, Kelly Nott, Lita Fice, Chris Stewart, and Jared Streets—deserve special credit. Thanks, everyone.

Shadow Man

*B*y the light of the moon, just past midnight on April 16, 1873, a man prowled outside Sacramento County Jail. He wore no hat, no shoes, a coat turned inside out, and a white handkerchief covering his face. Using a ladder, he climbed the south wall. From there he crept over the customhouse boiler, scurried to the kitchen roof, and jumped down to the prison grounds. This was nimble work, especially for a Civil War veteran wounded in the right ankle during the Siege of Port Hudson.[1]

Heading toward the jailhouse door, the man in the white mask drew a revolver. Then—after yanking on the bell pull—the trespasser darted out of sight.

Inside the jail, Deputy Sheriff Manuel L. Cross drew his big six-shooter. For the last several nights he had been expecting an attack and was ready for it. Or as ready as he could be. A former assayer from Truckee, the thirty-year-old deputy wasn't accustomed to midnight gunfights, but Sacramento County Sheriff Mike Bryte thought him more than capable. Cross was about to find out.

Banging open the jailhouse door with the muzzle of his gun, Cross stepped through the entryway. He paused, scanning. Carefully he walked down the brick pathway leading south toward the yard door at I Street. Five paces from the door, Cross looked back toward the rear wall. Cross spied the masked man in the moonlight, pointing a Colt revolver at the deputy's head. The masked man said something in a low voice, indistinguishable through the white handkerchief. It was the last thing he ever said.[2]

Cross wheeled and pulled the trigger. His first shot caught the intruder in the chest. Cross's next shot crashed through the white handkerchief, smashing into the man's teeth. Staggering, the fatally shot intruder dropped the revolver and lurched toward the jailhouse door. Cross continued to squeeze the trigger, but it was useless; his gun had jammed. Groaning, "Ugh! Ugh! Ugh!" the man stumbled inside. Leaking blood, he ran north down the hall, crashed into a brick wall, and toppled in front of Cell No. 5, which held a prisoner sentenced to be hanged next month. The man he had come to rescue: his brother, Charles J. Flinn.[3]

From the man's corpse were recovered a pearl-handled dagger, a hand-drawn map of the jail, and papers identifying him as William J. Flinn. Reporters learned William hailed from Lynn, Massachusetts—ten miles north of Boston—and was a former Union soldier, having enlisted in 1862 as a private in the 38th Massachusetts Infantry, commended for his bravery.[4]

Whether it was bravery or foolishness, Will had died trying to save his older brother, Charley, from a hangman's rope. Had Will known Charley as Californians had known him, the vicious criminal called "Mortimer," one wonders if Will would have crossed the country to rescue him—or to witness the execution.

Part One

SOWING THE WIND

Mortimer is one of the worst men known to the Police....
He will be captured, if it takes the department ten years to
accomplish it.

—Mark Twain, *San Francisco Daily Morning Call*

The Mortimer Gang in Virginia City

*I*n March of 1863 Charles Mortimer was released from San Quentin State Prison, having served a year for attempted robbery in San Francisco. About twenty-nine years old, he stood five feet eight inches tall, had auburn hair, striking blue eyes, and to his name possessed $2.50. After paying for passage aboard a ship to San Francisco, he was left with only $1.50.[1]

Mortimer entered San Francisco "utterly miserable," as he recalled in his memoir. Unable to find work, stealing food for sustenance was a possibility. The next day, Mortimer ran into Pete Goodwin, "a convict . . . discharged two weeks before." Goodwin had gone to the country to find employment but, thwarted, had returned to the city.

"He was tired, footsore and despondent," Mortimer reflected. "I gave him a quarter. My money gone, I walked the streets meditating over my prospects."

Mortimer's luck turned when he ran into a half-tipsy fellow with an easy disposition. Seeing a drinking partner in Mortimer, the man generously bought the two of them more liquor, until Mortimer's companion was fully drunk. Wisely, Mortimer counseled him to sleep it off, and the man took Mortimer's advice, allowing his well-spoken new friend to guide him to his lodging house.

"I undressed him, but in this act of kindness my hands slipped into his pocket and a few half dollars stuck to my fingers," Mortimer related. "In putting him to bed I gave him a good searching and found seventy-two dollars. I put five dollars into his stocking and some silver into his boot and left the house."

On the street, Mortimer caught sight of a poor woman leaning on a crutch with a little girl at her side. Asking for alms, she declared that she was starving. At that moment Goodwin appeared. Mortimer gave Goodwin some money but did one better for the woman. He took her to a restaurant and bought her a meal. Learning her name was Mrs. Smith, and that her husband was "a drunken brute," he gave her five dollars.

Outside the restaurant a sharp-eyed man was waiting. He asked Mortimer if he knew the woman. Mortimer responded that he did not. The man replied that she was a petty thief who had been discharged from the county jail only that morning. When Mortimer expressed his doubts, he showed his star. To the officer Mortimer declared that he was "more convinced than ever that she had told the truth." Inwardly, he may have recognized in Mrs. Smith something of a kindred spirit. Returning to Mrs. Smith, he instructed her "not to steal from the table as an officer was watching her; to eat all she wanted, and to carry off such food as was left; that I didn't care how it was with her, she had my sympathy."

Bidding farewell to San Francisco, Mortimer drifted fifty miles south to San Jose. He worked there for a few months, though whether through odd jobs or theft is unclear. In June 1863, however, Mortimer decided to abandon California. Like tens of thousands of other red-blooded Americans, dreams of riches lured him to Nevada Territory, where millions in silver were being mined from the Comstock Lode, and to a boomtown where a man of Mortimer's talents would be appreciated.[2]

Virginia City, it was called.

By the time Mortimer reached Virginia City—the "Queen of the Comstock"—he was nearly broke. Although Mortimer only had $1.50 by this point, he didn't fret, giving a dollar to a poor blind beggar. Perhaps Mortimer sensed how much money he could make in the boomtown. With more riches in silver located on the Comstock Lode than all the treasure in California's gold rush, it wouldn't be terribly hard for a man of Mortimer's disposition to seize his opportunity.[3]

By mid-1863, some of the most profitable mines on the Comstock Lode included the Gould & Curry, the Ophir, the Savage, the Potosi, the Hale & Norcross, the Belcher, and the Chollar. The riches generated by these and lesser mines supported not only Virginia City, but also Gold Hill just to the south. John Piper's Opera House was crowded seven days a week, as was the San Francisco Saloon. Thousands were commonly bet on billiards matches. The *Territorial Enterprise* and the *Union* reported steadily on mining accidents, saloon shootouts, famous visitors, and predictions that Virginia City, with its 2,800 wooden houses, would soon be as big as San Francisco. The population of Virginia City and Gold Hill combined was 20,000—large enough for Mortimer to operate.[4]

"Virginia City I found a very lively town and much excited over newly discovered riches in the mines," Mortimer recalled. "I saw many old convicts there from California."[5]

One such convict Mortimer spied was Harry "Blue-eyed" Thompson, one of the dozen men to have successfully escaped San Quentin during the mass breakout in 1862. Mortimer probably wasn't tempted by the fifty-dollar bounty on Thompson's head. But Mortimer determined that revealing he was out of cash would be a mistake. After all, if the others thought he might turn them in to collect the bounty money, they might take steps to silence him.[6]

With his financial distress potentially fatal, on the night Mortimer arrived in Virginia City he sought to rectify the situation, staking his claim. Instead of a mine, Mortimer's claim was "a well dressed man" with his hands in his pockets. Resolved "to do desperate work," Mortimer followed the man to a lonely spot.

"Stranger," Mortimer called, "can you tell me where I can find a lodging house? I have been to several, but they are all full."

The helpful man took his hands out of his pockets, pointed, and said, "You go down—"

"Silence!" Mortimer commanded, jerking a ten-inch blade close to the man's throat. "Silence, throw up your hands."

The man did as bidden. Working quickly, Mortimer reached into the man's right-hand pocket. As he suspected, the man had been carrying a derringer. Mortimer also found some loose change and a clasp purse "well filled" with gold. After Mortimer removed his gold watch, the man pleaded that it was "a keepsake." Moved, Mortimer returned it.

"Go on at once," Mortimer ordered.

The man fled, and Mortimer promptly went the other direction, down D Street, past the Gould & Curry works, a mile and a half farther to Gold Hill, and two more miles to Silver City. There Mortimer paid for a room.

Virginia City drew him back. That the boomtown attracted so many desperadoes did not surprise *Territorial Enterprise* reporter Samuel Clemens. A twenty-seven-year-old former Mississippi riverboat pilot, Clemens had reluctantly joined a Missouri militia before deserting the Confederacy and taking a stagecoach to Virginia City two years earlier.

Reflecting on criminal activity around the Comstock, Clemens noted, "Vice flourished luxuriantly during the hey-day of our 'flush times.' The saloons were overburdened with custom; so were the police courts, the gambling dens, the brothels and the jails.... The year 1863 was perhaps the very top blossom and culmination of the 'flush times.'"[7]

Not one to miss out, Mortimer returned to Virginia City a few days later, but by then he had made some alterations to his appearance. It did the trick, for if the man spotted Mortimer, he didn't identify him as the thief that had accosted him. Mortimer, on the other hand, recognized Pete Goodwin, reuniting with his partner in crime. Described by Mortimer as "a quiet sort of man," Goodwin nevertheless tipped Mortimer to a "good Indian" (slang for easy mark) staying at The Great Republic. That night, on D Street, they buttonholed him. "While Pete covered him with a pistol," Mortimer related, "I plunged both hands into his pockets, when he seized me by both wrists."

Mortimer's hands might have been useless, but his feet weren't.

"I gave him a trip backwards and, as he fell, the pants parted at the side seams and the whole forepart came off, my hands still in his pockets all the while," Mortimer recalled, his memory sharpened by his work as a tailor. While the man sat there, stupefied and barelegged, Mortimer and Goodwin "whacked up" (divided) their loot and separated.[8]

They didn't stay apart for long. Shortly thereafter, Mortimer and Goodwin teamed up again to rob a house in Six Mile Canyon near the quartz mill. Mortimer pilfered some jewelry and a watch chain. "Pete said he got nothing," Mortimer recollected. "Perhaps he didn't. He was on the side where the coin was."

After robbing the house, Mortimer headed south to Gold Hill. There he "chummed in" with "Blind" Tom Mitchell, a nearsighted cutpurse with a propensity for fighting. With their number now totaling three, it was time to establish a base of operations. The where of it was a stroke of genius: they would go underground. Within the American Ravine—two and a half miles south of Gold Hill and just west of Silver City—they discovered an abandoned 820-foot tunnel, once part of the Atlantic mine.[9]

Mortimer noted, "We boarded up the entrance to an old dry tunnel, about 100 feet in a back ravine, and furnished the cave with blankets and cooking utensils and grub. We got a trustworthy Spaniard to stay at the cave and take care of the place."[10]

After discovering the headquarters of "the Mortimer gang" in 1876, more than a decade after it served as their secret lair, the *Virginia Chronicle* provided diabolical details:

> This tunnel was arranged in an artistic manner to effect the death of any one entering in search of them. The entrance to the tunnel was blocked up by heavy bowlders so it would be hard for even one man at a time to effect an entrance. At a distance of 200 feet from the mouth of the tunnel a shaft had been sunk forty feet deep, with a moveable drawbridge.[11]

One day Blind Tom visited Gold Hill and returned to the hideout with three like-minded rogues: French Frank, George "Cockey" Wright, and John "Black Jack" Bowen, all who had recently traveled east from California. French Frank may have been Frank Largos, a Frenchman who had been arrested in 1861 for stabbing James Codeville in Sacramento. Wright and Bowen were better-known figures.[12]

Having been shot in the face while attempting to steal from a gambler, Wright bore a distinctive scar on his right cheek. On more than one occasion Wright teamed up with Black Jack, a Rhode Island sailor turned California highwayman. According to the *San Francisco Daily Morning Call*, partners Black Jack and Wright had at one point been sentenced to a ten-year stretch in San Quentin for highway robbery.[13]

A few days later the Mortimer gang further expanded when "Three-Fingered" Robinson joined them at the hideout.[14]

"We now numbered seven," Mortimer recalled, "and when night set in we would divide and pursue a course to suit us."

The Mortimer gang had an immediate effect. On August 25, 1863, the *Virginia City Evening Bulletin* commented that since July a virtual crimewave had struck, mostly manifesting through theft and robbery. "The band of thieves in this city will in a short time be almost strong enough to overpower the decent portion of the community," lamented the *Bulletin* reporter.[15]

Clemens, now using the penname Mark Twain and writing for the *San Francisco Daily Morning Call*, agreed with the *Bulletin's* assessment. In the September 3, 1863, edition, Twain noted that Virginia City was "infested with thieves, assassins and incendiaries."[16]

Although Mortimer declined to "detail all the adventures we had," he admitted that his inclination was for smaller capers while Wright, Frank, and Black Jack preferred more "high-toned" jobs, which led to strife. At the same time, Black Jack could be astounded by Mortimer's bold manner.

On one occasion Mortimer and Black Jack were walking past the Illinois lodging house when Mortimer had an idea. Leaving Black Jack on the street, Mortimer boldly walked in "as if I belonged there." Striding into the long room, Mortimer noted that the rows of bunks situated on either side of him made them seem like steamer berths. The bunks were filled with lodgers, some of whom woke up. To these men Mortimer engaged in conversation—but all the while he kept his fingers busy, pocketing their possessions. In due course he rejoined Black Jack on the street.

"Where have you been?" Black Jack demanded.

"In there."

"Why, there was some one talking in there."

"Yes, I and the lodgers."

"You! Why, what on earth did you talk about?"

"Oh! About politics, mines, religion, and one thing and another—showing what I got."

"Well, you've got a hell of a lot of cheek."[17]

In another caper, Mortimer and Blind Tom robbed a house of three hundred dollars. According to Mortimer, after robbing the house Tom "failed to divide fairly, and that led to a row." It was at this point that the gang broke up, Black Jack, Wright, and Frank moving on. Tom attempted to bury the hatchet a few days later, asking for Mortimer's help with a "good injen" who lived in Gold Hill but frequently visited Virginia City. Tom's plan was to rob the man at night when he was in the "Divide" between the two boomtowns. Mortimer agreed, shadowing the man as he entered the Divide. Between the darkness and Tom's poor eyesight, he lost sight of Mortimer and the intended victim. This fell neatly into Mortimer's plans.

Near a woodpile, Mortimer stopped the "good injen" using his knife as a "persuader." From the man Mortimer seized nineteen twenty-dollar pieces totaling $380, a watch, a chain, some small change, and a pistol. Just at that moment Mortimer caught sight of two men heading toward Gold Hill. Mortimer dashed away as his victim gave the alarm. Then they all gave chase. Had Mortimer kept running, they might have overtaken and overpowered him. But luck was with him.

"I jumped into a prospect hole and heard them run by me," Mortimer recalled. "Shortly after others ran back, all wondering where I'd gone to. I staid in the hole two hours, and then got home and kept close some days. I did not give Tom a cent and thus got even with him."

Betrayal and double-dealing seemed to be catching. In Dutch with Blind Tom, and with Frank, Black Jack, and Cockey Wright having left Virginia City for greener pastures, Mortimer turned to an acquaintance, "Limsey." Unbeknownst to Mortimer, Limsey had a secret plan to put himself in good with the police and place Mortimer back behind bars.

Speaking with Limsey, Mortimer was soon convinced to meet with some other fellow cronies. At a street corner four men passed them, one an officer who looked hard at Mortimer. Mortimer sensed there was some sort of silent communication going on between the officer and Limsey, whom he pegged as a "stool pigeon."

"I was on my guard in an instant and walked to an open lot," Mortimer remembered. "The officer turned and blew his whistle. I was now in the rear of some houses on the lower side of B street, on the block below the International Hotel. As I climbed up to the sidewalk, bang! bang! bang! went three shots."

Pressing on, Mortimer escaped. But he knew now it was only a matter of time. His gang had dissolved, the police had his description, and he'd narrowly escaped being shot to death. In other words, it was time to skedaddle.[18]

Twenty-four hours after nearly being shot in the back, Mortimer reached Hunter's Station in Truckee Meadows, twenty-seven miles north of Virginia City. But that wasn't far enough by half. With the days getting shorter, and having barely cheated death, Mortimer headed west to California.[19]

CHAPTER 2

Mortimer at Large

*M*ortimer made it to Sacramento in the last days of September 1863, just in time for the California State Fair. During this week, crowds flocked to the capital to bet on the horse races at Union Park Course, visit Lee and Ryland's circus tent at J and Fourth, and marvel at the displays of California industry. Silks, leathers, and glassware delighted patrons. Fairgoers were also pleased to see a groundswell of agricultural extravagances largely denied them since the South had seceded: cotton, tobacco, sugar, syrup, and molasses. Virginia City silver, extracted through California ingenuity, was also on display.

Commented the *Sacramento Bee*, "We ... feel assured that all who visit the Fair will be received and agreeably entertained."[1]

Doubtless, Mortimer was "agreeably entertained." Three weeks later, while lounging with Nellie Brannan, referred to by the *Sacramento Bee* as "a notorious English 'moll,'" in a rented Sacramento room on Second Street between K and L, Mortimer seemed on top of the world. The three policemen outside the door—Fred T. Burke, Fred D. Chamberlain, and Samuel Deal—had drastically different ideas about where Mortimer stood.[2]

The officers "entered my room and gave it a thorough overhauling," Mortimer complained. Although they found no loot, they did uncover a knife with a fifteen-inch blade. At that the officers exchanged knowing looks, but Mortimer figured possession of the knife should not land him in hot water. The policemen found no blood on the blade. Nevertheless, Burke placed Mortimer and Nellie Brannan under arrest.[3]

"I was kept in jail a week," Mortimer lamented, "while the officers tried to work up a job."[4]

As much as he could, Mortimer tried to hide his identity from the police. The *Sacramento Bee* reported that he went under the alias "Spencer" and had as his name "G. Mortimer."

Failing to pin anything substantial on Mortimer, the police eventually hauled him before Police Judge S. Solon Holl, having pushed back the trial date a few days. On November 4, 1863, Judge Holl sentenced Mortimer to ninety days in the county jail for violation of the "Vagrancy Act."[5]

"There was not the slightest evidence that I had done anything evil in the town," Mortimer griped. "I had money, my room rent was paid in advance, and I had not been in the city four weeks at a time for a year and a half. The true reason I was committed was because I would not act as a 'stool pigeon,' and because I had a short term in State Prison."[6]

Nellie Brannan was also brought before Judge Holl, officially for violating the Vagrancy Act. Although Mortimer described Brannan simply as "a woman," the papers certainly believed there was something amorous between Mortimer and "his Nellie." Along with being charged as a vagrant, Nellie was deemed "a dissolute person." The evidence brought before Judge Holl described Nellie as frequenting the shrubbery on the riverfront on R Street, a known hideout for thieves. Judge Holl judged her guilty on November 3. Along with Mortimer, Holl sentenced Nellie to ninety days in county jail on November 4.[7]

Mortimer's glib tongue may have served him well, for though he had refused to become a "stoolie" in Sacramento he became a "trusty" in the county jail. This allowed him the opportunity to get out into the street once in a while. Unfortunately, Mortimer's violent nature got the best of him. On the night of January 10, 1864, Mortimer was arrested for "pitching into and pounding" John Fleming. Two days later Judge Holl found him guilty, fining him thirty dollars or an additional fifteen days. After the sentencing, Mortimer remarked that he thought "the Judge was getting to be uncommonly lenient."[8]

In February, having paid his debt to society, Mortimer teamed up with highwayman Ike McCullum and headed twenty miles east to Folsom. They stayed in that one-horse town for a month before Mortimer determined he'd try his luck once again in San Francisco.

Mortimer was not alone in his desire to visit the cosmopolitan city, for of all the meccas in the Golden State, San Francisco was the place to be. With the furor of the Comstock Lode having died down, San Francisco's capitalists turned to real estate. The Cosmopolitan Hotel boasted the most luxurious rooms on the West Coast. Bay View Park now sported a racetrack. Treats could be bought at Ghirardelli's Chocolate and Coffee Company, jewelry at Otto Wiedero's Watchmakers, and American flags (supporting the war effort) at D. Norcross's Military Goods.

Mayor Henry Coon could also brag that, to get around, nearly every major thoroughfare was accessible by rail, courtesy of the San Francisco Market Street Railroad, the Omnibus Railroad Company, and the City Railroad. Lesser streets were often connected by horsecars. Ferries commonly shuttled crowds from San Francisco to Oakland and back. Along with the smell of fish guts and horse dung, opportunity was in the air. In total, San Francisco boasted 14,443 buildings and a population of 113,000.[9]

Mayor Coon was more reticent to speak of San Francisco's seedy underbelly. Along with the countless saloons, bordellos, and opium dens, the ports were a hubbub of criminal activity. In the early 1860s, people began referring to the northwestern harbor as "The Barbary Coast"—a nod toward North Africa's piratical coastline. San Francisco's Barbary Coast soon incorporated not just the waterfront from Broadway to Pacific, but the highlands of Stockton Street and almost the entire length of Dupont Street. Commented historian Benjamin E. Lloyd in 1876:

> Barbary Coast is the haunt of the low and the vile of every kind. The petty thief, the house burglar, the tramp, the whoremonger, lewd women, cutthroats, murderers, all are found here. Dance-halls and concert-saloons, where blear-eyed men and faded women drink vile liquor, smoke offensive tobacco, engage in vulgar conduct, sing obscene songs and say and do everything to heap upon themselves more degradation, are numerous.[10]

Shortly after returning to San Francisco, Mortimer met up with a pal, Rufe Anderson. Like Mortimer, Anderson had just finished a three-month stretch in the penitentiary. Slyly, Anderson introduced Mortimer to Tom Shears as a miner from Virginia City. It was a backstory Mortimer stuck with.

One evening in 1864 Mortimer was lounging in a San Francisco saloon, watching two men play poker. After a while he volunteered a suggestion.

"One got angry and dared me to bet on the game," Mortimer recalled, "at the same time pulling out a handful of silver and two twenty's."

Mortimer declined, apologizing for interfering with the game. To set things right he picked up the money and dropped it into the gambler's pocket. No one noticed the two twenties stuck to his fingers, and Mortimer, ever the gentleman, thought it wise not to further impede the progress of the game by bringing it up.

The gamblers continued to play for some time before the hothead missed the twenties. Enraged, the gambler accused everyone at the table of stealing his money. They denied it, suggesting the "honest miner" from Virginia City was the likely culprit. By that time Mortimer had vanished. A police detective soon began tracking him, and spoke to George Hoyt, a stool pigeon. Hoyt pointed out Mortimer to the detective, and Mortimer was locked up for a few days before being let out. "[T]he thing was *squared*," Mortimer reflected.[11]

Free once more, Mortimer traveled twenty-five miles south to a house in Belmont, San Mateo County, also frequented by Nellie Brannan. Mortimer made Belmont his headquarters, pulling various jobs in different locations. Known for cattle ranches and wheatfields, and with the railroad connecting Belmont to San Francisco completed that year, rural Belmont was the perfect place for Mortimer to lay low.[12]

"From there I radiated to different sections," Mortimer recollected. "As certain quarters would get too warm, I would operate in others."

Of this industrious period in his career, Mortimer recalled he "worked things lively" and had many a "frolic." His goal was to procure enough money for a "home stake."[13]

Looking for a big score, Mortimer took on the role of an eastern businessman who had just arrived in San Francisco. In this guise he invited a "fellow business-man" he met on California Street to a drink. Mortimer confided that he had a wife and baby, and "$5,000 to $8,000 to invest in some light established business here."

Over drinks, Mortimer offered to "buy in for the sake of keeping alive in business here as well as at the east" and that, having just been to the Cliff House (which he intimately shortened to "the Cliff") with some friends, he expected to "catch fits" from his young wife.

When asked where he lived, Mortimer glibly replied, "On Second Street. I say, if you're not engaged for an hour take a walk with me round to the house and we can make it all right with the little woman; we've been trying to manage about business, you know, and all that; you see, I'd promised to take the wife to the theater to-night, sure, and she'll be sadly disappointed; now, I'm not fit to go; suppose if she presses the matter I suggest you as an escort, eh?"

With a laugh the man—clearly intoxicated with spirits, the promise of easy money, and a night at the theater with another man's wife—agreed. They were near-ing the end of Second Street when Mortimer showed his true colors. "I astonished him by a close embrace around the neck, threw him to the ground, put his hat over his face and searched him." Mortimer quickly relieved his victim of a Eureka watch, a chain, and some coin.

"Keep quiet," Mortimer ordered.

With that, Mortimer went through a yard, hopped some fences, made it to a cross street, hurried down South Park, and turned onto Third Street.

Just then, on the corner of Third Street and Brannan Street, Mortimer overheard an argument taking place between two men. One man accused the other of being drunk and stormed into a nice house, leaving the other man on Brannan Street, opposite an open lot where the USS *Camanche*, an ironclad that had been shipped in pieces around Cape Horn, was in daylight hours being assembled. Approaching the man, Mortimer sympathized with him, "and he was soon well disposed to me," Mortimer recalled.

Believing he had lured the man into a false sense of security, Mortimer wasted little time. Unfortunately for Mortimer, when he tackled him, he found his intended victim was nearly a match for him in strength. Worst of all, a knife had appeared in the man's hand. He slashed at Mortimer, badly cutting his arm, slicing through the sleeve of his coat, and bloodying his left breast.

Fleeing in pain, Mortimer ran past the *Camanche* and the San Jose depot, and crossed behind some houses before slipping into a pool of stagnant water. "I was now in a bad fix; my clothing wet, heavy and stinking," Mortimer related.

Climbing onto the sidewalk, Mortimer dashed off but, in his haste, ran over a drunkard. The drunkard sat up and asked Mortimer where he was. Generously, Mortimer agreed to help the lost man to his lodgings.

"I got him there with little trouble," Mortimer scribbled. "Of [*sic*] him I got a dry suit of clothes. We started out together again, but at the door I left him—it was best for him. It was best for me, for he was to go with me to my room and bring my clothing back."[14]

After that wild night, where he'd beaten and robbed a man, been slashed while attempting to rob another man, and stolen a drunkard's clothes, Mortimer made the twenty-five-mile journey south to Belmont. He lay low for a week or two before venturing out again.

From Mortimer's memoir it can be determined that he was in San Francisco during the first week of July 1864. On June 30 Mortimer may have teamed up with Rufe Anderson in burglarizing the posh home of real estate developer Colonel Thomas Hayes on Van Ness Avenue, part of the ritzy Hayes Valley neighborhood. After slipping through a window, Anderson (and possibly Mortimer) filched a fur coat worth $250 and several other items. Suspecting Anderson of the burglary were veteran detectives Isaiah W. Lees and George W. Rose—both of whom would play vital, yet starkly different roles in Mortimer's criminal career.

Lees, born in 1830 on Christmas Day in Lancashire, England, was called by William Pinkerton "the greatest criminal catcher the West ever knew." Joining the San Francisco police department in 1854, he employed the system of police work pioneered by the reformed French ex-convict Francois Eugene Vidocq, who championed criminal records, disguises, and employing stool pigeons. With a list of arrests that spread from San Francisco to New York City, Lees was promoted to captain of detectives in 1858 and was roundly considered one of the finest officers in the state.[15]

One of Lees's detectives was Rose, who was used to dealing with dangerous men. Born in Massachusetts in 1831, Rose had served on the San Francisco Police force for a decade, seven of those years as a detective. Known for his energy and efficiency, Rose was particularly experienced at handling Chinatown toughs, having been stabbed in "China Alley" and in another instance assaulted with a cleaver.[16]

On July 2, two days after looting the Hayes house, Anderson had just entered the Miner's Restaurant when Lees and Rose appeared. After arresting Anderson, the detectives recovered some of the stolen property.[17]

In the early morning of July 6, 1864, Mortimer was two miles northwest of Hayes Valley, passing by a cellar saloon on the northeast corner of Kearny and Clay, called the Pioneer Liquor and Billiard Saloon. By choosing that street to walk down, Mortimer had unwittingly placed himself a stone's throw from a simmering feud. Around half past two in the morning, that feud came to a boil.[18]

According to *San Francisco Morning Call* reporter Mark Twain, whose residence was listed as 32 Minna Street, three-quarters of a mile southeast of the saloon, the seeds of the feud had been planted a few nights earlier. It all began on July 3 when John Barrett, a hot-headed volunteer soldier, had been tossed out by the co-owner of the cellar saloon, John A. Wyman, presumably for drinking too much. On the street, Barrett's fellow soldiers mocked him, and Barrett was heard to curse that he would "get even." Later that night Barrett came back with a few soldiers and "wanted to whip everybody in the house." Eventually he was induced to leave.[19]

At 11:00 p.m. on July 5 Barrett returned to the Pioneer Liquor and Billiard Saloon. The dive was crowded with patrons and waitresses. Wyman was friendly enough with the soldier, and Barrett responded by ordering a drink rather than threatening violence. For drinking companions Barrett had with him David Hunter, an *Alta California* printer, and John McGowan, a cab driver from New York, about thirty years old, who literally lived across the street. Around midnight the trio left the saloon but returned at 1:30 a.m. and continued to hit the sauce. An hour later, deep in their cups, McGowan said to Hunter, "Let's take a drink."

Witnesses reported McGowan also pushed Hunter toward the bar. Armed, intoxicated, and prone to rage, McGowan's aggressive action triggered something in Barrett.

"I have seen enough of that," Barrett snarled. From his sheath, which bore his name, Barrett drew a new Colt revolver and pointed it at McGowan. Before Barrett could fire, Charles Lauterbach—Wyman's partner in the Pioneer Liquor and Billiard Saloon—spoiled his aim by grabbing his arm. When Barrett squeezed the trigger, the bullet slammed into the floor. Pandemonium broke loose.[20]

After the gunshot rang out, Mortimer witnessed "waiter girls and men" boil out of the cellar saloon like army ants. But where other men fled from danger, Mortimer sensed opportunity.[21]

While Mortimer descended into the watering hole, Barrett shook off Lauterbach. Reported Twain, "McGowan ran behind the counter, and Barrett fired again, the ball passing through the counter."

"For God's sake don't shoot!" McGowan shouted at Barrett.[22]

But Barrett's blood was up. As McGowan retreated toward the far end of the counter, Barrett followed him with his pistol. It was at that point Mortimer appeared, catching sight of Barrett "standing in the center of the room, but near the bar," his pistol in his hand. Mortimer saw Lauterbach leap over the counter. "As he jumped the soldier fired but missed him," Mortimer recalled. The ball passed over the counter, bored through the partition, and lodged in the Clay Street wall. Lauterbach then dashed out the Clay Street exit, rushing south toward city hall. Meanwhile, Barrett lost sight of McGowan.[23]

Noticing Mortimer, Barrett asked him "where that son of a bitch went to."

"Didn't you see him run out?" Mortimer asked, referring to Lauterbach.

"No," Barrett said, "that's not the one; I'll find him."

Drawing near the bar, Barrett called out, "I've found him."

McGowan had been cowering on a sack of oysters. Taking careful aim, Barrett squeezed the trigger one last time, putting a bullet through the middle of McGowan's forehead, killing him instantly.

"I was alone, save for the soldier," Mortimer recalled. Thinking quickly, Mortimer suggested the soldier go at once to the provost guardhouse.

"All right," Barrett agreed, and left through the Kearny Street door.

In an instant Mortimer passed by McGowan's corpse and emptied the till into his pockets. Moments later Lauterbach returned with lantern-jawed Police Captain William Y. Douglass, who lived a half-mile south of the saloon at 20 Geary Street, and several other officers. "The officers rushed in now and I walked out," Mortimer noted.[24]

In the police inquest that followed, and the report Mark Twain wrote up for the *San Francisco Morning Call*, Mortimer's presence and secondary crime went unnoticed and unreported.

Although Mortimer's various crimes netted him enough money for the "home stake" he desired, he frittered it away rather than purchasing property. "[I]t went the way of the rest," Mortimer bemoaned, "just as all money got in that way does."[25]

One way Mortimer tried to save money was through cheating the railroad, paying for a short ride, happening to miss his stop, and getting off at the destination he actually desired. According to an investigative journalism piece Twain later composed for the *San Francisco Morning Call* on Mortimer's life of crime, in late July or early August of 1864, Mortimer attempted to swindle the San Francisco & San Jose Railroad (S. F. & S. J. R. R). Mortimer bought a ticket from San Francisco to San Mateo when his actual destination was four miles farther south, in Belmont. Unfortunately for Mortimer, the train conductor Michael N. Nolan—who lived a half-mile from Twain at 112 Sutter Street—was no dummy.

Noted Twain, "Mortimer . . . paid his fare to San Mateo, in the morning train . . . and then tried to slip by and go on to Belmont, but was detected by Mr. Nolan, the conductor, who put him ashore, and had a rough time accomplishing it. Mortimer swore he would remember the treatment he had received and kill Nolan for it the first opportunity he got."[26]

Part of Mortimer's stolen lucre went to helping out George Sibley, who had served a year in San Quentin for attempting to burglarize a house on Tehama Street. Once free, Sibley briefly joined the US Navy, serving aboard the steam-powered sloop-of-war *Saranac* before deserting. On the day they crossed paths, Sibley was penniless, hungry, and suffering. Mortimer described him as a "gutter snipe."[27]

"I supplied his wants," Mortimer recalled, though he would soon regret that act of charity. A few days after they fell in together Mortimer and Sibley were walking together when an officer appeared.

"Sibley, I want you," the officer told him. "I can make $30 by returning you to the Saranac."

"It will be in greenbacks; they are worth forty cents each," Mortimer said, offering more money to let Sibley go.

"To this he agreed, and it was so fixed and 'squared.'"[28]

Shortly after bribing this officer, another policeman began "dogging" the pair. For safety, Mortimer took Sibley to Belmont. Deciding to put more mileage between themselves and the San Francisco police, the two boarded the night train for San Jose, twenty-seven miles away. With its population of about six thousand, San Jose could offer Mortimer delights that rural Belmont could not, such as those found at the luxuriant Continental Hotel on Market Street: a swank saloon, fashionable guests, and coquettish women. But luck was against them. When the train ran off the track, Mortimer was badly injured.[29]

Instead of pressing on to San Jose, the knaves returned to Belmont, Sibley having agreed to care for Mortimer until he recuperated. Instead, Sibley went on a bender. After spending his last dime, Sibley pawned his own clothing and shamefully slunk up to Oakland. To Mortimer's regret, that would not be the last he heard of George Sibley.[30]

Six weeks after Mortimer deftly robbed the Pioneer Liquor and Billiard Saloon, a sensational robbery occurred in San Francisco, which would come to be known as the Myers pawnshop robbery. Mortimer probably was not the perpetrator, still recuperating in Belmont from the injuries he'd sustained in the railroad accident. However, the robbery significantly affected the climate in San Francisco, stirring up the public to pressure Chief of Police Martin Burke to order his subordinates to put more criminals behind bars.

On August 17, at about 2:30 p.m., Harris H. Myers—who had been born in 1800 in Prussia—left his pawnshop at 632 Commercial Street to attend some business. To manage the shop in his absence, Myers left in charge his nineteen-year-old son, Henry. When Myers returned at about 3:00 he found the pawnshop in a state of extreme disarray. Word quickly spread that a violent crime had occurred. At 3:15 Myers's pawnshop was crowded with policemen, doctors, and reporters. Of the police, the most capable was Captain Lees. Of the reporters, the most capable was Mark Twain.

Now twenty-eight years old, Twain cut a fine figure: five feet nine inches, handsome, with a full head of auburn hair, and greenish-blue eyes beneath bushy eyebrows. Having recently traded Virginia City's *Territorial Enterprise* for the *San Francisco Daily Morning Call*, Twain was looking to make a splash as a crime reporter. The Myers pawnshop robbery was just the ticket.[31]

Noted Twain in the *San Francisco Morning Call*: "[Myers] found pools of blood here and there, a knife and double-barrelled shot gun on the floor ... several trays of watches, diamonds and various kinds of jewelry gone, the doors of the safe open, its drawers pulled out and despoiled of their contents—disorder visible everywhere, but his son nowhere to be seen!"[32]

Myers had investigated when he heard a groan coming from a back room. Following a trail of blood, Myers located his son, Henry, lying insensible, drenched in a spreading pool of blood. Behind his right ear was a terrible indentation, the skull fractured.

Twain, Lees, and the others quickly learned Henry was alive and conscious but could only speak incoherently. Henry ultimately recovered, but the memory of who struck him never returned. Along with the crack in his skull, the detectives noticed indentations on his throat, made by the left hand of the assailant. The police determined that neither the knife nor the shotgun had been used, and that after Henry had been struck his assailant dragged him to the back room. Myers testified that the robber, along with attacking his son, stole eight thousand dollars worth of jewelry and money.

No one had seen the assault take place, but a man came into the shop and, according to Twain, told Lees that at about that time he saw "a man in Kearny street, running as if destruction were at his heels; that he broke frantically through a blockade of wagons, carriages, and a funeral procession, sped on his way and was out of sight in a moment."

The witness noted that the running man carried an improvised sack made of an old calico dress, which he grasped by the neck, bulging as though full of about two-dozen eggs. As for his appearance, the witness described the running man as "thick set, about five feet seven or eight inches in stature, wore dark clothing, a black slouch hat, and had a sort of narrow goatee."[33]

Could this have been Mortimer? Despite not claiming the robbery as his work, the description of the fleeing man is a close match to a photograph of Mortimer, number sixty-four in the Rogue's Gallery, then hanging in Chief of Police Burke's office. Accompanying the photograph was a description of Mortimer: "5 feet 6 inches; weight, 160 pounds; hair, light; eyes, blue; complexion, light; full face, red cheeks, good looking; has a crucifix, with lighted candles, three pierced with arrows, on his right fore arm, printed in red and black ink, and on his left arm the letters C. J. M.; also, on one arm, the name of Flinn."[34]

Considering Mortimer was actually two inches taller than the Rogue's Gallery claimed, the resemblance is striking. Whatever Mortimer's involvement, the Myers pawnshop robbery fascinated the public. Reported Twain, "[A]t no time, from three o'clock in the afternoon, yesterday, until midnight, was there a moment when there was not a crowd in front of Meyer's store, gazing at its darkened windows and closed and guarded doors."[35]

Mortimer, too, remarked on the effect of the robbery: "Several other little affairs followed, and all these, one after another, excited the people; the more so as the officers could not 'work up' the cases. The public gave the Chief of Police fits, the Chief gave it to the officers, and they in turn stirred up the 'stools.'"

Despite the criminal climate having become more dangerous in San Francisco, Mortimer couldn't stay away. Having finally recuperated, Mortimer decided to try his luck once more, and on the night of September 1, 1864, he was in the Bay City, observing the body of Sam Wells arrive aboard the *Chrysopolis*. A beloved member of the California Minstrel troupe, Wells had died on August 26 in Virginia City when he'd been thrown from his horse. His dying wish was that he be buried in San Francisco's Lone Mountain Cemetery and that his fellow minstrels should bear the body.[36]

"The night Sam Wells' body arrived from Virginia City, I was in the crowd and saw a man fall," Mortimer recounted. Police officers rushed to the man and so did Mortimer. Mortimer helped the drunkard up, and when the policemen accused the man of falling down drunk, Mortimer defended him. The man denied it as well. "I locked arms with him and as we walked along he took in more whiskey. At Union Square we sat down upon a dray and he soon fell asleep."

No slouch at robbing sleeping men, Mortimer lifted from him a finger ring, a "nice" pearl breast pin, and some coin. Mortimer left him, but the story did not end there. Noted Mortimer, "The papers said the man had been knocked down and robbed by two highwaymen who stood over him with knife and pistol and took his hat, pants, coat and boots. If so, others must have 'cleaned' him after I left."[37]

Mortimer must have suspected he would have a harder time dodging headlines in the weeks to come, for his next scheme could potentially put well over a thousand dollars in his pockets and would assuredly take all of his wits to pull off.

This time Mortimer set his sights on Mayor Coon's right-hand man.

The Wiggin Affair

Charles Louis Wiggin was going places.

Born in Maine around 1832, Wiggin first appeared in *The San Francisco Directory* in 1860, giving his vocation as a seaman. Wiggin quickly traded the sea for city hall, clerking for Mayor Coon. Versatile, well-liked, and a member of the People's Party, Wiggin aimed to join the state assembly, the election slated for September of 1865.[1]

On September 2, 1864, Wiggin was glad-handing with a party of well-heeled friends whom he had invited for a drink at the Pony Express Saloon, on the corner of Commercial Street and Kearny Street. Unbeknownst to Wiggin, a fellow New Englander and lover of ships was also at the bar, paying undue attention to the mayoral clerk.[2]

It wasn't by chance Mortimer was at the Pony Express Saloon. He and a "friendly" police detective had earlier walked there. "[H]e showed me some chaps carousing and said they had 'good money' and would run all night," Mortimer recalled, "and if I'd stick to them I'd probably find a 'good injen.'"

Trusting that a fortune could be made, Mortimer ingratiated himself with Wiggin and the others, carousing with them until daylight. Only then did the revelry cease. "I spotted my 'injen,' and when the party broke up I walked on with him," Mortimer related. After nearly three-quarters of a mile, they reached Wiggin's house at 9 Minna Street. There, Mortimer bade him good morning and took off. But while Wiggin went to sleep, Mortimer stayed active. In his memoir he noted that, back in town, he "got breakfast, cleaned up, shaved and had my head rubbed, and by seven in the morning was back at the house."[3]

Mortimer rang the bell, and a servant girl, described by Mortimer as a "charming young lady," opened the door.[4]

"Good morning, madam," Mortimer greeted.

"Good morning, sir," she responded.

"I have called per agreement to see Mr. Wiggin on a matter of business."

"I don't think he is up yet."

"I did not expect to find him up. I am aware of the time he came home this morning, you see," Mortimer said, smiling.

The young lady left Mortimer to consult the lady of the house. Upon her return, she said, "I will show you to his room."

The young lady led Mortimer up the stairs, where a "gent" scowled at Mortimer as he passed downstairs. Shortly thereafter, the young lady pointed to a closed door.

"That is Mr. Wiggin's room."[5]

"I am greatly obliged to you, madam," Mortimer said. After she was gone, he entered the room and locked the door behind him. Presumably so that no one could peek, Mortimer also hung his handkerchief over the keyhole.

According to Wiggin, Mortimer then chloroformed him. Interestingly, this tidbit did not find its way into Mortimer's memoir. Whether or not Mortimer deemed it necessary to use a rag or pocket handkerchief doused with trichloromethane to knock Wiggin unconscious, both men agree Mortimer proceeded to steal all the money and jewelry he could find. This included a heavy pearl ring from Wiggin's finger, Wiggin's gold watch and chain, which bore a solid gold Masonic emblem, $600 in gold coin from a purse taken from his pocket, and $260 in greenbacks from his pocketbook. All told, Mortimer estimated the jewelry worth about $640, making this a $1,500 score.

At the foot of the stairs, Mortimer once again ran into the charming young lady.

"How does Mr. Wiggin feel this morning?" she asked, smiling.

"I find him very much as I expected," Mortimer replied. "He has a severe headache and is going to try to sleep it off. Good morning."

"Good morning, sir."

Flush, Mortimer shared the wealth. He went first to Howard Street, where he gave some of the stolen money to a poor woman and some destitute children. He next visited the house of a certain detective (very likely the same crooked detective who had tipped him to the party at the Pony Express Saloon) and gave the man two hundred dollars. Afterward, he headed south to Belmont.[6]

When Wiggin groggily awoke, he determined that he'd been robbed. Making a quick inventory of the room, he found his money and jewelry had vanished. The checks in his pocket book had been pawed through but, evidently, the burglar had left them after noticing they were payable to order and unendorsed. Valuable mining stock had also been left, though if Wiggin took any comfort from that it was likely threaded with panic. Wiggin knew he had to report the robbery to the police if he had any hope of recovering his property, but the inquiries they would ask could be sticky. To answer questions, such as "Where were you last night? What time did you return home? Why didn't you wake when the stranger entered your room? How much money did the robber take? Why did you have so much money on you?" would reveal that Wiggin perhaps wasn't as upstanding a citizen as he pretended.

Certainly, as a potential candidate for the state assembly, and with the election a year away, Wiggin did not want to suffer the embarrassment of revealing he'd been so inebriated that he hadn't even woken when a robber slipped his ring off his finger. Given that revelation, the press might also dig into what he was doing with over eight hundred dollars in cash and where that money had come from. Could it be that at the Pony Express Saloon certain movers and shakers in San Francisco had ponied up the majority of that money, bribing Wiggin to support their policies? In Wiggin's case, was the term "mayoral clerk" synonymous with "bagman"? Was drunken Charley Wiggin really the sort of man one wanted to see elected?

By the time the police arrived, Wiggin had his story straight. The word he used— and reporters, policemen, and historians parroted—was "chloroform." That the robber had rendered Wiggin unconscious by using the foul-smelling organic compound neatly explained why Wiggin hadn't put up a fight and why he was so groggy. As for the money, the *Sacramento Bee* reported, "Mr. Wiggin had taken the money home with him for the purpose of purchasing drafts in the morning to remit to his family at the East."[7]

Whether or not the chloroform assertion was a lie, reporters ate it up, and the fact that Wiggin was completely intoxicated was never examined. Mortimer's rendition leads one to believe that Wiggin fabricated the chloroform angle, for Mortimer does not mention it (in fact, in none of Mortimer's crimes does he ever describe using chloroform). During the robbery of Wiggin, his exact words were "I went in easily, closed and locked the door, hung my handkerchief over the keyhole, and went quietly to work, Mr. Wiggin sleeping sweetly."[8]

If the police doubted the chloroform story, they kept it to themselves. Officer Ben Bohen, in an interview conducted by *San Francisco Chronicle* in 1870, repeated that Mortimer had chloroformed Wiggin. In *Celebrated Criminal Cases of America*, published in 1910, former San Francisco Chief of Police Thomas S. Duke also described Mortimer chloroforming Wiggin. The two corresponding accounts demonstrated that if rumors of an alternative theory existed, those rumors had short shelf lives.[9]

Although the reporters didn't look hard at the mechanism through which Wiggin was made unconscious to his own robbery, the San Francisco police opened a vigorous investigation, operating on the assumption that the same man who robbed Wiggin may have also committed the Myers pawnshop robbery.

Naturally, policemen questioned the young lady who had led Mortimer up the stairs to Wiggin's room. According to the *Alta California*, "The girl can give no description of his appearance, and thus far the police have no clue to go by."[10]

This seems unlikely. By Mortimer's admission, the young lady had not simply let him in, but checked with the lady of the house. She would have looked him over before determining she needed to check on the proper protocol. Furthermore, she had another conversation with Mortimer just after he left Wiggin's room. The likelihood is that the police instructed the newspapermen to report the girl as being no help for three reasons: to protect the girl from any possible retaliatory action of the robber, to sooth her fears, and to lure the thief into a false sense of security. Although

Mortimer had cleverly changed his appearance between leaving the Pony Express Saloon with Wiggin and entering Wiggin's abode, between the young lady and the scowling man Mortimer passed on the stairs, the police would have had a good description of Mortimer's present appearance.

It didn't take long for the police to see Mortimer's handiwork in the Wiggin robbery. Recalled Bohen, "Bystanders said a man who answered to Mortimer's description was drinking at the bar at the time.... We could see Mortimer's smooth finger-tracks right through the job."[11]

Less than a week after the robbery Bohen caught sight of Nellie Brannan, who he remembered as "Ellen Brenn" at a McClellan for President ratification meeting in San Francisco. Noted Bohen, "Ellen was Mortimer's pal, and we knew he couldn't be far away."[12]

San Francisco's finest caught a bigger break when Detective George Rose arrested George Sibley, and Sibley turned stool pigeon. Promising to cut Sibley loose, Rose got out of the deserter the whereabouts of Mortimer's Belmont headquarters. Sibley also advised the detective to search the house for "clues" of Mortimer's various robberies. Rose took the information to Chief Burke, who on Friday morning, September 8, 1864, dispatched Rose to Belmont.[13]

Later that day, Mortimer, Nellie Brannan, and an old man were within Mortimer's house when a knock came at the door. While the old man answered the knock, Mortimer immediately stowed himself away. It was good that he did, for two men were at the door: a stagecoach driver and Detective Rose. Rose asked for Mortimer, and Nellie responded that he was "in the City."

"This was all he wanted," Mortimer recalled. "He was brave enough when he had only a woman to deal with. He said he wanted to look through the house. She objected, but he did not mind her."

The Fourth Amendment be damned, Rose began searching the house. In due course, he uncovered some of Mortimer's ill-gotten gains. "As he found one article of jewelry after another, I thought his fun had gone on long enough, and showed myself," Mortimer admitted. "He pretended he wanted to arrest me, but when the stage driver's back was turned, he told me it was only for a blind. He denied having found the jewelry, but finally owned up to it, and said if I'd own up it would be better for me, and so tried to laugh the matter off."

Convinced that Rose intended to arrest him, Mortimer determined to "put my wits to work to prevent his return to San Francisco, as he intended on the afternoon train."

To have a private conversation, Rose and Mortimer walked to a nearby park. There Rose read him a list of articles stolen from Harris Myers's pawnshop. Mortimer possessed a lady's watch and chain that closely resembled one on the list. After returning to the house, Mortimer clandestinely placed it where Rose would be certain to stumble upon it. Finding the watch and chain, Rose reacted with "great glee," believing it to be the one from Myers's shop, and that he had caught the man who'd assaulted and robbed Henry Myers back in August. Mortimer also recalled Rose bragging that "he would get the reward offered."

As for the rest of the jewelry, Mortimer claimed he had "planted" it in San Jose.

"You have got me in a bad fix; now if you will be easy with me I will 'turn up the plant,'" Mortimer told him.[14]

Lured by the promise of buried treasure, Rose traveled with Mortimer to the Belmont depot and boarded the afternoon train. After rattling twenty-five miles southeast, they disembarked in San Jose, in Santa Clara County.

"[W]e went out when it was dark to the spot I described," Mortimer noted. By the time they reached their destination, about one and a half miles from town, it was 9:00 p.m. The place matched the description Mortimer had given. If Mortimer hoped this would lower Rose's guard, he was mistaken. Rose kept his hand on his holstered pistol, and Mortimer knew he had another one under his buttoned coat. Mortimer then tried to light some matches, purposefully failing. It fell to Rose to show Mortimer how it was done, bringing his hand from his pistol.

"The moment his match blazed, I garroted him," Mortimer recalled. With Mortimer's hands around his throat, squeezing the air from him, Rose reached for his pistol. No dice. Mortimer threw his full weight upon him and, having the advantage over the detective, cautioned him not to try for it. But the moment Mortimer eased up, Rose went again for the pistol. Mortimer tackled him once more, resulting in the pistol coming loose and landing behind Rose.

"I . . . took out my penknife, opened it with my teeth, and told him I did not want to hurt him, but as I was master of the situation, and should disarm him and take what property he had of mine and let him go."

Rose, believing Mortimer meant to kill him, pleaded, "For God's sake, think of my poor mother."

"I think most of my own mother," Mortimer replied, "but I don't want to hurt you."

With one pistol lying on the ground behind Rose, and with Rose's buttoned coat obstructing his reach for his remaining pistol, Mortimer knew he held the upper hand. Boldly, he went for Rose's fallen pistol, but as he did so Rose made a quick dive for it.

"I gave him a very severe hug and shoved the blade into his neck," Mortimer related. Catching him with the flat of the blade, Mortimer missed the carotid artery, instead carving into his windpipe.

"I had been as mild as I could with him," Mortimer reflected, "and had often cautioned him to not resist. He must have thought I would not or could not do him injury. I must then have been almost insane, thinking what he had forced me to do after I had tried to avoid it."

After forcing Rose to the ground with a bleeding neck, Mortimer reached inside the detective's coat and took his pistol. Mortimer also recovered the property that Rose had taken from him in Belmont. Afterward, he rolled Rose on his stomach to get at his back pocket. As he did so, Rose grabbed for his fallen pistol, succeeding in getting ahold of it. This further enraged Mortimer. After a short struggle, Mortimer took the pistol from Rose and used it to bludgeon him. When Rose shoved a hand in his assailant's face, Mortimer responded by biting Rose's little finger with ferocious strength, all but severing it. Finally, Mortimer used the pistol to crack Rose over the head hard enough to fracture his skull.[15]

Mark Twain, who wrote up the attack for *San Francisco Daily Morning Call*, described it somewhat differently. According to Twain:

> The prisoner watched his opportunity while the officer's back was turned for a moment, or while he was digging for the hidden treasure, and knocked him down by striking him in the back of the head with a stone; he then took the officer's knife from his pocket and cut his throat with it, severing the windpipe half in two; next he thrust the blade into his throat and twisted it round; then, to make the murder sure, he took Rose's revolver and struck him across the forehead with it, inflicting a ghastly wound.[16]

Twain also reported that after ten minutes, while Rose lay on the ground, an unfamiliar voice called out, "Hallo, my friend, what are you doing there? Anything the matter? If you're ailing, my farm-house is close by."

When Rose raised his head, the man spoke again, this time using his real voice.

"Oh, so you're not dead yet!" Mortimer exclaimed. "I was afraid so; you've hunted me out, my man, and you can't live."

Using the pistol, Mortimer once more beat Rose over the head.[17]

The *San Francisco Bulletin*'s version was even bloodier. After Mortimer, disguising his voice and pretending to be a farmer, lured Rose into raising his head, Mortimer stabbed him in the throat while crying out, "Goddamn you; you know too much. While you live, I am not safe, and you must die!"[18]

Bohen provided different details. "Rose started with him to the place designated in Santa Clara, and after getting a pick and shovel, started to work. Mortimer managed to get behind Rose at one time, and immediately seizing the chance, 'jumped' him. He managed to get Rose's revolver and beat him with it until he thought there was no more need of it."[19]

Indisputably, Mortimer then robbed Rose of forty dollars, dug up his "plant," and vanished.²⁰ These subsequent stories are known because Rose, after Mortimer left, defied the odds. Instead of dying quietly, with a fractured skull, a slashed throat, and a finger mostly bitten off, he stubbornly clung to life. When he regained consciousness sometime that night, he was stunned, confused, and weakened by blood loss. Unable to stand, Rose crawled nearly a mile to the nearest farmhouse, owned by Mr. Trenneth, reaching it around midnight.

According to Twain, Trenneth and his family "sat up with the wounded man all night, and did everything they could for his relief." Doctors who came to the house on September 9 initially supposed he could not survive his injuries. Along with amputating Rose's bitten little finger and bandaging his slashed throat, the doctors counted several blows to his head: one on the top of his head, two behind the left ear, and several on the forehead. But Rose's strength slowly returned, and the next day he was deemed well enough to travel.

"A man of his nerve and resolution requires more than one fatal wound to kill him," commented Twain.

The Trenneth family furnished him with blankets and bedding to make him more comfortable, and on September 10 he was placed on the evening train, conductor Nolan taking special care to see that he made it to San Francisco in good health.²¹

By this time the San Francisco police station had become a hornet's nest of activity. Mortimer was now the chief suspect for the Wiggin robbery, the Myers pawnshop robbery, and had beaten Detective Rose to within an inch of his life, making him the most wanted man in the Bay Area. Chief Burke posted a two hundred dollar reward for "the apprehension of Charles James Mortimer" and sent telegrams to the interior towns where they determined Mortimer was likely to flee. William Gray, a pal of Mortimer's, was sought for questioning. Burke also dispatched Captain Lees and a posse of police officers to Belmont. Bohen noted that Lees needed little prompting.

"We've got to get that fellow, and we'll start right now," Lees declared, before rounding up a posse including Jim Bovee, Alfred Clark, John Connolly, and Bohen. Between the reward, the conviction that Mortimer was responsible for the Myers pawnshop robbery, the Wiggin robbery, and leaving Rose for dead, the officers were out for blood.²²

Although Twain felt certain the police would ultimately hunt Mortimer down, he did not necessarily think it would happen overnight, opining, "Mortimer is one of the worst men known to the Police.... He will be captured, if it takes the department ten years to accomplish it."²³

After taking a special train to Belmont, the officers spread out. "At the first trace of him we separated," Bohen recalled, "and I made south and took up guard against a tree, with a six-shooter ready, for we thought he had to come that way. I held up that tree all night."²⁴

At daybreak Bohen moved on to a roadhouse, kept by a Dutchman, where the officer suspected Mortimer might have holed up. When the door opened, Bohen caught sight of the Dutchman, pale-faced, quivering with fear, and holding a revolver.

"Who ist dat?" asked the Dutchman.

"The San Francisco Police," Bohen replied.

"Ach, tank Got!" the man replied. He'd been worried that Bohen might have been Mortimer, but Bohen—who by his own admission dressed as something of a dandy at the time, and on that day was in his Sunday best—could only be what he claimed. Having had a sleepless night, Bohen was grateful for the coffee the man offered him.[25]

Meanwhile, Lees and the others placed under arrest the old man who had been with Mortimer earlier that day (Nellie Brannan likely already having lit out). Although Lees had his men scouring the countryside, they had little luck hunting Mortimer in Belmont, and Lees returned to San Francisco. On September 16, Twain reported that Officer Jim Bovee had also returned "without having been able to obtain the slightest clue to his whereabouts."[26]

Small wonder, for Mortimer first headed instead to Santa Clara before braving Belmont. On Franklin Street, Mortimer entered the Cameron House—a two-story brick hotel next to a saloon and a stable—and approached an acquaintance he referred to as "old man Allen." Although Mortimer was armed with his penknife and two pistols he'd taken from Rose—which Twain described as "an old five shooting revolver, and a new six shooter"—Mortimer wanted his own pistol.

Twain also reprinted Mortimer's description in the Rogue's Gallery, adding a few details of his most recent appearance: wearing a soft hat, having a recently made knife wound on one arm, a slight bruise on his nose, a black eye, and sporting a "large coarse goatee and moustache, sandy color, dyed black." Twain additionally listed some of Mortimer's mostly stolen possessions: a knife, both of Rose's pistols, $600 in gold coin, $240 in greenbacks, a Master's Mark (signifying his membership in the Freemasons) with a sextant engraved on one side, a sailing ship on the other, and the words "Chas. L. Wiggin, Cal. R. A. Chapter No. 5," and two gold watches, one which read "Marine Time Observer," attached to a heavy gold chain with hands clasped over a heart, and the other an E. S. Yates & Co. lever watch, No. 22045, in a gold hunting case with "Eureka" on both sides.[27]

Mortimer was about to add one more possession to that list. Allen, relinquishing the pistol he'd borrowed from Mortimer, asked what had become of Rose.

"Gone on another chase," Mortimer replied.

Afterward, Mortimer made for the train depot. Armed for battle, Mortimer rattled twenty-three miles northwest to Belmont. On board, Mortimer learned that George Rose had crawled to a farmhouse and told his story. He now knew that he was being hunted.

From his car, Mortimer could see men on the road eyeing the train. Nevertheless, Mortimer got off at Belmont and met with two men he knew, then took a little-used byway. Even this was too conspicuous. Crawling through the chaparral, Mortimer made it to a hillside where he could view his surroundings from concealment.

"I soon saw armed men going to and fro," Mortimer recalled.

Scouring the countryside were officers under the direction of Sheriff Keith, along with bands of vigilantes hoping for fame and a share of the two hundred dollar reward Chief Burke had posted. Mortimer laid low. When night fell he made his move, starting "for the Montie or Monte," Mortimer related, referring to Belle Monti, a subdivided section of Belmont that translated to "Pretty Mountain." When the fog rolled in, Mortimer got lost, but he reached the mountainous section of Belmont at dawn.

"Here I saw the men approach, both armed," Mortimer noted. "I passed around the point of timber, crawled in and fired on them, on which both beat a retreat. I afterwards learned one was shot in the foot and one in the hand."

Between the gunshots and the cries of the wounded, other armed men soon appeared, forming a mob. Recognizing that to stay where he was would only result in his being shot or hanged, Mortimer made for a marshy lake surrounded by tule at one end of the willow forest, crawling through the brush and the brackish water for a mile, losing the mob.[28]

Meanwhile, on September 23, 1864, Sheriff Keith sent a telegram to the San Francisco police, notifying them that Mortimer was still at large and armed, having shot one man in the hand and another in the foot while eluding capture on the outskirts of Belmont. Detective Jake Chappell—a tough officer who had made headlines the year before for tracking down Sterling A. Hopkins and the $1,700 worth of money and jewelry he'd stolen in Virginia City—immediately traveled south to aid in the manhunt.[29]

The following day Chappell sent Lees a discouraging telegram, the contents of which Twain shared the following day, "that no traces of the missing scoundrel could be found, and that it would be useless to send down a larger force to hunt for him."[30]

The problem—and this was what Mortimer had been counting on—was that between the marshy lake and the dense willow forest, the officers and vigilantes would be stumbling around the countryside with little chance of finding him and a better chance of shooting one of their own by mistake. Furthermore, with the countryside full of pigs, sheep, fowl, cattle, and creek water, Mortimer would not go hungry or thirsty. Twain concluded, "The only sure method of catching him lies in burning the willows; but as this would probably result in the destruction of the crops thereabouts, the farmers will not permit it to be done."

Lees tried as best he could to help matters in San Francisco. He and Chappell joined forces with Henry H. Ellis, a sterling detective who would ultimately become San Francisco's chief of police. Seemingly catching a break, they arrested an old associate of Mortimer's, Sam Markle, alias "Sam Wilson," alias "Sam Biercla," alias "Slippery Sam." But about Mortimer's present whereabouts, Sam was of no help, and Lees let a Sacramento officer escort him to California's capital to answer for his crimes. Rumor had it that from Belmont Mortimer traveled southwest through the wilderness to Spanishtown (later renamed Half Moon Bay) and Pescadero.[31]

While the others hunted for Mortimer on the coast, Twain caught a train to San Jose on September 25, presumably on the assumption that Mortimer had headed southeast. Of the six thousand inhabitants of San Jose, Twain determined Mortimer was not among them.[32]

Naturally not, for instead of hanging around the scene of the crime Mortimer headed north. Making it to San Mateo, he stayed there until the next night. With the posses searching for him south, Mortimer determined his best course of action was to make a midnight run for San Francisco, where he could lay low while plotting a course of action. Avoiding the railroads, he snuck twenty miles to the Bay City. There, he holed up for seven or eight days. In the papers, he read with interest about Rose's convalescence.

"Mr. Rose is now sufficiently recovered to be about again," Twain wrote in the September 29 edition of the *San Francisco Daily Morning Call*. "He left yesterday to hunt for Mortimer, and has made up his mind to catch him."[33]

With Rose on the warpath, Mortimer knew he either needed a new identity or a new territory. Ultimately, Mortimer decided on both.

CHAPTER 4

Highwayman

*I*n the fall of 1864, Mortimer—claiming to be George Foster from Salt Lake City—arrived in Napa. There to greet him was an old friend, John "Black Jack" Bowen, and George Shanks, a deserter from the Fourth California Infantry who went by the alias "Jack Williams."[1]

With police activity abuzz in San Francisco, sixty miles to the south, the trio hid out in Napa, keeping mostly to themselves. A fortnight after Mortimer's arrival, he and Shanks left Black Jack behind, stealing two horses and riding out of Napa.[2]

"The roads were all guarded half an hour *after* we left," Mortimer noted.

Riding through the mountains, they made it to the plains near Woodland. From there, the two cut a circuitous route, traveling over 350 miles while committing highway robbery on the desolate roads around Knight's Landing, Marysville, Oroville, Colusa, Red Bluff, Shasta, and Yreka, the county seat of Siskiyou County. There, only 250 miles from the Oregon border, Mortimer and Shanks fell in with an escaped convict from Nevada State Prison, Tom Boulton. While Shanks and Boulton got drunk, Mortimer determined he'd had enough of their company, and headed southwest.

After twenty miles, Mortimer reached the small mining town of Fort Jones in Scott Valley. "Here I made a chap get up out of his room in an out-house, and told him boldly I had come to rob his employer, Mr. Donahue, and made him give me a description of the dwelling house," Mortimer recalled.

The chap's name was Bob Ferry, and he liked the idea of his boss being robbed, asking to "stand in" with Mortimer.

"I thought I knew my man and consented," Mortimer reflected. For the next several months, he and Ferry would be as thick as thieves.

Although Mortimer had planned on committing the robbery that night, he postponed it until the next night, and in the intervening time fell in with a man named Mack before proceeding to Donahue's house. Leaving Mack standing watch, Mortimer and Ferry scoped out the Donahue residence. They returned to find Mack had disappeared. Fearing treachery, they abandoned the job. Sticking around Scott Valley, they robbed the Ohio House a few days later, then in November "chummed in" with an escapee from Oregon State Prison in Portland, William Richardson. That night they stayed at the home of "Cherokee Mary," who kept a notorious rendezvous spot and hideout for highwaymen, about nine miles southwest of Yreka.

Over the next few days, the three highwaymen may have reflected on their good fortune. It was common knowledge that over two hundred of Siskiyou County's red-blooded patriots had joined the US Army, lending their aid in the war against the Rebellion. The three companies consisted of Company M, Second Cavalry; Company A, Fifth Infantry; and the Siskiyou Mountaineers, Company F. With the eighty-three cavalrymen deployed in Nevada, Utah, and Colorado, the eighty infantrymen stationed in Arizona, New Mexico, and Texas, and the sixty-seven mountaineers sent to Fort Jones to fight Humboldt Indians, the desperadoes seemingly had the run of the place.[3]

So long as the Siskiyou Mountaineers didn't catch their scent.

Needing provisions, some nights later Mortimer and Ferry snuck down from the mountains to Dutch Charley's storehouse. For the goods they desired to take, neither man intended to pay—but they almost paid with their lives.

"As I stepped in I heard a cap snap, and I at once dropped," Mortimer recalled. "When all was still I struck a light and there stood a gun in a framework, with a string from the trigger to the door. I had sprung the trap, but the powder was not dry."[4]

Steamed that one or both of them might have been killed, Mortimer and Ferry "took all we wanted and destroyed all we could." Mortimer estimated this included several hundred dollars' worth of goods. They also took the gun with them. It was with satisfaction that Mortimer recollected this effectually "burst" Dutch Charley. Rejoining Richardson, they went to a store on McAdams Creek owned by M. Rosenberg, a patriotic American who had donated provisions to Union soldiers. Entering the store at seven in the evening, the trio noticed that it was crowded. Mortimer remembered eight or ten men present. Irrespective of the witnesses, they progressed with the robbery, raking in over a thousand dollars' worth of goods.[5]

Recognizing it was past time to skedaddle, the highwaymen lit out for Sailor Diggings, a small gold-mining town in Oregon with a long history of outlawry. Two days later, riding alongside the Klamath River near Reave's Ferry, they were overtaken by half a dozen or more men on horseback. All were armed to the teeth.

Surrendering, Mortimer, Ferry, and Richardson were lashed to their horses, the posse leading them back to Fort Jones. That night Richardson managed to "slip his harness" and escape. Mortimer and Ferry were not so lucky.

"Bob and I were taken to Yreka and lodged in jail," Mortimer recollected. "Here we lay three months."

On February 7, 1865, Mortimer and Ferry were hauled before Judge Alexander M. Rosborough, a South Carolinian who had fought the Creek Indians in Alabama and the Seminoles in Florida before turning to the law. Stern and upright, Rosborough did not like to see highwaymen trample his laws, sentencing Bob Ferry and Mortimer—under the guise "George Foster"—to three years in San Quentin State Prison.[6]

Before being taken south, they were locked in Siskiyou County Jail in Yreka with six other prisoners. Three of them were Chinese. The other three were white men. One of the white men was an army deserter named Kaifer, going under the alias McGuire, with only a few days left on his sentence. Another was Ritchie, who wasn't under sentence but only indictment. The last was Thomas King, an Irishman who on July 2, 1863, had murdered saloonkeeper James Duffy in French's saloon on the south fork of the Scott River, plunging a dagger into his heart. Rosborough had found King guilty a year ago, in February of 1864, but the case was under appeal in the California Supreme Court, and King had been languishing in jail since the day of the murder.[7]

All that changed on February 8, 1865.

Because there were only five cells, jailor E. A. McCullough determined the most trustworthy of the prisoners should be placed in the hall as a trusty. Unsurprisingly, that man was McGuire, whose sentence was almost up and had inspired confidence by revealing to McCullough the prisoners' previous plots to escape. McCullough should have known better. A little before eight o'clock that night, Mortimer and Ferry convinced McGuire that rather than being released he would be convicted and shot for desertion. Believing he had no choice, McGuire removed the wire from the lid of a tin water bucket and used it to pick Mortimer's lock.

Working quickly, Mortimer used the wire to pick the locked cell doors of Ferry, Ritchie, and King, leaving the Chinese alone. Unfortunately, there was a fly in the ointment.

"Ritchie refused to join them," McCullough recalled, "stating that he was not afraid to stand his trial, that he would be acquitted."

Determining if Ritchie wasn't with them, he was against them, the others knocked him down and bound and gagged him. With the door to the hall too securely fastened to pick, Mortimer instructed McGuire to call for water.

"After closing up for the night I never gave drink to any but those whose terms had nearly expired," McCullough explained, "or who were in jail for light offenses, and then with great caution."

With a cup of water in hand, McCullough opened the door just wide enough to pass it through. As he did so, McGuire asked for some matches. Almost as soon as the words had left his mouth, Mortimer, Ferry, and King jerked the door open wide and surrounded and pinned McCullough.

"I made an effort to give the alarm, but was prevented . . . by Foster choking me," McCullough related.

Pulling him into a cell, they tied his hands and feet and gagged him with a handkerchief. Mortimer took his pistol but told McCullough he'd leave him his watch and purse. Mortimer also arranged a blanket for McCullough to lie on, and temporarily removing the handkerchief, gave him a sip of water. According to McCullough, Mortimer "said he wanted to leave me as comfortable as he could consistently with his own safety."

As the prisoners made to leave, McCullough heard one of them say, "Crooks will be back soon with Charley. Hurry up," referring to Sheriff Andrew D. Crooks and Undersheriff "Charley" C. W. Pindle.[8]

The last thing Mortimer told McCullough was that he had arranged the fastenings on Ritchie just so that in an hour or two he'd be loose and could come to his aid. Once outside the hall, McGuire stole a revolver McCullough had left on the head of the bed. Then, with their leg irons still on, Mortimer, Ferry, King, and McGuire fled Siskiyou County Jail, heading southwest.[9]

Only twenty minutes passed before their escape was discovered. All of Yreka was notified, and posses began hunting for the escaped prisoners. Around dawn Ferry made it about nine miles southwest to Cherry Creek, despite his leg irons, when he was captured by John Hendricks's posse. King also fled southwest, but weakened from his nineteen-month incarceration, didn't get very far. At about 2:00 p.m. the next day, William Short and Charles Brown found the murderer hiding in an overgrowth of manzanita near a brickyard, only a short distance from Yreka, with one of his leg irons partially sawed off.

As the days passed, and the rural police realized Mortimer and McGuire must have traveled outside the radius of Yreka where the townsfolk could help, Sheriff A. D. Crooks organized a company of manhunters. Crooks's new band included Jesse Sherman, Livy Swan, A. V. Burns, J. Babb, and a few others. With the trail having gone cold, they reasoned their best bet was to anticipate where the escapees were heading. Considering the others had been traveling southwest, they determined they'd been fleeing to Cherokee Mary's. As it happened, they were right on the money.[10]

A few days after the escape, Mortimer—having shed his twenty-five-pound leg irons in the first hour—reached the infamous hideout. "I knocked and she came to the door and gave my hand a squeeze," Mortimer related, "but I was so hungry and worn out I did not understand it, and so stepped in."

As Mortimer did so, a gun was placed to his head. Mortimer stepped back, slammed the door close, and took off running for the road. But he didn't run fast enough. "Three shots were fired, one of which hit me in the back of the neck and down I came," Mortimer remembered.[11]

The ball had grazed his jugular vein, broke his right lower jaw, and lodged in his cheek. As the posse returned Mortimer to town, they determined there was little danger of him dying from the gunshot wound; instead, the greater danger came from the lynch mob that formed in Yreka, wanting to see the highwayman dangling from a rope. Law officers managed to convince the townsfolk to postpone the hanging a day. The next morning, McCullough's write-up of the jailbreak in the Yreka papers demonstrated that the escapees hadn't beaten McCullough. In fact, they'd only robbed him of his weapons, sparing his money and his watch, and made him as comfortable as possible. That "cooled them down," Mortimer reflected.[12]

Unfortunately, Judge Rosborough wasn't in a forgiving mood. Annulling his previous sentence, he condemned Mortimer to seven years' hard time. McGuire, who made it all the way to Fort Jones before deeming escape impossible and surrendering, was sentenced to two years. Ferry's sentence was increased as well. As for King, it was still in the hands of the California Supreme Court, but his eighteen hours of freedom couldn't have helped his cause.

In the meantime, Rosborough ordered Sheriff Crooks to transport Mortimer to San Quentin. The last stretch brought them by boat to the San Francisco waterfront. Night had fallen by the time they docked, and although the state prison was just ten miles north across the bay, Crooks decided to lock his charge in the station house and deliver him to San Quentin in the morning. Mortimer urgently tried to dissuade Crooks, insisting they could sleep comfortably enough on the boat. Suspicious of his intentions, Crooks refused the prisoner's entreaties.

Entering the station house, Mortimer had his face muffled, concealing his features. But as Crooks and Mortimer passed Detective George W. Rose, standing near the door and conversing with Police Captain Stephen H. Baker, Rose recognized the prisoner from his figure and walk.

"Mortimer, by God!" shouted Rose.

Enraged, the nine-fingered detective drew his pistol.[13]

CHAPTER 5

Gilchrist's Scheme

Sheriff Crooks, who had no idea what was happening, was caught flatfooted when Mortimer seized him. "I grabbed hold of him and kept him close to the front, 'facing the music,'" Mortimer noted.

With Mortimer using Crooks as a human shield, Rose couldn't get a clear shot at his nemesis. This tactic bought Mortimer enough time for Captain William Douglass and Officer Brown to close in on Rose. Douglass, a Forty-Niner from New York who had been with the San Francisco Police since 1853 and, as the *San Francisco Examiner* put it, "stood for law and order," wasn't about to allow Rose to gun down an unarmed prisoner. Not on his watch. Together he and Brown (who may have been Andrew D. Brown, David Brown, George F. Brown, or W. P. Brown, all of whom were employed as San Francisco policemen in 1865) grabbed Rose and hustled him out the station house door.[1]

"It was done quickly, but not a moment too soon," Mortimer reflected. "I was almost in the act of dropping Crooks, for he was shaking like an aspen leaf."

Mortimer was placed in irons so heavy they made the ones he was fitted with in Yreka look like toys. These were thirty-two-pound monsters, with riveted wristlets, and leg irons with a heavy bar between them. It might have seemed extreme, but they were taking no chances.

Word quickly spread that the infamous Mortimer was back in town and in police custody. A crowd swelled to see Mortimer placed inside a stagecoach by the police. Among those in the crowd was Rose, who could only glare impotently at his bête noire. A teamster named George "Cockeye" Stanton was also in the crowd, who muscled through and cried out, "Where is the son of a bitch?"[2]

At the dock an even bigger crowd formed, all wishing to personally see the man who had supposedly beaten Myers, robbed Wiggin, and pistol-whipped Rose "sent across" to San Quentin.

"Now began my seven years of prison life," Mortimer recalled.

Upon his return to San Quentin State Prison, commencing on March 15, 1865, it took the combined efforts of two smiths half an hour to strike off the irons. Commissary James J. Green, who had represented the Republican Party in the California State Assembly in 1861 and was considered by Mortimer to be "a good man and an officer," took Mortimer aside and gave him a piece of advice. Mortimer's reputation would not count for or against him here, and if he behaved and followed the rules, Green would do everything he could to make Mortimer's stay as easy as possible. Mortimer told Green that he would "join in nothing to get up an excitement, but I would not promise not to leave, if I had a good chance to regain my liberty."[3]

Mortimer was given a berth in Cell 18, which he shared with three other prisoners. By night Mortimer enjoyed singing, reportedly having an excellent singing voice and knowing a wide repertoire of songs. By day Mortimer returned to his old vocation as a tailor in the state tailor shop, sewing burlap sacks for Union soldiers. History had seemingly repeated itself. "With the exception of the convicts being better fed, better clothed, and the officers showing a more humane feeling toward the prisoners, matters were much the same as when I was first there," Mortimer noted.[4]

Mortimer's skill as a tailor again served him well. In recompense for his toil, Mortimer made about fifty dollars a year—less than half of what convicts in Nevada State Prison made, which needled some residents of San Quentin. Convicts, most of whom ate in the dining room, also complained about the food. "Those who had means to afford it, could eat elsewhere than in the dining room," Mortimer explained. Rather than hoarding the paltry amount he earned, Mortimer shelled out the money to eat more comfortably in the tailor shop.[5]

One evening in mid-January 1866—after Mortimer had served about eight months of his seven-year sentence—a new meal was introduced to the prisoners: cornmeal mush. Mortimer was eating "supper" in the tailor shop with two others, so did not witness the ruckus that was made in the dining room when the large body of convicts discovered that their so-called dinner consisted of wretched, semisolid lumps of cornmeal.[6]

It may be that some of the outrage was genuine, and that the "mush break"—as the attempted jailbreak would be called—was spurred by the barely edible rations. Mortimer, however, dished that the ringleaders of the mush break merely used the cornmeal supper as an excuse to rile up the prisoners, focus their rage on the unsuspecting guards, and make good their escape.

Spilling the beans in his memoir, Mortimer added, "Many of the 'cons' made known their dislike to the dish, and used this as the excuse for the attempt to regain liberty."[7]

At dinnertime, the prisoners—about six hundred of them—filed into the dining room as usual. The only difference was that several of the boldest convicts were the last to enter. This meant that they happened to be standing near the door when the officer in charge of the dining room, James Fitzpatrick, stepped inside.

"As soon as he did so," Mortimer related, "he was caught hold of by some three or four 'cons.' . . . The course the prisoners intended to pursue, was to keep the officer in the dining room till dark as a protection, and then 'every one for himself' in the effort to scale the wall during the night."

Mortimer commented that it was a good night for it, being very dark and periodically raining hard. But it was not to be.

"[Fitzpatrick] made some resistance and an outcry. At that moment a convict came rushing in with a large knife and rescued the officer. This act of treachery was unsuspected. He was a traitor to his 'kind.'"[8]

Shocked, the bold convicts loosened their grip when they saw one of their own coming toward them with a knife, and Fitzpatrick broke the hold and made it out the door. The "traitor" followed. As he did so one of the prisoners raised a club, smashing him over the head.

"It was well dealt," Mortimer noted, "but did not bring him down. If it had, there and then he would have 'passed in his checks.'"

Shortly after the "traitor" followed Fitzpatrick out the door, the alarm rang for all prisoners to return to their cells. In the tailor shop, Mortimer's companions were doing just that. Mortimer didn't like it. "I told them I'd not take the chances of being shot by those crazy guards, as we did not know how things stood and we might be turned loose upon by the guards at any moment. Just then two shots were fired and that fixed them not to leave the shop."

As for the events unfolding in the dining room, J. J. Green pulled off a double act, imploring the guards not to shoot, and ordering the prisoners to peacefully return to their cells. One guard by the lower gate disobeyed. "He blazed away into the dining-room windows, but fortunately did not hurt anyone," Mortimer recalled.

Things went worse for the men in the brickyard.

About a dozen or so prisoners, hearing the alarm bell, crossed the brickyard to be admitted and return to their cells. "They were all standing huddled together and quietly awaiting the gate guard's pleasure to let them enter," Mortimer recollected grimly. "While thus standing he turned loose on them a heavy charge of canister, killing five or six outright and wounding others, some quite severely."[9]

For a couple of the ringleaders, the horror had just begun. On January 22, 1866, a few days after the mush break, the guards determined that the lion's share of the blame could be pinned on two convicts: George Robinson and George Wingate. Mortimer paid no special attention to Robinson. Wingate was a different story. Having grown up in the Boston suburb of Charlestown, Wingate may have inspired some affection from his fellow Bay Stater. Like Mortimer, Wingate had worked a legitimate job in California as a cabinetmaker before turning to crime. In October of 1864 Wingate was arrested for stealing embroidery from the Washington Street store where he used to work. Later that month, Wingate was formally indicted, along with Mortimer's old partners in crime George "Cockey" Wright and George

Sibley. In late November Wingate was judged guilty and sentenced to four years in San Quentin.[10]

For his involvement in the mush break, Wingate was tied to the "Ladder."

"The man who did the whipping was a powerful man," Mortimer remarked. "Many old stagers said that they were the heaviest laid in that they had any knowledge of. Some of the men's backs and sides were masses of corruption for months after, and some did not leave the hospital till they went feet foremost to the grave yard. I am thinking of one in particular—his name was George Wingate."[11]

According to the *San Francisco Chronicle*, which took special note of the incident, "Wingate . . . was fastened to the diabolical place of torture and his flesh mutilated in a horrible manner. Mortification and dropsy set in and the man died."[12]

Mortimer described the terrible details. "After struck fifty he was cross ironed and put into the dungeon and was kept there several weeks. He was then removed to the hospital, at which time his back was alive with maggots, and was horribly offensive. Others were nearly as bad, but weathered the storm; yet most of them were broken down."[13]

George Robinson was one such convict who broke down under the pain of torture. Three years later a newspaperman for the *Chronicle* noted that though Robinson survived the brutal whipping, he had been "insane ever since."[14]

Mortimer allowed that the cruel punishment may have been inadvertent. "The whipping master told me that he never realized that he was punishing men so hard," Mortimer recorded, "and seemed to regret his position." This may have curbed some anger against the whipping master, but the guard who had gunned down the prisoners in the brickyard, for no apparent reason, couldn't simply explain it had been a mistake. Resentment built to such a level that he was forced to leave the prison until passions cooled. As for the "traitor" who rescued Officer Fitzpatrick from the clutches of the prisoners, he was soon made a full trusty, and was pardoned about a month later.[15]

Shortly after the mush break, Mortimer's past came back to haunt him. The seven years Judge Rosborough had sentenced him to had been for his exploits in Northern California as a highwayman and the subsequent jailbreak. So far charges of robbing Charles Wiggin and assaulting Detective Rose were pending, and additional years could be added to Mortimer's sentence. In San Francisco, Wiggin—now a state representative, elected in September 1865—was shown a ring that he identified as one that Mortimer stole from him on the morning of September 3, 1864. Mortimer had his doubts about the ring.

"It was claimed to be found in my house," Mortimer griped. "If Rose had that ring I must have overlooked it, as I have said, when I throttled him."

Rather than immediately trying Mortimer for the crimes he'd committed in 1864, the prosecutors bided their time, possibly to collect more evidence against him. With nothing but time on his hands, Mortimer worked from San Quentin to have his case overturned. To this purpose he became "very intimate" with George Taylor, a one-time member of the "Rattlesnake Dick" gang of outlaws.[16]

"[W]e agreed to work together," Mortimer reflected. "I was to help him, and when he got out he would aid me. In due time he was pardoned on the condition he would leave the State within thirty days. This he did not do and was brought back. In a short time he was pardoned again. It was said he had done some service to the State as a 'stool pigeon.'"

If Taylor made good his pledge to help Mortimer while free, it did not result in the Wiggin case being overturned. As the years passed, the prospect of being once again found guilty continued to hang over Mortimer's head.

In early 1867 Mortimer had reason to gloat when "Cockeye" Stanton—who had called out, "Where is the son of a bitch?" during Mortimer's last arrest—was imprisoned for killing an African American named Samuel Brown in a saloon brawl on Pike Street.

"[H]is curiosity was fully satisfied," Mortimer noted sardonically.[17]

The following year Mortimer was moved to Room No. 2, the larger quarters, a factor of the growing prison.[18]

Reading the San Francisco papers, Mortimer learned that in May 1868, Detective George Rose had been dismissed from the San Francisco Police Department. The police commissioners were cleaning house, and when it came to light that Rose had been paying another officer to walk his beat and was likely "on the take"—generally only venturing into Chinatown to collect his cut for turning a blind eye to the ubiquitous gambling halls, opium dens, and houses of ill-repute—the axe fell on the nine-fingered detective. For his part, Officer Bohen agreed that Rose was a rascal, summing up the life-and-death struggle between Rose and Mortimer in San Jose in pejorative terms: "Rose went down there to trap him, but Mortimer was the smarter rogue of the two."[19]

On the subject of Rose, Mortimer scrawled, "I will not detail the trouble he got into. At any rate, he had trouble, and I'm not the one to say if he was right or wrong—I do not know."[20]

Even without his star, Rose was loath to give up playing cops and robbers. In December 1868, when Raphael Castro's Spanish ranchero, eight miles outside of Santa Cruz, was robbed of $6,300, the former police detective personally looked into the matter. The main suspect was John Melville, who had married one of Castro's granddaughters. Melville had supposedly gambled away a fortune in Sacramento, raising eyebrows as to where the money had come from. Locating Melville, Rose delivered him to the law. On January 18 Melville was convicted of grand larceny and sentenced to four years of hard time. Santa Cruz County Sheriff Charles H. Lincoln transported the prisoner eighty miles north to San Francisco, reaching the Bay City on January 20, 1869. Shortly thereafter Melville was made a guest in San Quentin State Prison.[21]

According to the *Santa Cruz Weekly Sentinel*, at some point during this time Rose led Melville on an hours-long walk "for the purpose of ascertaining his guilt in the crime for which he was convicted." Controversially, during this walk Rose determined Melville was actually innocent of stealing Castro's money. The truth may have been much stickier.[22]

Mortimer noted that in 1869 "a man came over for four years for larceny from Santa Cruz County...whom I will call Jim." Mortimer let on that of the money "Jim" stole, three thousand dollars was unaccounted for, and the common belief was that "Jim" had planted it. That "Jim" was actually John Melville adds up. Both "Jim" and John Melville were incarcerated in San Quentin State Prison in 1869, had been sentenced to four years for larceny, had robbed upward of $3,000, and hailed from Santa Cruz County. Strikingly, if Melville had not lost all of the $6,300 while gambling in Sacramento and had instead planted $3,000 of it before being arrested, it would account for Rose's walk with Melville and sudden change of heart. After all, Rose had taken a walk with Mortimer in 1864 in hopes of making him turn up his plant, and though it did not go the detective's way, in 1869 Rose may have figured Melville was no Mortimer. In all likelihood he left his coat unbuttoned. If a deal was struck between Melville and Rose, a significant part may have involved Rose making public his belief that Melville was innocent.

Sensing blood in the water, the *Sentinel* ridiculed the former police detective for his assertion that the arrest of Melville, which he himself had facilitated, had been a miscarriage of justice. The *Sentinel* described Sheriff Lincoln as efficient and capable, Rose as less than useless. Ultimately, this criticism may have eaten at Rose. He soon left California altogether, trading San Francisco for Salt Lake City. Time would tell if that decision would be for good or ill. Whether or not he had any of the planted three thousand dollars was up for debate. As for Mortimer, if he desired the missing money that John Melville/J. M./Jim was rumored to have planted, circumstances conspired to put him in the hunt.[23]

The man who sought to use Mortimer as a pawn in his own game was none other than Captain of the Guard Robert C. Gilchrist. Gilchrist, born in Pennsylvania during the late 1820s, had been swept into San Quentin during the Democratic wave that dominated California politics in the late 1860s. "His reputation as officer varied—at times he was in favor with the public, and then again he would be in a fog," Mortimer noted.[24]

Just prior to Melville's arrest, Gilchrist had made great strides within and without San Quentin. On December 6 Gilchrist wrote to Dr. William T. Lucky, the principal of the state Normal School, declaring that he was "trying an experiment to-day, for the first time in this prison. I have just started a school, and notified all the prisoners who cannot read or write to assemble in the dining-room.... My object ... is to try and have you get me a good supply of spelling books, small slates, pencils, pens and papers."

Five days later the *Examiner* published the letter, including a glowing write-up of Gilchrist: "Captain Gilchrist is spoken of in high terms as a kind man, both by the convicts now in prison and many who have been discharged, as well as by those who are acquainted with him."[25]

But while Gilchrist earned favor with the public and many of the prisoners, to Mortimer he showed his true colors. Hearing of the planted three thousand dollars, he instructed his bookkeeper to determine where the money had been hidden. Gilchrist's bookkeeper and Mortimer were friendly, and Mortimer was persuaded to help in what Mortimer called "Gilchrist's scheme."

"I then took lead in the matter," Mortimer recalled. "When I came to talk to the Santa Cruz man ... my feelings warmed towards him, for I found him one of the boys of the old school. I at once warned him of the Gilchrist plot."

Having thrown in together, Mortimer and "Jim" hatched a plan to one day rob the Santa Cruz Treasury. "We finally agreed to meet on the outside world at some future time and arrange the matter," Mortimer noted.[26]

Meanwhile, in the spring of 1869 both Mortimer and Gilchrist found themselves within the pages of the *San Francisco Chronicle* after a reporter visited the prison in March. Of the ten hardened criminals who the reporter felt were noteworthy, Mortimer was the first one mentioned. "[H]e is well known as a bad and desperate man ... now he runs a sewing machine for the benefit of the State. He looks healthy, and says the world owes him a living."

As for Gilchrist, he was described favorably. By refusing to act as the whipping master, and by seeing that the prisoners were educated, it was said that he had brought about a noticeable change "in the conduct of the men stained with guilt and hardened by crime."[27]

Mortimer didn't buy Gilchrist's act, recalling the duplicitous manner with which he tried to use him to ferret out where "Jim" had planted the treasure. Mortimer recalled, "A few months later the Supreme Court granted him a new trial." That Melville was granted a new trial in September 1869 also corroborates the theory that "Jim" and John Melville were the same person.[28]

"[Gilchrist] was very sore about it," Mortimer remembered, "and threatened to make it hot for Jim if he was sent back. He also held me responsible for his failure, but he could not fix it on me then. Jim did not come back." Coincidentally, John Melville was acquitted of the crime on January 6, 1870, walking out of the Santa Cruz Courthouse a free man.[29]

Shortly after Melville had been released from prison, Gilchrist puzzled out how he'd failed to get ahold of the planted money. "Gil," as Mortimer disparagingly referred to him, "then began to make my prison life a little more unpleasant. I stood this patiently, but kept my eyes open. It was very essential that I should keep quiet for if I made one misstep Gilchrist would have my 'benefit' taken from me, which now amounted to eleven months."

Friends of Mortimer warned him that, given the least provocation, Gilchrist intended to strip him of his "benefit"—time off for good behavior. As the time of his release neared, Mortimer became more and more careful. At the same time, Gilchrist became more and more desperate.

"He finally began to despair; he then set his stools to work to put up jobs on me, but I outgeneraled them all," Mortimer boasted.[30]

As the months passed, prisoner and jailor continued to carefully watch each other. Convinced Gilchrist meant to deny him his benefit, even without provocation, Mortimer hinted to the turnkey, Len Harris, that it would be in Gilchrist's best interest to count Mortimer as a friend. After all, any newspaperman worth his salt would love to print a story from the infamous Mortimer. In October 1870 the *Chronicle* even ran a long exposé on Mortimer's life of crime, interviewing Officer Bohen. "He is a bad egg, and wants a deal of tender watching lest he should break," Bohen concluded.[31]

A potential follow-up article, where Mortimer exposed how the "honorable" Captain R. C. Gilchrist was actually a two-faced schemer, as rotten as any convict in San Quentin, would certainly make good copy. Faced with this possibility, Gilchrist "cooled off a little," Mortimer reflected, but still continued to oppress him.[32]

Inevitably, things came to a head. "In about three months the thing became so rough I told all I knew about Gilchrist to some guards, and so it all came out," Mortimer related. "Mr. Shone of Petaluma was one of the men who knew all about it. The result was Gilchrist locked me up in solitary confinement for the last three months of my time, and no one was allowed to speak to me."

Of all the cells Mortimer had occupied in San Quentin, he liked his private room the best. At the same time he noted that this served Gilchrist's ends as well, for no citizen was able to speak to Mortimer. Eventually—having served six years—Mortimer's time was up. He was taken from his cell and exchanged his prison stripes for civilian clothing. It was there that "Captain Gilchrist came in and talked as rough to me as he dared to, but he cooled when I warned him, when the guards' backs were turned."[33]

On the day Mortimer was discharged—Mortimer does not give the exact date, specifying only January 1871—he was paid the standard three dollars. He was also arrested by Police Captain James Towle, who had previously done a stretch as the captain of the guard at San Quentin. The matter was the Wiggin case.

Mortimer was lodged in the San Francisco City Jail, where his jailor, one of the many men with the surname "Kelly" on the police force, treated him "with great kindness." Mortimer retained George W. Tyler as his attorney, whom Mortimer described as an able counselor. Small wonder Mortimer liked him, for Tyler made the most of George W. Rose staying in Salt Lake City rather than coming back to San Francisco to testify against him. With the prosecution unable to call their key witness, Tyler managed to have the case indefinitely postponed.[34]

"When I was discharged Mr. Kelly gave me some money and advised me for my best good," Mortimer recollected. "He wished me to get employment, to keep steady money afterwards. I paid a little back, but I owe him much yet. And if I never pay it, I beseech him to forgive the debt."

After leaving the city jail, Mortimer called on his attorney, Tyler. Tyler, too, gave Mortimer some money and good counsel.

"I then went into the world," Mortimer scribbled.[35]

Edmund Mortimer, locked in the Tower of London, declared in Act 2, Scene 5 of Shakespeare's *Henry VI, Part I*, "Even like a man new haled from the rack, / So fare my limbs: with long imprisonment." Charles Mortimer, weakened by his years of incarceration, felt much the same. "I was bewildered," he admitted. "I must have felt and appeared much as a cat does in a strange garret."[36]

Mortimer tried to find employment at several San Francisco locales. One such was Michael Short's tailor shop on the corner of Commercial and Leidsdorff. When Short asked Mortimer where he last worked, Mortimer lied, giving the name of a different tailor shop. Short told him he employed a man who had worked there, and that Mortimer should come to work the next morning. Realizing his lie would be found out when he met the other employee, Mortimer did not show up to work in the morning.

While roaming the city Mortimer ran into an old acquaintance who invited him to his room. Mortimer stayed there for a few days. While there, he learned that a sick woman named Tilly was in a nearby room. Mortimer called on her and learned her story. She'd been brought from Petaluma to San Francisco by a woman named Silvey, who operated a bordello in Petaluma. When Tilly had gotten sick, Silvey took her to this house, paid a week's rent, and left her to fend for herself.

"I went and got a physician for her, Dr. Johnson, and at her and others request I watched with her that night," Mortimer recollected.

That evening a knock came at the door. After Tilly asked Mortimer to see who it was, Mortimer opened the door to find standing before him an old acquaintance, Joe McQuillan, then working as a longshoreman. McQuillan had a bundle with him and wished to leave it in the room. Tilly permitted him to do so. The next morning Mortimer went to a drugstore to bring back medicine for Tilly. When he returned he found two police officers waiting inside her room: James Gannon and Daniel Coffey.

Gannon and Coffey placed Mortimer under arrest. The bundle, it was revealed, contained clothing stolen from a printer at the *Chronicle*. Mortimer tried to explain that it wasn't his, and Tilly backed up his story, but the policemen "declared that too thin" and brought him to the station house. They kept him there for over a week. Meanwhile, Tilly, the landlady, and some others found the printer at the *Chronicle* and told their side of the story. Afterward, the printer refused to press charges, and Mortimer was freed. Calling on the printer to thank him, Mortimer learned that the policemen had been angry with the printer.

At large again, Mortimer still had the same problem: lack of gainful employment. "Long confinement had me weak and I could not do hard work," Mortimer related. "My purse was light and I was at a loss what to do."[37]

Hounded by the police and shunned as a jailbird by the good citizens of San Francisco, Mortimer ultimately decided to take on the role that suited him best: playing the villain. Entering a political meeting, he attempted to lift a man's watch but failed. The unsuspecting man left with a group of others and headed to a saloon on Kearny Street. Mortimer shadowed him. Afterward he walked up Geary Street toward Union Park (present-day Union Square).

"I overtook him and walked and talked," Mortimer related. Mortimer noted that the man gave his name as "Henmerman." Although no one by that name appeared in *The San Francisco Directory*, it is likely that between Mortimer's memory and the man's drunken slurring, this was actually Richard Hemmelmann, whose dwelling on the corner of Battery and Pacific was a mile northeast of Union Park, in the direction he was walking. That Mortimer elsewhere gave his name as "Mr. H." also inferred that Mortimer might have been a bit unclear on the man's real name.

Mr. H told Mortimer that he had been a pioneer in the 1850s, had been part of the San Francisco Vigilantes, and kept a broker's office near Dunbar Alley, on Washington Street. Ultimately, they reached Mr. H's house, a small, framed building ten feet from the street.

"I bid him good night and he went in. I then discovered that I had a watch and chain," Mortimer recalled. Mortimer lamented that he might have returned the watch and chain to Mr. H, but, unfortunately, because of the man's history as a vigilante, it might not have been safe to do so.

A few nights later Mortimer entered a saloon on Montgomery Street to have a drink. There he acquainted himself with Lieutenant William Stanton, stationed at the Presidio, and a major. The soldiers joined Mortimer for a "social glass," but when they suggested another Mortimer excused himself by saying it was his bedtime.

"But before parting Mr. Stanton's watch and chain had got into my possession. It was useless to think of restoring it to him that night," Mortimer reasoned, "as he seemed determined to make a night of it regardless of my counsels."[38]

Mortimer "met with one or two like adventures" until April 29, 1871. On that day William Randolph Hearst, the future media tycoon, celebrated his eighth birthday in San Francisco. In New York City, Robber Baron Jay Gould was found in contempt of court for refusing to hand over the Erie Railway Company books. And in Paris, where the antireligious army of radical socialists known as the Paris Commune had enacted a revolution, heavy fighting poured into the streets.

But none of that was anything to Mortimer. For on that particular night the most significant event of his life took place, one that sent him careening on a trajectory filled with lust, love, betrayal, murder, and tragedy. For that was the day he first met Carrie.[39]

CHAPTER 6

Lovestruck

*T*hat Mortimer considered Kate Dunn's saloon the pits didn't stop him from approaching it. At about 11:30 p.m. on April 29 Mortimer entered the notorious Kearny Street saloon, his eye lighting on Kate's newest girl. "She looked tired and sick," Mortimer recalled. But there was something about her. At midnight the front of the saloon closed, and about ten or twelve of the patrons and girls went to the back rooms. By chance, Mortimer sat next to the new girl. After calling for drinks, the pair engaged in conversation. Some time passed before the new girl asked if she could lay her head on Mortimer's shoulder. Mortimer obliged. "[S]he felt so tired," Mortimer wrote, "but could not leave till the customers did."[1]

Mortimer quickly learned the girl's name was Carrie and that she and her two-year-old baby boy had arrived in San Francisco about ten days earlier with a blacksmith. They took rooms across from Kate Dunn's saloon, but the smith soon abandoned her, stealing her watch, chain, and thirty dollars. To her name, which she claimed was Spencer, she'd been left only $1.50 to support her and her child. To make ends meet she'd ventured into the saloon on April 26. Kate told her she'd have an easy time picking up customers. Attractive, long-legged, and about twenty-four years old, this was likely true.[2]

"I frankly told the 'new girl' she was in one of the worst holes in the city, and in a bad business," Mortimer related.

When Carrie asked his business, Mortimer replied that it was "not better than hers," that he was a "cross-man," having been just released from San Quentin. When Carrie asked if he had a woman, he replied he did not. When she asked if he would take her as his woman, Mortimer replied he would see.

"She was as yet inexperienced in the calling she had entered upon. I advised her while yet there was time to try and get a place in some family in the country. I begged her to reflect, and think of the life she was going to lead before her child."

A sucker for hard-luck cases, Mortimer promised he would help see her established and would not quit till he succeeded.

"Have you a room for the night, Carrie?" Mortimer asked.

"Yes," Carrie replied. "I have two or three dollars and room, but can't I go to your room tonight?"

"No," Mortimer answered, "I have some business to attend to, but I'll see you in the morning. Come now, go to your baby, and rest assured I will do by you as I have promised."

Mortimer then left to "look after a small 'job' . . . in the 'Valley.'" At dawn he made it to the Pacific Lodging House on Kearny Street. Walking to his room, he heard through a door a child "crying as though its little heart would break." Mortimer knocked on the door. When there came no answer he tried the door. Finding it locked he looked through the keyhole. There was no key. Unhappily, he left the situation alone. But on his way to breakfast he ran into Carrie, who had her child in her arms. She'd been visiting the room of Billy Lear, a "cross-man" who had served one prison stretch, and had left the child alone. Mortimer asked her if she'd like breakfast.

"Yes," Carrie answered.

"I got cake and playthings for the child and put it in my room, and took Carrie to breakfast. On our return we talked over her future. I soon found how poor she was." Carrie had all but one dress, no cloak or shawl, an old alpaca, and few undergarments. The child had even fewer possessions, just the clothes on his back. Mortimer got from Carrie that she also had "two loathsome diseases; one was at its worst form."

"Charley," Carrie cried, "help me—pity me! I do not know what to do or where to go. Help me, and I will devote the balance of my life to your happiness. You may find women better educated, but you will find not one who will be more true to you than I will be."

Reflecting on all the pain he had suffered over the last several years, Mortimer was moved to pity. His heart having warmed toward her and her child, that same day—Sunday, April 30—he led them to Mrs. Deneson's on the corner of Broadway and Pinckney Place. Mrs. Deneson was "a poor, but good woman," Mortimer judged, and the room he rented was superior to Kate Dunn's and the Pacific Lodging House. There he found her good doctors, Johnson and White. Along with the two diseases she knew about, they diagnosed her with another illness. All of this reduced her to a low level. Mortimer nursed her day and night.

"Her condition called for the kindest of care," Mortimer reflected, "and had she been some devoted friend of long years standing, I could not have done more for her."[3]

Carrie certainly needed a caretaker just then. Caroline Jones had been born in 1847 in New York to William Daniel Jones and his wife. When Jones caught gold fever in 1849, he took his family with him to California. Their lives as argonauts didn't pan out, and by the late 1850s the Jones family was living in a farmhouse on Westside Road, Dry Creek, outside Healdsburg, whose population was eight hundred. Despite her good country upbringing, at fourteen Carrie became involved with an older man, J. R. Wardell, also known as Wordell or Weddle. When Carrie became pregnant, her parents reluctantly agreed to the shotgun wedding, and on August 26, 1862, fifteen-year-old Carrie married thirty-two-year-old J. R. in Santa Rosa. The marriage lasted all of two years.

Having a penchant for attracting lusty men with checkered pasts, Carrie drifted south, taking on the name Spencer. In time she gave birth to two more children, bringing her brood to three. One died, one was elsewhere by the time she met Mortimer, and the last she struggled to keep fed.[4]

Within a couple months of Mortimer seeing to her needs, Carrie partially recovered, although Mortimer was now somewhat sick himself. Mortimer thought traveling would prove "beneficial"—and he hadn't forgotten the pledge he and "Jim" had made to rob the Santa Cruz Treasury. In June 1871, after leaving the baby in the care of someone in San Francisco, they headed eighty miles south, shuffling between Santa Cruz, Soquel, and Watsonville. Carrie now went by Carrie Mortimer. Although technically a common-law marriage, in the first week of July the lovers honeymooned with John Melville in Soquel, for whom Mortimer began working.[5]

Melville later recalled, "He came to me sick and I gave him shelter. . . . He made mention of Mr. Effey's jewelry store and said it was a rich thing. He was posted about the town. . . . He promised he would commit no depredations while at my house."[6]

Regardless of Mortimer's promise, William Effey's jewelry store on Santa Cruz's Front Street was soon burglarized. On July 4 Mortimer and Carrie were arrested in Watsonville by a Mr. Nevils in connection with the jewelry store break-in. Apparently, the evidence against them was too thin. Let go, the lovebirds—Charley a jailbird and Carrie a soiled dove—migrated north. According to Melville, on either the 2nd or 3rd of August, Mortimer and Carrie left Santa Cruz County for San Francisco.

Calling on the child, they learned that he had been missing for weeks.

"I then exerted all my energy to find her child. I traced him to the station house."[7]

Mortimer appealed to Chief of Police Patrick Crowley, a forty-year-old New Yorker of Irish ancestry who sailed to California in 1850, and in 1866 defeated Isaiah Lees for the position of chief. Crowley knew Mortimer well, and when he realized that the child's mother was living with the notorious thief, Crowley refused to give him any information on the child's whereabouts. Crowley's motivation, according to Mortimer, was to settle some old scores. The wily chief figured that so long as the baby was lost to them, somewhere in San Francisco, Mortimer would likely be kept busy searching for him.[8]

"He was correct, for if we (more properly speaking, I; for I truly believe I felt warmer and more earnest desire to find the child than its mother did—he was a pretty boy two years old) had recovered the boy, I should have left the State that Fall and never returned to it."

Although Mortimer claims he was more desirous to find the child than Carrie, it is strange that he does not name the child in his memoir—unless it was his desire to protect the innocent. As it happened, Mortimer and Carrie abandoned San Francisco (and the search for the boy) in the fall, heading to Sacramento.

"I wished to stop roving and try a different mode of life," Mortimer reasoned.[9]

Mortimer didn't mention—although the *San Francisco Chronicle* did—that in late September a bench warrant was issued in San Francisco for his arrest, and that his trial was slated for September 29. The likelihood is that this was the Wiggin robbery again resurfacing; even without Rose to testify, the police wanted to keep Mortimer tied up in the courts as much as possible, forcing him into plain sight rather than allowing him to operate in the shadows.[10]

Despite the warrant for his arrest in San Francisco, Mortimer and Carrie made it to Sacramento unmolested, renting a hotel room near the corner of K and Tenth.

The capital had certainly changed since Mortimer had last seen it. In February of 1864 Sacramento boasted a population of about 12,500. Although not as populous or prosperous as San Francisco, by the fall of 1871 Sacramento's population had doubled to 25,000, and the evidence of industry could everywhere be seen. Cobblestone pavement had been introduced to curb flooding. The domed capitol building dominated the formerly empty grounds between L and M, and Tenth and Twelfth. Blacksmiths, butchers, and stablemen now had over fifty saloons in which they could wet their whistles. The young men who had gone West had made Sacramento a thriving metropolis.[11]

Commented Mark Twain, "It was in this Sacramento Valley . . . that a deal of the most lucrative of the early gold mining was done. . . . It was a driving, vigorous, restless population . . . none but erect, bright-eyed, quick-moving, strong-handed young giants."[12]

Perhaps as a testament to his desire to go straight, instead of spending a few days working the Sacramento saloons, Mortimer decided to leave early the next morning for the lower Stockton and river roads, eight miles away. His intention was to meet a Mr. Foster who lived thereabouts and with whom Mortimer had an agreement. Mortimer had thought it best to leave Carrie behind at the hotel, later bringing her back when Foster had business in Sacramento. Carrie thought differently. Insisting that she come along, Carrie eventually wrangled Mortimer's consent, even though it meant she would have to walk.

Halfway to Foster's, Carrie revealed why she'd insisted on going: she had filched one of the landlady's dresses. Mortimer thought it "a foolish trick" and griped that when he went to town, someone might recognize him and cause trouble.

Sure enough, three or four days later Mortimer accompanied Foster to the capital. Nearly thirty minutes later the landlord accosted him. He wanted that dress.

"I put on a bold face, denied all knowledge of the matter, but he was not to be shaken in that way," Mortimer lamented. "[U]nless he could be indemnified he was going to make trouble."

Mortimer knew that if a search warrant was produced the dress would be found in their room. Seeing no other option, Mortimer offered twenty-five dollars for the dress. The landlord agreed and, pledging he would repay him, Mortimer borrowed twenty-five dollars from Foster. This money he handed over to the landlord.

"I swear I am ashamed to say it, but Mr. Foster never has been paid," Mortimer recalled. "The work I was wanted to do came hard on me at first, but I was resolved to do my best, and I think I should have given satisfaction, but Mr. Foster thought we were a weak team for his business. He thought Carrie too delicate, lazy or something also."[13]

Having struck out at the outskirts of Sacramento, Mortimer and Carrie pushed twenty-three miles east, trying their luck near the Cosumnes River, on Jackson Road. Acting as the main thoroughfare in the late 1840s and 1850s between Sacramento and the flourishing southern mines, Jackson Road continued to be vital in the 1870s, linking the capital with the ranches and farms irrigated by the Cosumnes River. On Jackson Road, under the alias of Butler, Mortimer found work as a lumberjack, chopping a tree for Barney O'Neill, described by the *Sacramento Bee* as "a too genial rancher."[14]

O'Neill noted that "Butler" seemed unused to work. After two or three days, O'Neill's new lumberjack brought in a woman, who introduced herself as Carrie Jones of Amador County.[15]

After four or five days their footloose nature got the best of them. "One day I concluded to leave for Sutter in the next morning," Mortimer noted. Only twenty-five miles east, Sutter Creek was at this time still called "Sutter." This was the heart of the old gold rush, where two thousand men and women eked out a living, many of whom still brought gold out of the mines. Mortimer saw no reason some of that Sutter gold couldn't find its way into his pockets.[16]

That evening Mortimer traveled three miles to Blair's country house, on the river, and made arrangements with a man who, after extensive haggling, promised to take them there by wagon. Within a half-mile from where he'd been staying on Jackson Road, at about three in the morning, he ran into Carrie. Mortimer expressed surprise at meeting her at that time. Carrie, of course, accounted for her actions.

"I went through the drawers in the room we were sleeping in, and found a lot of money," Carrie explained.

Shades of the dress Mrs. Mortimer had filched less than two weeks ago, Mortimer had to caution her that "it would be missed." This time Mortimer reasoned he could put the money back before anyone noticed.

"I knew the money was there," Mortimer told Carrie, and explained that once he'd shuffled her off to where she could not be implicated in the crime, he intended to double-back and steal it. Carrie didn't like this, however, insisting on keeping the money.[17]

At least that's the way Mortimer told it.

A reporter for the *Sacramento Bee*, writing a year and a half later, agreed that, yes, in the fall of 1871 Mortimer and Carrie worked for Barney O'Neill for a few days. But as to Carrie having committed the crime, the reporter's story diverged: "The last day Charley went to a neighbor's; caroused and gambled all day and night; and early the following morning returned to O'Neill's house, with all his evil passions inflamed by his long course of grog, entered through a window, rifled the drawers and, with Carrie, started out."[18]

Regardless of which of them burgled O'Neill's drawers, Mortimer knew it was time to hotfoot it out of town. They made it to Blair's, but things were slow. Getting the team situated took time. Husband and wife settled in for a pensive breakfast inside the country house as the sun grew higher in the sky.

Meanwhile, O'Neill became suspicious when he found Mortimer and Carrie absent. On entering their room, he found it ransacked. Mounting a horse, O'Neill set off for Blair's, riding up to the country house just as Mortimer and Carrie finished breakfast.

"I have been robbed! I have been robbed!" O'Neil cried out. "That damn bitch has robbed me and ran away."

Blair, who saw no reason to keep Mortimer's whereabouts a secret, admitted they were in the house. When Barney O'Neill stormed inside he made "a terrible fuss," as Mortimer described. "Carrie and I finally got him to our room. I got some whisky. We talked matters over and Carrie gave up the money, and we made arrangements with Barney to take us over to Sutter. We all got into a wagon and were driven back to Barney's. Barney and I sat beside each other in the bottom of the wagon, and while on our way I managed to get about sixty dollars of money out of Barney's pocket."

Drinking freely, Mortimer and O'Neill were intoxicated when they reached his place. O'Neill managed to hitch up the team before climbing into bed and falling into a drunken stupor. Leaving him snoozing, Mortimer, Carrie, and two others started for Sutter. They'd made it about two miles when they came upon a two-hundred-yard stretch of water. Attempting to ford it, they were nearly through when one of the horses lost its footing. Mortimer and the others rushed to drag the horse to dry land. Once on the other side, they failed to coax the horse to its feet; apparently it was sick. One of the men mounted a horse and rode back to O'Neill's for help.

Mortimer, afraid O'Neill might discover he'd been robbed again, wasn't about to wait for the rancher's return. To the man tending the sick horse, Mortimer stated that he would take Carrie to a farmhouse a half-mile off and return. This was only half a lie. Reaching the farmhouse, they got a man to drive them about twelve miles northeast to Latrobe. From there they boarded a train car back to Sacramento proper. In the capital they stopped at a brick hotel between L and K for a couple hours while arranging to take a ship to San Francisco.[19]

"The lady let Carrie go in her bed room to arrange her clothes," Mortimer recalled. "While there she went through some of the drawers and took two little savings banks—such as children have. I expected every moment to have trouble about them. There was no possible show to get them from her without others in the setting room would notice it."

To Mortimer's great relief, they managed to board the ship without anyone the wiser.

"She will do most anything," Mortimer reflected. "She has the nerve, but she has very little forethought—her caution is small."

The day after arriving in San Francisco they left for Healdsburg, eighty miles north of the Bay City. The likelihood is they took the train, for it connected San Francisco and Healdsburg earlier in 1871. They stayed in that small town the night they arrived, the next day traveling six miles up Dry Creek to her father's farmhouse.

"Her father and brother did not give her a very warm reception," Mortimer commented.

One evening Mortimer and Carrie whiled away the hours with Carrie's sister, who lived a mile away from her father's. They returned at about ten o'clock at night, finding the doors locked. When no one answered their knocks, Mortimer and Carrie went to the barn and slept in the hay. At some point, Carrie's brother intimated, in a private conversation with Mortimer, that Mortimer did not know his sister as well as he did. Two days later, Mortimer and Carrie left for greener pastures. "Her father bid her a somewhat cool farewell—none of the others did," Mortimer recalled.

From her father's farmhouse Mortimer and Carrie headed south, stopping a couple of miles from Healdsburg at the Stewarts. Mortimer assisted Stewart in building a house in town. When it was habitable, the family moved in. Leaving Carrie with Mrs. Stewart, and with his goal to raise enough money that they could afford their own place, Mortimer got a job at Elias Jacobs's tailoring shop. Having monopolized the tailoring business in Healdsburg, Jacobs could afford the three dollars a day wages he paid Mortimer. Unfortunately, while Mortimer returned to his oldest profession, Carrie may have returned to hers.[20]

"Carrie got into some fuss there," as Mortimer remembered. On top of that, Mrs. Stewart heard the neighbors' stories of Carrie's conduct when she'd previously visited Healdsburg. This was news to Mortimer, who had believed Carrie when she'd told him she'd always conducted herself properly in town. In any event, Mrs. Stewart tossed Carrie out. With nowhere to go, Carrie turned up at the tailor shop. Mortimer let her stay at his boardinghouse.

Four or five days later the landlord told Mortimer he'd have to find another place to stay. Mortimer demanded an explanation. It wasn't what he wanted to hear.

"He told me the boarders were talking about my wife's conduct while I was at work," Mortimer recalled. "He told me there was no chance for a doubt in regards to the truth."

That night they moved to Hicks's boardinghouse. They stayed there for all of four days before the landlady told Mortimer they had to move. Mortimer asked Hicks what the problem was. It was more of the same. "He told me Carrie was making so free with the boarders that it was giving the house a bad name. He allowed me time to get a place. I commenced to drink and neglect my work."

Mortimer spent two or three days intoxicated. Healdsburg had proved hopeless. He didn't have the money to rent and furnish a house, and all the boardinghouses were shut to them. After the liquor wore off Mortimer and Carrie returned to San Francisco.

Fortunately, things had worked in his favor in the Bay City. Mortimer's attorney George W. Tyler managed to get the Wiggin case thrown out. The charge that had been hanging over him for years was finally lifted. But other than that there was little to celebrate. With his funds low, on about January 10, 1872, Mortimer rented a room for and Carrie and himself in the "Valley," on the corner of Hunt and Third.

With his money running out, and having failed abysmally to walk the straight and narrow, Mortimer returned to the crooked side of the street. On the night of either January 11 or 12 he filched a gold watch and nearly two hundred dollars. Not long after he sent Carrie to Santa Cruz to check on something connected with the treasury job he was still planning. On January 18 Mortimer was three-quarters of a mile north of his rented room, in the Russ House on Bush and Montgomery, when he heard about "a good thing" in Virginia City. Carrie returned from Santa Cruz on January 21. Although the weather had been too cold for her, she'd found prospects in Santa Cruz brighter than Mortimer had expected. Feeling Virginia City might actually be the better score—and possibly needing a longer break from his wife—Mortimer next sent Carrie to the Comstock Lode.[21]

On January 26 Mortimer chummed in with a man named Ferguson. In Mortimer's room they drank freely. The next morning, leaving Ferguson in his room, Mortimer stopped by Wells Fargo & Co. and the post office. As he expected there was a letter waiting for him from Santa Cruz. It stated that he and another convict Mortimer was acquainted with—whom Mortimer gave the alias "John Folensbee"—were to rendezvous in Alameda. Afterward, they were to travel to Santa Cruz, and on the night of February 2, between eight o'clock and half past nine, they were to be in the vicinity of the Santa Cruz Treasury. Sauntering back to his room, Mortimer fell in with a man, and together they entered a saloon.

"While there I had occasion to feel in my breast pocket for something and drew out a six-inch blade knife in a scabbard," Mortimer scribbled.

If Mortimer intended robbery, his companion was too quick for him. The man seized Mortimer and cried out that he'd been assaulted. In a rush Mortimer was taken to the station house and locked up by Officer Michael Fitzgerald. That same day, while incarcerated, Mortimer was visited by an old "con." The man asked him who was in his room. Mortimer told him it was Ferguson, and to not meddle with him. But the convict paid no heed.

Sometime later Ferguson appeared. His watch and chain had been stolen, and he accused Mortimer of stealing it. Mortimer demonstrated that if he'd desired his watch and chain, he could have stolen it long ago. Mortimer also told Ferguson that if he didn't press charges, he'd see it was returned, but if he insisted on pressing charges, he'd never see it again.

Ferguson left him, but he soon returned, telling Mortimer that the policemen were forcing him to make the charge. Mortimer begged him not press charges, declaring he'd be put in jail for six months to a year if he did so. While Ferguson mulled it over, Mortimer was taken to Police Court.[22] As Mark Twain noted, this was a brick building, about twenty-four by forty feet in size, with a noticeable lack of ventilation.

"Police Court . . . smell[s] like a polecat, like a slaughter-house . . . like a graveyard after an earthquake," reported Twain.

Twain went on to note that—within this "Black Hole of Calcutta"—there was a collection of "drunken filthy loafers, thieves, prostitutes, China chicken-stealers, witnesses, and slimy guttersnipes . . . four feet deep, a solid mass of rotting, steaming corruption."[23]

While in Police Court Ferguson's inner pendulum swung toward Mortimer. He swore that he could not be sure if Mortimer had taken the watch and did not want him prosecuted.

Seeing the robbery angle disintegrate, and unable to make the assault charge stick, Mortimer was released. Together he and Ferguson went to Squarza's punch rooms at 120 Leidesdorff Street. As they entered, Mortimer spied his old friend who had robbed Ferguson in his sleep sitting in one of the reading rooms. At once the man got up and left, leaving a package on the table. Mortimer and Ferguson sat down at his table. Opening the package, Ferguson found inside his watch and chain.

"We parted on best of terms," Mortimer noted. "I have seen him once or twice since, but not to speak to him."[24]

Later that day, January 27, Mortimer tried to return to his room, but the landlady refused to admit him. Ferguson, as it happened, had soiled the bed. Adding fuel to the fire, the officers had informed her that Mortimer was a thief. If she doubted this, all the officers had to do was show her the third page of the *San Francisco Chronicle*, which contained a brief description of Mortimer's latest misadventure: "Chas. Mortimer was arrested yesterday charged with stealing a watch from a drunken man, whom he was 'seeing home.'" Mortimer was only allowed to gather his things after paying expenses: five dollars. Afterward, Mortimer walked the city until dark—Mortimer's favorite time to be out.[25]

"I overtook a man in the evening on Battery street, near Market, going towards Broadway," Mortimer recalled. "We got acquainted and wakled [sic] together. He talked about steamboats, and I was much *interested*. Finally I left, with a watch and chain better off than when I met him. I stowed that safely away. Not being sleepy I looked around further."

Venturing into a saloon, Mortimer began chatting amiably with a "gent" who had been hitting the sauce with gusto. Walking out together, they stopped at the corner of Stockton and Geary. There, Mortimer pointed out the back of a residence, claimed it was his, and invited the man over. It was while they were approaching the rear of the house that the man slipped and fell.

"I lifted him up very indignant," Mortimer recollected, "and told him I could never take a man before my family in that condition. I helped him up, but in doing so my hand accidentally slipped into his pocket and his purse stuck to my fingers. I could not shake it off till I put my hand into my own pocket. I sat him against a wall, but in the act his watch and chain got tangled in my fingers, too. My friend took a nap and I took a walk."

Approaching morning, Mortimer was walking up Kearny Street when he happened to see Carrie, having just returned from Virginia City. She reported that the criminal plan Mortimer was hatching on the Comstock looked promising. Content, Mortimer and Carrie booked a room on Montgomery, north of Broadway. On January 31 Mortimer went across the Bay to Alameda, meeting up with "John Folensbee." He and his old companion determined they would travel separately to Santa Cruz, pledging to meet two days later at the agreed upon time and place. Mortimer also got word to Carrie's uncle, Bill, himself a fellow pickpocket. Planning to be gone some time, Mortimer hoped Uncle Bill would look after his niece.

From Alameda, Mortimer made it to Santa Clara, where he stayed the night with a friend from San Quentin, "Henry Foster," also in on the plot. The next morning they hitched a two-horse team and started for Santa Cruz and, if all went according to plan, the greatest score of Mortimer's criminal career.[26]

The Santa Cruz Treasury Job

Mortimer—armed with a Colt six-shooter, a Sharps four-shooter, and a knife—reached Santa Cruz on February 2, 1872, at about six o'clock in the evening. After paying his friend one hundred dollars for the ride, he ventured to a saloon in the upper part of town. Next, he visited a watering hole near the Flatiron Building, at 1550 Pacific Avenue, before walking diagonally down the street to a third saloon across from the Franklin House. There he took his third drink of the evening. Afterward, Mortimer crept a little less than a quarter mile southeast. At eight o'clock he was at his post, near the corner of Pacific and Cooper, watching the "Cooper House."[1]

Built in 1866 by Santa Cruz pioneers John L. Cooper and William F. Cooper— distantly related to author James Fenimore Cooper—the two-story structure was made of yellow brick, located a quarter mile west of the San Lorenzo River and a mile north of Monterey Bay. With stone trim, a white picket fence, and wooden plank sidewalks, the Cooper House served as Santa Cruz's first courthouse, and certainly its opulence reflected the pride the residents of Santa Cruz felt for it. On July 20, 1867, the *Santa Cruz Sentinel* noted, "No finer courthouse for the money was ever erected in the State." The next year further improvements were made, including the installation of a twelve-light chandelier in the dead center of the building and the addition of cocoa matting to the courtroom floor. It was no small wonder the building was so luxurious, for along with inhabiting the County Courthouse the Cooper House also boasted the Santa Cruz Treasury.[2]

From Mortimer's position outside the Cooper House, he kept his eyes on a shadowy figure he could see moving about the treasurer's office, partially illuminated by a light therein. A little before nine o'clock, a dozen or so men strolled out the courthouse doors and began walking in Mortimer's direction. Mortimer nonchalantly sauntered up the street. Returning, he was joined by Folensbee at nine o'clock. As it happened, Folensbee bore bad news.

Their man in Soquel, who had written the letter that put them together, had completely backed out. Although Mortimer sardonically dubbed him "John Doolittle" in his memoir, this was almost certainly "Jim," better known as John Melville. Folensbee explained that Doolittle, having spent time in San Quentin, determined that after the robbery he would be the first person the police would question. His best course of action, therefore, was to take no part in the caper. Instead, Doolittle planned to spend the night playing poker with friends, establishing an alibi. This left only Mortimer and Folensbee to pull off the job.

Mortimer shared his observations: a dimly lit individual in the treasurer's office, and the men who had left the courthouse scant minutes ago.

"How many were there?" Folensbee asked.

"I don't know," Mortimer replied. "Eight, ten, or a dozen—perhaps more."

"It don't matter whether they are in or out," Folensbee declared. "We must make an effort to beat this county out of a few cases to-night. I think I'll hang the bloke up."

"Yes, we must do the job to-night, if ever," Mortimer agreed, expressing concern that if Doolittle tipped off the "cops" they might be "collared." "There is no telling but that he has done so already."

"No, I am sure he was sincere in what he said to me," Folensbee reasoned. "He has been sent across twice, and he now weakens on the turn. You keep your lamps peeled on the place; I am cold, and will go and get a drink."

Mortimer resumed his watch on the Cooper House. Twenty minutes later Folensbee reappeared. To get a better look at the figure in the treasurer's office, Folensbee crept up to the windows. While Folensbee made his inspection, Mortimer kept his eyes on a man slowly leaving the Cooper House while engaged in conversation with S. W. Blakely, the County Treasurer, who was still inside. Shortly afterward, Folensbee returned to Mortimer's post, and the two compared notes. Folensbee had spied Blakely through the window.

"I think I'll hang Blakely up," Folensbee stated, warming to his task.

"No, don't you do so; you will have to be severe, and may silence him so long as to jeopardize ourselves," Mortimer said, cautioning his partner against "hanging" or "garroting" Blakely. "I feel satisfied there is no one else in the building, and we had better quit the business if we can't handle one man without hurting him. We will keep near the front door, and when he prepares to leave the office we will then suit ourselves to our circumstances."

A few minutes after ten o'clock, Blakely opened his office door. Before leaving, he stepped back inside to turn down the gas in the lamp—but at that moment someone caught his arms from behind. Almost simultaneously a pistol was jammed into his neck, and Blakely heard the gun cock.

"I wished B. to hear the 'music' of the click of the pistol," Mortimer scrawled, "to convince him that we meant business."

To Blakely, Mortimer said, "Keep quiet, and you shall not be hurt; it's the money we want, not you."

"I'll keep quiet; don't hurt me," the treasurer begged. Blakely could now see his assailants. One was taller than the other. Both wore hats and handkerchiefs to disguise their faces. Other than that, Blakely couldn't tell them from Adam.

When Mortimer told him to open his mouth, Blakely complied.

"I gagged him with handkerchiefs," Mortimer remembered. "Folensbee then led him to the vault-room. I put my pistol into the scabbard and locked the office door. I then went to the vault-room, closed the door, lit the dark-lantern, and then directed Blakeley to open the vault and safe, which he did."

Blakely hesitated when asked where the money was, before pointing toward a drawer. Inside was revealed silver.

"Damn the silver," Folensbee swore. "We want the gold. Where is it?"[3]

After Blakely opened the inside door, Folensbee helped himself to twenty-dollar gold pieces, stuffing the money into a barley sack and a leather bag Mortimer had brought with him. Leaving Folensbee to his work, Mortimer simultaneously watched the treasurer and inspected the front of the building to see if they'd been discovered. After securing the money, they stepped out of the vault room.[4]

"What shall we do with the bloke?" Mortimer asked.

"Slough him up with the gopher," Folensbee answered. Blakely probably had little idea that Folensbee was suggesting they lock him up in the vault, but Mortimer had spent years in San Quentin and along the mean streets of Sacramento and San Francisco. He knew the lingo. Still, he was worried that Blakely might perish in the vault.

"It's so close. Is there not danger of him scruging?" Mortimer asked.

"That's his affair. We must have the coast clear."

"I thought we could buck him and leave him in the room, and still be safe," Mortimer admitted to Folensbee. "But it is better to be sure than sorry. If the alarm should be given it would be all day with us, for there is a standing Vigilance Committee in this county."

Turning to Blakely, Mortimer tied his hands behind his back to ensure he couldn't open the vault or make noise by pounding. When Folensbee ordered him into the vault, Blakely did as commanded. The doors were then closed on the treasurer.

Rid of Blakely, Folensbee admitted, "Charlie, this swag is quite heavy. I'll put part of it in your sack and we'll whack it outside."[5]

While Folensbee loaded up the treasure, Mortimer went to see that all was quiet outside. Satisfied, the pair "sallied forth." At the edge of town, near a creek, Mortimer and Folensbee dumped the contents of their sack on the ground. Rolls of twenty dollar pieces—five hundred dollars in each roll—fell out. They counted and divided the money. According to the *Santa Cruz Weekly Sentinel*, all told the robbers stole $16,757. Mortimer thought the figure high, noting in his memoir there had been a little less than fourteen thousand.[6]

"I suppose you have your intended course laid out?" Mortimer asked.

"Yes," Folensbee replied. "I intend to take the coast route to San Francisco to-night, and to-morrow I'll go over to the ranch at Alameda."

"Very well. I'll return the way I came," Mortimer told him, "and if all goes well with me I will go over to your place Sunday to see that you are all right. But if I should not make my appearance you will then know that something has gone wrong with me. You must then ascertain without a moment's delay the nature of my trouble and come to the rescue. I will do likewise with you."

Separating, Mortimer soon found Henry about a mile from town, pacing by his team of horses to keep warm. Mortimer considered Henry a "staunch and true" friend and knew him to be a family man. That he'd mixed Henry up in the robbery, even though it had been successful, weighed on Mortimer. He pledged he would make it right. In the meantime they set off over the mountains.

"I laid down in the wagon and slept, and nearly $7,000 in coin composed my pillow," Mortimer reflected.

Near Los Gatos they reached a place familiar to Mortimer. There they stopped, Mortimer planting about four thousand dollars. The rest Mortimer kept with him in the wagon. Ultimately, they reached Henry's ranch.

"Take this, $1,000," Mortimer said to Henry. "Be cautious how you act and talk. In a short time there will be a great excitement about this matter, and there will be many spies about. You must avoid all suspicious actions."

Henry pledged that he would be careful, and that afternoon Mortimer set off for Mountain View. At dusk on the night of February 3—one day after the sensational robbery—Mortimer reached San Francisco. Having $2,000 on his person, he stashed $1,500 of it and called upon his former lawyer, George W. Tyler, with the intention of paying a debt.

"Where have you been the past three or four days?" Tyler asked him.

"Why do you look at me in that way?" Mortimer shot back. "And why do you think I have been anywhere?"

"You have been absent from the city, this I know," Tyler replied coolly, "and I should like to know where you have been."

"I have been at San Mateo, Redwood City and thereabouts," Mortimer lied.

"Have you not been in Santa Cruz County?"

"No, sir, I have not. Why do you ask?"[7]

As an answer Tyler handed him a copy of the *San Francisco Evening Bulletin*. By then the story had disseminated all over California. Two men had robbed the Santa Cruz Treasury and thrown S. W. Blakely, bound and gagged, into the vault they'd emptied. A janitor had discovered him in the morning. The work looked professional, the handiwork of what the newspapers called "San Francisco experts." None other than Captain Isaiah Lees was on the case.[8]

"What do you think of that?" Tyler demanded.

"I don't doubt but that it is correct."

"Yes, and you were one of those two masked men."

"I regret that you are mistaken," Mortimer lied glibly. "For I am in very great need of a few dollars to-night, and my principal business with you this evening is to see if you could not lend me a few dollars for a few days."

"Well, who do you think the parties were? You are somewhat acquainted with that class of men."

"Well, it's my opinion that Blakely did it, and the two masked men are only a blind."

"But he could not lock himself in the vault, and him tied."

"He must have had an accomplice," Mortimer reasoned. "Some confidential friend, perhaps his wife. She would answer the purpose, and in most cases would prove most reliable."

Gradually, Mortimer felt Tyler's suspicions lessen. The conversation eventually turned to other matters, and—after borrowing three dollars to help sell the act—Mortimer soon left, puzzled over where Tyler had first learned he'd been away from San Francisco. More than ever, Mortimer decided it would be best not to let on that he was flush with cash. He also thought it prudent to stay away from Carrie until he had his affairs in order.[9]

That night Mortimer called on a friend or two before taking a room for the night. The next morning, February 4, Mortimer once again visited Tyler to get the latest on the Santa Cruz robbery case. Mortimer must have enjoyed spinning whodunnit theories with the lawyer, discussing the tricks of the trade while maintaining the illusion he'd been fifty miles north of Santa Cruz the entire time. Later that day Mortimer crossed the Bay to Alameda. Folensbee wasn't there, but his sister-in-law said he'd just missed him; he'd been gone for about an hour.

"Satisfied of his safe return, I passed the day visiting some of the fair sex, and having a general good time," Mortimer recalled. "My money flowed like water."

In San Francisco the next day, Mortimer divided his time between business and pleasure. He also resolved that he needed a better hiding spot for the four thousand dollars he'd planted near Los Gatos. Henry was a friend, sure, but four thousand dollars was a lot of money—and he knew the particulars of that night. Best to remove the temptation altogether. For that purpose, on the morning of February 6, Mortimer headed south for Santa Clara. There he found the Santa Cruz robbery was on everyone's lips, and he was thoroughly delighted at the many theories bandied about. The most popular theory was that it was an inside job, just as Mortimer had suggested to Tyler. It had even come to light that Blakely was a gambler, and in debt. In short, he had means and motive. Doubt was also cast at whether or not Blakely could have opened the vault from the inside with his hands tied, had he really wanted to. Everybody seemed to think that had they been in Blakely's position, they would have acquitted themselves better.

As much as Mortimer would have loved to weigh in, he had work to do. Borrowing a horse from Henry, he rode out to his plant, recovered the stolen loot, and returned to the ranch. Wednesday morning he began walking northwest to Mountain View, planning to catch a train car for San Francisco. However, when he passed some men who looked at him hard, his hackles raised. When a farmer offered him a ride, Mortimer quickly accepted, going with him to Mayfield, where their paths diverged. Crossing the valley—alone but for the fortune in stolen money—Mortimer made it to the foot of the mountains and continued on for two or three miles. It was there that he noticed two men on horseback making a beeline toward him.

"I thought it best to take no chances, and so I went up the mountain, and got a position where I could see and not be seen," Mortimer recalled. "The men stopped and looked up the mountain in my direction. I could plainly see they were disappointed at the course I had taken. I could also make out that it was their intention to intercept me at some other point."

Mortimer watched one of the men "lope" off in the direction they seemed to think Mortimer had taken. The other trailed behind at a walk. Mortimer changed course, hiking along the backbone of the ridge. At about two in the afternoon, he reached the ranch of an old friend near the outskirts of Belmont.

"I got him up and got some food, transacted a little business, and pretended to start for San Mateo," Mortimer related. "When he went back to bed I went around his barn and stowed away in the hay, where I lay till night again, when I again set out for San Francisco."

At some point during Mortimer's walk to San Francisco, he stashed the four thousand dollars in another hiding spot. On the morning of February 9, he reached the rooms he and Carrie shared. At the door he gave the signal, and Carrie let him in. This was the first they had seen each other since January, and they wasted little time getting to it.

"When I had refreshed the inner man I went to bed," Mortimer remembered. But Carrie wasn't about to let him sleep without getting some answers.

"How came the wild oats in your hair and whiskers?" Carrie demanded. "And why are your clothes so dirty?"

"If I should tell you, you would doubt me. So the best way is ask no questions."

Carrie wasn't having it. "Why did you not come home last Friday, instead of sending Uncle Bill? He came here with $100, and said you sent it, but couldn't come home, as you had some business to look after. If it was only an hour or two, you could and would have come if you cared for me. I understand you perfectly. Well, you have some woman; that is what takes you away from home so much. You may find better educated women, but you will find no truer one that I am to you."

"It is a very bad habit of yours to be dreaming while you are awake," Mortimer deflected. "Please give it a rest."

But it was no use. Carrie, as Mortimer recognized, was in the mood to lecture, and nothing would talk her out of it. Mortimer's absolute exhaustion ultimately won the battle.

"I finally went to sleep," Mortimer recalled, "with her tongue still going."

When Mortimer awoke he noticed that Carrie had gone through his pockets, finding a couple hundred dollars—"more than I had on leaving home"—and more in silver. Mortimer also determined that, sweetly, she had brushed his clothing. "I soon convinced her that to her and her alone I was devoted," Mortimer related.[10]

That some members of the "fair sex" in Alameda could have claimed differently seemingly didn't bother Mortimer. After all, so long as Carrie never found out about his indiscretions, what could it hurt?

CHAPTER 8

Ringers

*T*he weeks after the Santa Cruz Treasury job should have been good ones for Charles Mortimer. Striding down the Bay City streets with Carrie on his arm and Uncle Bill at his ear, Mortimer could play the family man. With the police chasing their own tail, having arrested poor S. W. Blakely for robbing his own treasury, Mortimer had little to fear on that account. Mortimer also had no need to find employment, having more money in his pocket than at any other time in his life. Naturally, Mortimer still "worked" as a pickpocket from time to time, happening to find a watch or a purse here or there that had somehow become stuck to his fingers, but he no longer operated with the same sense of desperation as when he'd been starving and penniless. Instead, it appears at this point in his life Mortimer mostly committed petty crimes for the fun of it—that and to teach Carrie the ropes.

Initially, Carrie showed promise. Shortly after Mortimer returned from Santa Clara, Carrie and Mortimer took in two thieves, Charley Nightly, an old convict who was sick, and Uncle Bill, who Mortimer stated also "needed help." One evening while out, Mortimer and Nightly spied Carrie in the company of a stranger. After watching them for some time, Mortimer and Nightly crossed their path.

"It was a surprise to Carrie," Mortimer noted, "but she had her wits about her. She gave me the 'office'—a cough—and went up Russian Hill to a dark, quiet spot."

While Carrie and her beau "got into a very earnest conversation," as Mortimer described it, Mortimer and Nightly surprised the man, robbing him of his money.

"Nightly did the searching," Mortimer recalled. "When we took account of the stock, Nightly did not bring to light nearly as much coin as Carrie knew her beau had."

Mortimer tried to reason with the old con, but Nightly stubbornly maintained he hadn't pocketed any extra lucre. Mortimer didn't believe him but, as it was in the past, "thought the least said the soonest mended."[1]

It was appropriate for Mortimer to have used a tailoring metaphor, for a few days later Nightly suggested they rob Louis P. Redwine's tailor shop on Mission of two hundred dollars, the money being in a man's pockets. Mortimer liked the idea, but the timing wasn't quite right. As the days passed Mortimer noticed that more and more of his own money was disappearing, including a new coat. This was the last straw.

He told Nightly it was time to change quarters. Although Nightly complied, Carrie proved equally difficult to manage.[2]

Around February 19, 1872, Mortimer was in Oakland on business. When he returned that night on the last boat, he found Uncle Bill and Carrie in their rooms. Carrie related that earlier that evening she had been strolling through San Francisco when an older gentleman with whom she was mildly acquainted spotted her and joined her. In due course, Carrie stole the watch off the "old Yank," thinking it was gold. When she realized it was silver she chucked it into a vacant lot. Later, having cooled down, she retrieved it.

If Carrie thought this would impress Mortimer, she was mistaken. Mortimer told her he did not like her attempting that sort of robbery and that she was not qualified for it.

"Suppose," Mortimer continued, "he had followed you and have kept you in sight, and it is an easy matter to keep a woman in view, he would have his property, have got an officer, traced you to the house, and we would all have been taken to the station house. You would have got six months in the County Jail, while Uncle Bill and I would have to lay in the station house a few days, if not do worse. All our hands would be tied. But if I was at liberty I could be of great help to you. Perhaps be the means of saving you from the County Jail. Under no circumstances never bring any property that's not honestly got into the house we are living in."

"Why don't you say what you think?" Carrie demanded. "You think I am 'green,' and that I have not got 'nerve.'"

"I say to you just what I think and just what I mean," Mortimer responded. "It would be very bad policy for me to use deception with you in such matters in particular. That man would certainly recognize you if he should meet you in the course of a month or two, and he would have you arrested. The detectives would say that after he had missed his watch he came and gave a description of the woman, and they wrote it down. They would read the same to you. You would see that it answered your description. The 'Yank' would have some friend come and say that he saw you and him walking together that evening. Now, in the face of all of this what would you say?"

"I would say that I was walking with him, but I did not take his watch, and in fact, did not know he had one," Carrie answered.

"No. In a case like this your only chance would be to say decidedly, and stick to it to the last, that you have no recollection of having ever seen him before, and you are positive you never took a watch from any person."

"Carrie, Charlie is right," Uncle Bill chimed in. "He is advising for your own and his best good. There was Mary Cockney—Jack's woman. She did not go into the business till after she became a grown woman. But she took to the business and became an expert. She has made a large amount of money. When the last time she went home to London she had four or five thousand dollars."

The next day Mortimer was gone on business. He later recorded the conversation that took place between Carrie and Uncle Bill in his absence.

"Uncle Bill, whenever you go out on the 'dip,' I do wish you would take me along with you," Carrie implored. "I do want to see if I can't learn to do that kind of business."

"Very well, if Charley don't object, and the 'push' is a proper one for a woman to be in, you may come," Uncle Bill conceded.

"We will keep Charley in ignorance of our little arrangement until such time as I shall become an expert and get away with some good trick; then we will give him a surprise," Carrie suggested.

This was too much for Uncle Bill. "Carrie, you must at all times look for Charley for advice. When you commence pulling the opposite way from him, he will become dissatisfied and everything is sure to go wrong. You should bear in mind that what he knows, it took him years to learn, and for some of his knowledge he paid dearly."

"Yes, I know all this," Carrie admitted, "but sometimes when Charley gets a little angry with me, he tells me that I am dull and stupid, and I want to convince him to the contrary."

"Very well. The quickest and most sure way for you to accomplish that, is to listen to his advice."[3]

A few days later a "push," or large crowd, sprang up, a perfect opportunity for Carrie to learn the art of being on the dip. Although Mortimer and Uncle Bill recognized it was "imprudent" to linger overly long in the Bay City, to them the celebration of Washington's 140th birthday—February 22, 1872—was too good to pass up. Along with the marching band, parade, and civic speeches, what made this celebration of Washington particularly memorable was the laying of the cornerstone of San Francisco's new city hall.

Built just northwest of Market and Eighth (on the site of the present-day San Francisco Library), city hall was complete but for a 6.5-ton slab of granite—five feet, four inches long, three feet, eight inches wide, and three feet, seven inches thick. To keep the cornerstone aloft, heavy ropes and three heavy derricks were employed. To give the crowd a grand view of the ceremony, a vast amphitheater had been erected, capable of fitting a crowd of seven thousand. Those who could not find seating within the amphitheater lined sidewalks, stood atop rooftops, and looked on from neighboring sandhills.[4]

One especially active member of the crowd was Mortimer.

"At about noon February 22, 1872, Frank Gibson, his wife, Jack Prentice, Carrie and myself met at a place agreed upon," Mortimer recalled. "We had a sociable time for about an hour. We all then went to the ground where the ceremony was to come off."[5]

At 1 p.m., when Mortimer and his party and the grand procession led by Brig. Gen. John Hewston Jr. reached the new city hall, seemingly all of San Francisco was there to take part in the festivities. In particular, many of San Francisco's less reputable citizens were interested in the contents of the copper casket—a time capsule of the sort that King Tut might have created—that was to be placed beneath the cavity the granite cornerstone fit.

To be fair, it wasn't just the thieves who coveted the copper casket. The contents of this literal treasure chest included US currency, coins made of silver, gold, and nickel, a lead impression of the Great Seal of California, a specimen of rich silver ore, a silver plate with the engraved names of Grand Master Leonidas E. Pratt and Mayor William Alvord, and a piece of stone from Solomon's Temple in Jerusalem. Contemporary newspapers, maps, and almanacs were also included—but these somehow did not excite as much attention.

Ordered to control this chaos was Police Captain William Douglass. The police, noted the *Chronicle*, "had to fly in a very lively manner" in order to prevent thieves from making off with the copper casket. Boldly, some of the more enterprising criminals scrambled over the railing with pencils in their hands, pretending to be reporters, in hopes of being allowed to remain. "But bearding 'the lion in his den'— the Douglass in his hall (particularly in his new City Hall)—didn't work very well," quipped one actual reporter for the *Chronicle*. "The Captain has as sure an eye for a reporter as he has for a burglar or a highwayman." One by one, the false reporters were ordered off or hauled way.

A little after 2 p.m., the grand master of the ceremony, Leonidas Pratt, said to the grand treasurer for all to hear, "Brother Grand Treasurer, it has been the custom of the Craft, upon occasions like the present, to deposit within a cavity in the stone placed at the northeast corner of the edifice, certain memorials . . . so that if, in the lapse of ages, the fury of the elements, the violence of man, or the slow but certain ravages of time, should lay bare its foundations, an enduring record may be found by succeeding generations, to bear testimony to the . . . industry of the Free and Accepted Masons. Has such a deposit now been prepared?"

"It has, Most Worshipful Grand Master," the grand treasurer theatrically replied, "and the various articles of which it is composed are safely included within the casket now before you."

In due course, the contents of the casket were read to the crowd, the casket was moved into the cavity, and the cornerstone wrangled into place. When the cheering and the music ceased, John W. Dwinelle—a Forty-Niner who had served as the mayor of Oakland, championed the establishment of the University of California, and successfully argued in court that an African American child could not be denied an education based on his race—gave a rousing speech.

"Oh, people of California," Dwinelle lustily implored, "cherish San Francisco! She is not merely one of your jewels, but she is the very crown of your glory—*all* gold and jewels."[6]

Although many of the thieves present would have liked to have looted the copper casket as *their* crowning glory, Mortimer had no such ambition. He had already plundered the Santa Cruz Treasury, after all. Other than the caper he was planning in Virginia City, small-time jobs would be his bread and butter.

"When the people began to gather we divided up," Mortimer noted in his memoir, "and commenced to work—picking pockets—and did not stop till we were obliged to, from the scarcity of pockets."

Mortimer noticed another pickpocket at work, whom he admired professionally. "The little Gipsey was there on her own hook. It was amusing to observe her movements. She reminded me of a humming bird in a flower garden. I think she must have made a good harvest. Uncle Bill, Carrie and I could not complain."[7]

As for their own harvest, Mortimer and Uncle Bill taught Carrie how to operate as part of a three-man team. "Where the crowd is not compact enough," Mortimer noted, "one 'knuck' (pickpocket) stands in front and close to the side of the victim, that the other 'knuck' is at work on. The object of this is to screen the working party. The working party put his fore and middle finger into the pocket, his thumb on the outside; by working his fingers he draws the pocket up till the purse touches his fingers; he then draws the purse out with fingers." Mortimer also related that if the victim was a man, the pickpocket could signal the party in front of him for help, whereupon that person would step on the victim's foot as though by accident.

Watches were acquired in a similar manner but required an extra step. "The pickpocket behind the victim slips the watch out of the pocket, holds the watch in his hand, catches the ring between his thumb and forefinger and gives it a twist," Mortimer explained. "The watch is then separated from the ring and the chain is then lowered down. If it is not prudent for the party that took the watch to move away, he passes the watch to the man in front, who, all the while, has his back toward the victim, and he walks away and puts it in some safe place." Watches stolen in this manner, consequently missing their ring and chain, were known as "ringers."

All told, on Washington's 140th birthday, Mortimer, Carrie, and Uncle Bill brought in one hundred dollars, a gentleman's watch, and a lady's watch, both of them ringers. Shortly afterward, the trio moved to a nice, quiet place on the corner of Clementina Street and Fifth Street.[8]

One Sunday in early March, Mortimer was asleep in bed when Uncle Bill burst in. From Bill, Mortimer got the particulars of the excitement. Carrie, learning that Uncle Bill was going to see a funeral procession, had insisted on coming along. The procession was to start at the Grand Hotel (a stone's throw from present-day Ghirardelli

Square). Carrie and Uncle Bill were less than a quarter mile from the Grand Hotel, near the corner of Howard and New Montgomery, when a man approached Carrie—the "old Yank" whose silver watch Carrie had stolen several weeks earlier.

"Madam, I am quite sure we have met before."

"I think you are mistaken," Carrie replied.

"I know that I am not," the Yank replied, "and I insist on your coming with me to the Police office."

"I'll have *you* arrested if you don't go about your business," Carrie countered.

"Sir," interjected Uncle Bill, "how dare you talk in that manner about my niece. Sir, I'll cane you! Begone!"

While Uncle Bill and Carrie walked back to the house, the Yank followed them from the opposite side of the street. Ultimately Bill determined the wisest course was to leave Carrie in the street, make his way to the house, and seek Mortimer's assistance.

"He won't be shaken," Bill concluded. "He is looking for an officer, and she is trying to avoid them till you come."

Mortimer roused, hot-footed it up Fourth Street and beyond Folsom, and passed by Carrie as though he didn't know her. But his lips moved all the same.

"Don't notice me," Mortimer told her. "Go down to the bridge, get on the horse cars and ride as far as they will take you. When you get off, you continue to go out of the city. Do as told."

For once, Carrie followed orders, walking toward the horse cars. From the other side of the street the Yank and Bill followed. The four of them got on the same car, Uncle Bill and Carrie sitting and talking together. The Yank posted himself at the front of the car, his eyes following their every movement. Mortimer remained at the rear. Filled with adrenaline, Mortimer couldn't resist swiping a few valuables, keeping his "fingers busy." At the end of the route, the four of them left the car. When Carrie and Uncle Bill had strolled some thirty rods from the horse car, the Yank ran after them. Catching hold of Carrie, he began pulling her back the way they'd come. That's when Mortimer appeared, asking what the trouble was.

"This woman stole my watch."

"You're hurting my arm," Carrie pleaded.

"Let go of her arm and let me hear what this is all about," Mortimer instructed.

While the Yank explained he pulled a complaint and a warrant from his pocket. Mortimer looked them over before asking, "Are you an officer?"

"No, but I am going to arrest this woman and I want you to assist me."

"Yes, I will assist you. It's my opinion you are an imposter, a pimp, and want to kidnap this lady," Mortimer declared. "I think those papers are like yourself—frauds."

While the Yank grabbed hold of Carrie, Mortimer hit him square in the nose, tripped him, and flung him to the ground.

"He now understood that he had better make tracks, so he took my advice and did so in double quick time," Mortimer related.

From there, Mortimer, Carrie, and Bill walked about a mile to the beach, which offered a good view of their surroundings. About an hour later Mortimer noticed three men approaching. Using a field glass, Mortimer confirmed his suspicions. It was the old Yank and two policemen. Fortunately, Mortimer knew the Barbary Coast like the back of his hand. Thinking quickly, he hired a boat.

"Bill, Carrie and I got on board and we soon spread our canvas to a nice breeze," Mortimer recalled. "We sailed away until night fall. We then landed two miles further up, at the little cove at the Five Mile House."[9]

Named for being five miles from the new city hall on Market and Eighth, Five Mile House was a saloon, a boardinghouse, and the southern terminus for the San Francisco line. To Mortimer's party it was also salvation. From Five Mile House they walked to Folsom Street, boarded a car at about 10 p.m. and, instead of passing the night in "the Tanks"—the new prison beneath the front of city hall—slept in their Clementina home.[10]

"For the next two weeks we passed the time very pleasurably and pleasantly at home, Oakland, and San Mateo," Mortimer reflected. Good things cannot last forever. Having been recognized by the Yank once, Carrie became preoccupied with the notion that he would recognize her again and was very careful and concerned whenever out.

One day Mortimer said to her, "Carrie, I am going to hunt that old Yank up and send him his watch, then he may quiet down."

"No, he shall not have that watch," Carrie declared, "after the manner he treated me that Sunday."

"I am inclined to think he got the worst of that day's work," Mortimer reasoned, "and he will be less likely to let you off so easy the next time he meets with you. He now knows you so well that he can give a good description to the officers."

Carrie was adamant, stating, "He shall not have the watch."

"Very well," Mortimer capitulated. "Have it your own way and see how you will come out."

As strained as the relationship was between Mortimer and Carrie—Carrie jealous, vindictive, and untrusting; Mortimer irascible, secretive, and philandering—things were harder for Uncle Bill. He was sick, and though Mortimer did not identify his ailment or describe the symptoms, it appeared to be mortal. Mortimer had tried, and failed, to get Bill admitted to St. Mary's, but while there had a talk with the head physician. The man predicted that even if Bill had an operation, he wouldn't live more than a fortnight.

Nevertheless, Bill held on, spring turning to summer.

Two and a half months after the escape from the Yank, Carrie had a hankering to visit the other side of San Francisco. Mortimer told her to take Powell Street. Carrie said she would. By nine o'clock that night, when Carrie had not returned, Mortimer sensed trouble. Making it to the front of city hall, Mortimer called through the grating of the sidewalk, shouting "Carrie!" into the depths of the Tanks. When the reply was answered, Mortimer recognized the voice. Carrie had been arrested.

When Mortimer asked what she'd been arrested for, Carrie replied, "The Yank."

"What does he and others say?" Mortimer asked.

"Yank says it's so, and the officers say the same."

"What do you say?" Mortimer inquired.

"I never saw him before."

"I know you never did. Some one will call to see you in the morning at 8—go to sleep now. I must go. Good night."

"Oh, don't go, don't—but good night."[11]

The next morning Mortimer had a lawyer for Carrie. When her case went before the Police Court, Carrie's lawyer made mincemeat of the Yank's contention. Described by Mortimer as "very amusing," even the *San Francisco Chronicle* was tickled by the proceedings, publishing the story on May 2, 1872:

> An aged individual complained of Carrie Spencer, alleging that she had robbed him of a watch valued at $20. Carrie was walking airily up Montgomery street, when the ancient party espied her and joined her. He says that they were principally engaged in "star-gazing" and discussing the topics of the day. Suddenly the demoiselle remembered she had forgotten something, and started off, leaving her antiquated admirer to discover shortly after that he was minus his watch. The examination of the complaining witness was lengthy and ludicrous, and the complaint was dismissed, on motion of the Prosecuting Attorney.[12]

Mortimer ultimately got from Carrie that she had decided against taking Powell, wishing instead to look through the windows of the prostitutes on Dupont Street. It had been on the corner of Montgomery and Dupont that the Yank had grabbed her, forcing her to the police.

A day or two after Carrie's release, Mortimer was inside Kate Dunn's saloon. According to his memoir, he'd been taking an evening constitutional and, happening to find himself outside the notorious Barbary Coast saloon, went in to chat with Jack Dunn. "While we sat talking together there was some man that made himself more or less obnoxious," Mortimer recalled. "I had some words with him, and he went away."

A half hour later, however, the stranger returned. Mortimer could tell he was trouble waiting to happen. Having no wish to fight, Mortimer was in a pickle, for the only door out of the place was the front door, near the stranger. Eventually, Mortimer walked to the front door, hoping to quietly slip outside. But Mortimer wasn't quiet enough. When the stranger saw him, a knife appeared in his hand, and he slashed at Mortimer, cutting a five-inch slice through the left side of Mortimer's coat and vest. Mortimer's response was equally violent, giving him "a blow which tumbled him into the street."

Bolting out the door, Mortimer ran hell for leather toward Broadway, bare-headed and pursued by a crowd. Suddenly police whistles blew all around him. After three blocks Mortimer dashed into a claustrophobic alley on the side of Telegraph Hill. When he spied an open door, Mortimer darted into it. Unfortunately, it proved to be an unlit outhouse, only three by four feet. When the mob reached the alley, led by three or four policemen, a citizen from an open window called out, "He's in there, in there. Yes, yes, in there. I saw him go in."

Mortimer heard the policemen shout, "Come out! We are limbs of the law, and we command you to come out."

When Mortimer did not respond, the police fired their pistols, the bullets ripping through the outhouse door. After a few moments of silence, the police barreled in. Unlatched, the door flew open, the officers falling in a heap. When they lit matches, Mortimer—perched on the rafters above their heads—saw the policemen had their pistols out. The man in charge was Officer Michael Dunlevy, described by Mortimer as "a tall man and having very keen eyesight."

Spotting Mortimer above him, Dunlevy cried out, "There he is! Up there! Get ready!"

Just as their pistols turned upward, Mortimer shouted, "Dunlevy, don't shoot! I'll surrender."

Placed in their custody, Mortimer was taken to the station house and made a guest there overnight, while Dunlevy and the others attempted to "work up the case." The following day they informed Mortimer that they had the man who'd accosted him in custody, and Mortimer ought to have him arrested.

"Look and see if he didn't cut you somewhere," one urged Mortimer.

"No, he did not," Mortimer lied, refusing to turn traitor, "and I would not know the man if I should see him. Still farther, I did not see him have a knife."

Although the police didn't like it, with Mortimer refusing to press charges, they released him after a few hours. Going directly home, Mortimer ran into Carrie on the street, looking as miserable as someone just come from a funeral.

"Well, Carrie, what are you crying about?" Mortimer asked.

"Where have you been?" she countered.

"I have been locked up in the station house."

"That's not so. You have been off with some woman, and you can't deny it."

"You can believe me or not. Please yourself. The next time you get in the station house I'll come to the conclusion you are off with some man, and let the matter rest at that. Where is Uncle Bill?"

"He went to the hospital his morning. Dr. Hoff told him that if he would get into his ward he would operate on him."

Dr. Oliver Hoff, with his office at 208 Stockton, less than a mile from their Clementina home, may have been respected in his field, but Mortimer placed more trust with the head physician at St. Mary's, who thought an operation would not save Bill. Nor did it. In his memoir Mortimer noted that though they sought to make Bill "as comfortable as we can," his death was "horrible." But if there was a silver lining to the terrible death of Uncle Bill, it was that he'd lived long enough to see Old San Francisco in all her glory, and his friend and nephew-in-law, Mortimer, in all of his.[13]

Before it all came crashing down.

Figure 1. Charles Flinn, alias "Charles Mortimer," circa 1873. Courtesy of the John Boessenecker Collection.

Figure 2. Carrie Mortimer, circa 1872. Courtesy of the John Boessenecker Collection.

Figure 3. Sacramento County Sheriff Mike Bryte. Courtesy of Thom Lewis of the West Sacramento History Society.

Figure 4. Charles Flinn, circa 1858. Courtesy of the Sacramento Police Department.

Figure 5. Will Flinn, 1873. Courtesy of the Sacramento Police Department.

Figure 6. Mark Twain, 1872. Wikimedia Commons.

Figure 7. Samuel C. Denson, circa 1910. Courtesy of the Center for Sacramento History.

Figure 8. Ben Bohen, circa 1863. San Francisco Call, *May 6, 1900.*

PART TWO

REAPING THE WHIRLWIND

I knew Mortimer as a professional thief and criminal, a bold, unscrupulous man.

—Isaiah W. Lees, *San Francisco Examiner*

The Murder of Caroline Prenel

"C'est la vie!" was a phrase well-known to Josephe Caroline Prenel.

"Caroline," as she went by, was born on November 1, 1826, to Jean Baptiste Constant Prenel and Marie Jeanne Claude Bietry in Valoreilles, a small village in France. Despite Caroline having three brothers and three sisters, it may be that the village's size—so small that nearly two centuries later it only sported a population of about one hundred people—spurred her decision to see the world.[1]

Although not listed in *The San Francisco Directory*, by 1871 Caroline had made a name for herself as a woman of the town and was living in a small brick house at 115 Waverly Place, just outside Chinatown. She had money, nice furniture, jewelry, and elegant clothing. She liked to drink and liked the company of men—particularly those who enjoyed drinking with her and were generous with cash gifts.[2]

Unfortunately, the most prominent man in her life—Henri Bec—had a temper. Meeting in January 1871, the two had become friendly, but they often fell to quarreling. At one point, while arguing about money, Bec had attempted to slash Caroline's throat with a knife. A cook by trade, the Frenchman was used to wielding a cleaver. In June 1871 Caroline reportedly attempted to drown herself. She recovered, but by May of 1872 she was in the throes of a depression. Small wonder, for by this time Caroline and Bec were living together, though they kept separate rooms. On Friday, May 17, Caroline's neighbor, Minnie Lorch, saw Bec chase her up the stairs. Caroline later gave Minnie fifty-eight dollars to hide for her. For the next two days, Minnie could hear Bec and Caroline arguing about the money. Finally, on Wednesday, May 22, Caroline retrieved the fifty-eight dollars from Minnie and deposited it in the French Savings Bank a half mile southeast at 401 Bush Street.[3]

Banking the money didn't spare Caroline from Bec's temper. Later that day he confronted her. During the ensuing struggle, Minnie overheard Caroline shout, "Judas, you traitor, you strangle me!" before her words were smothered.

Two nights later, at 7 p.m. on Friday, May 24, Bec came to the house. When Caroline told him she had "company," he left. An hour later, Bec returned. This time it wasn't clear if Caroline was still "entertaining," but she shooed him away nevertheless. A little after she had chased off Bec, Caroline was at Owen Gaffney's saloon at 824 Clay Street, about 120 feet from her house. In the sitting room she conversed with Gaffney about her money troubles. As her English was filtered through a heavy French accent, anyone catching snatches of their conversation may have heard the words "money," "house," and "hidden" and come to the wrong conclusion.[4]

As it was, a man had been observing the Frenchwoman—which wasn't anything new for Caroline. Detaching herself from Gaffney, she sat down next to the stranger who had been watching her and engaged him in conversation. About thirty-eight years old to her forty-six, he was mildly handsome despite the scars and a slightly receding hairline, with tattoos on both arms and a look of self-assurance in his blue eyes. He called himself Charles J. Mortimer.[5]

How Mortimer had ended up that night at Gaffney's saloon was quite the tale, involving the police, two newfound, lowdown friends, and, of course, Carrie.

A couple days after Mortimer had been stabbed and shot at outside Kate Dunn's saloon, he and Dick Owens, who lived a quarter mile north of Mortimer's at 805 Mission Street, went on what Mortimer called "a prospecting tour." Before leaving he told Carrie he'd like her to remain in the house, as they planned to be back at about 10:00 p.m., and afterward he might like to go out with her. Carrie promised she would.

That night, while crossing Pine and Dupont—a little more than a mile north of Dick's place—Mortimer spotted a couple on the opposite side of the street, walking toward Pine before turning up Stockton. The woman Mortimer recognized as Carrie. The man, who was wearing black clothes and a plug hat, and who had beautiful black hair and a Napoleonic mustache, was none other than Christian A. Uhrig, the German American street inspector of San Francisco. Having never met the man, Mortimer didn't recognize him—but he did recognize what Carrie was up to.[6]

From their manner Carrie and Uhrig appeared to be "deeply interested" in each other's company. At the same time, he sensed the gentleman, who Mortimer thought might have been a Jew, appeared a bit distracted, as though he expected to come across someone at any moment and wished to avoid the meeting. Every so often he would glance behind him, and when he got to a street corner he would look cautiously about before hurrying across.

"What is the matter, Charley?" Dick asked.

"Didn't you notice that man and woman that just turned up Pine Street?"

"Not particularly. Did you know them?"

"Yes. The woman is Carrie. Don't she obey orders well? I told her to remain at home until we returned. I presume that as soon as we turned the corner after leaving the house, she also left the house. Let us go to the other side of the street and 'shadow.'"

Mortimer and Owens shadowed the couple up Pine Street toward Lone Mountain Cemetery. They quietly discussed their plan. Either they would come up behind the man and "throw the wing," or pass them, turn around, and "hang him up in that block"—both slang terms for garroting. As the couple passed the corner of Powell and California, Mortimer and Dick took California to head them off by turning onto Mason Street. But when they looped around, the couple was nowhere to be seen. They concluded Carrie and her beau must have climbed the steps to a vacant lot, where sly couples were known to take part in "stargazing." Searching for the pair, Mortimer and Dick stumbled over banks and into pits for a good fifteen minutes, disturbing three or four stargazing couples who "stampeded like young mustangs." Finally, at the corner of Mason and Pine, they determined they had lost their birds and it was time to wander back. They reached Mortimer's place around 10:30 p.m., and sat on the doorstep, waiting for Carrie. Eventually she returned.

"Well, old lady," Mortimer greeted, "you seem to be determined to have things your own way."

"Charlie, don't get mad with me," Carrie entreated. "I felt lonely, and I thought you would not care if I went out for a short walk. I have only been around the block. I have not been away from the house but a very short time."

"I am aware you have not been absent long. At least not so long as you will be if those detectives fasten anything on you. This last affair you got out of without much trouble. The evidence was not very strong against you, but it was enough to convince the most of people that you were guilty. And the same evidence again would make a much stronger case against you."

While Carrie mulled that over, Mortimer said, "Come, Dick and Carrie, let us go into the house."

Inside, over liquor and cigars, Mortimer told Carrie that he and Dick had seen her with the gent on Powell. Carrie admitted it and presented a gold watch and chain she had stolen from Uhrig. Mortimer initially let it pass, but the next morning asked for the details.

"I told her I knew every move in the business," Mortimer recalled. For someone of Carrie's small experience in knucking, he did not believe she could have filched the watch without allowing Uhrig to come very close. Carrie said that she had stolen it from his pocket and that he'd been distracted by the sound of men tumbling into holes on the vacant lot and the sight of couples running away.

"Carrie denied the man had taken any improper liberties with her," Mortimer recollected, "and so I let it pass, though convinced she would be arrested very soon."

As for the watch and chain, although Mortimer judged its value at two hundred dollars, he fenced it for fifty dollars, knowing he'd certainly be arrested if he took it to a proper pawnshop. Mortimer also learned that Dick Owens was in trouble. He and his wife, Julia, had robbed a woman on Broadway. With the detectives looking for him, Mortimer told Dick he could lay low with them.

In early May, Dick returned the favor by helping Mortimer and Carrie move to a quiet place on Greenwich Street, midway between Taylor and Jones. From this "old black frame house," as he described it, Mortimer enjoyed the splendid sights. Facing the bay, he could plainly see the ships at sea, as well as Fort Alcatraz, the hills of Saucelito and Marin, and, looming in the distance, Mt. Tamalpais, only ten miles from San Quentin State Prison. "Take it all in all, I was much pleased with my new home," Mortimer reflected, "but I was destined to have the bitter as well as the sweet. Alas! more bitterness than I had ever tasted in all my life."

During this period Dick and Julia were frequently in the company of the Mortimers and were often fighting. Lack of money, punctuated by an overabundance of drinking, led to some lively rows. Things came to a head on Friday, May 24, 1872. Julia came to visit, drunkenly telling them Dick was in trouble and imploring Mortimer to let her borrow ten or fifteen dollars to help him. Mortimer told her he would see her that evening and do the best he could. Later that afternoon, to get away from Julia and their neighbors—who had suffered through Julia's histrionics before and were plainly gossiping about them—Mortimer locked up the house. Afterward, he and Carrie took a room at Mrs. Deneson's, on the corner of Broadway and Pinckney Alley.

Telling Carrie to remain there until he returned, Mortimer went to Market Street "on business." On his way back, he took Dupont Street. While crossing Washington Street, he spotted Owen Gaffney standing in the doorway of his saloon at 824 Clay Street.[7]

"I went into his saloon and took a drink," Mortimer recalled. "I then took a seat in the sitting-room. In a few minutes there came in a woman and sat near me. Owen was chafing her about the French, etc. He called her name Caroline."

Eavesdropping, Mortimer picked up that Caroline was French, that she was somewhat under the influence of whiskey, and that she had some money at her house. Sizing her up, Mortimer could tell she had a very similar figure to Carrie. After striking up a conversation, Mortimer and Caroline "got quite intimate," as he related, "and she asked me to go to her house."

Planning on robbing her, Mortimer told Caroline he would meet her there. Shortly afterward, he followed her to her house at 115 Waverly. Entering, Mortimer found Caroline in a very cheerful mood. Caroline insisted that he undress and go to bed. Mortimer promised he would, but he'd like a drink first. Caroline thought that a splendid idea and that when he came back with liquor, she would go to bed with him. Mortimer left for a grocery store on the corner of Clay and Dupont, buying a bottle of whiskey. When Mortimer returned he found Caroline already in bed. Rousing, she led Mortimer to another room, where they both took a drink. Before long Caroline was in Mortimer's lap, speaking to him about her life. Having worked in San Quentin's tailor shop with the French convict Augustus Hipolite for three years, Mortimer was accustomed to the pitch of the Romance language. Even still he had trouble comprehending Caroline.

"I could not understand much she said," Mortimer recalled, "but I saw that it was a relief to her and I listened."

Caroline suggested they take a last drink and then go to bed "and talk." After the drink they fell into bed together. A minute later someone came to the back door. Caroline got up and gave the woman something. Mortimer suggested another drink, and when the glasses were poured, drank lightly himself. They returned to bed, and within a half hour of "talking" Caroline was asleep. Mortimer then proceeded to search the house. Not finding any money, he dressed and left, taking the whiskey with him.

At 9:30 p.m. Mortimer reached the corner of Broadway and Pinckney Alley. Mrs. Deneson was still up, about to go to bed. She told him that Carrie had begun to think he wouldn't return. Mortimer made something up, bade her good night, and went to find Carrie. To Carrie, he told her he'd met Caroline at Owen Gaffney's, had gone back to her place with the intention of robbing her once asleep, but when she fell asleep he couldn't find the money. For some reason, Mortimer left out that Caroline had been in his lap and that he had been naked in her bed.

"Carrie accused me of unfaithfulness—this I stoutly denied," Mortimer wrote in his memoir.

Perhaps to demonstrate that there was nothing special between him and Caroline, Mortimer told Carrie that because she was about the same size, if they robbed Caroline of her clothing, Carrie might have a whole new wardrobe. Unsurprisingly, Carrie liked the idea. With the whiskey in hand, they left Mrs. Deneson's.

"We went directly to Caroline's house, went in, closed the door and locked it . . . we went in like we belonged there," Mortimer recalled.

Inside, Mortimer lit a match. Pointing out Caroline's sleeping form to Carrie, Mortimer told her that she was in a drunken sleep, and they would have time to look over the place. But Carrie proved to be more interested in the lack of clothing.

"Charley, you lie," Carrie said, her finger in his face, "if you say you have not been with that bitch."

Mortimer tried to dissuade her, but the more he did so the louder Carrie became. He attempted to convince her to keep her voice down, that someone would hear. Eventually, Mortimer determined the best course of action was simply to leave. But Carrie was in no hurry to follow. As if knowing what was about to happen, Mortimer took a drink straight from the bottle while Carrie went to the bed and shouted, "You bitch, you—!"

That roused Caroline. According to Mortimer, the surprised Frenchwoman rose and fell headfirst out of bed, her legs on the bed and her head smacking the floor. In a murderous rage, Carrie positioned her foot over the back of Caroline's neck and stomped down hard.

Hearing something outside, Mortimer cautioned Carrie that there was someone at the back door. Mortimer and Carrie did not know it, but this was Henri Bec returning home. Finding the back door locked, Bec went around, climbed the stairs, and tried the front door. It too was locked. Hearing voices, Bec surmised Caroline must have company, so instead of unlocking the door with his key he left.[8]

This frightened Carrie, and she allowed they should leave. Distracted, Mortimer failed to see Carrie strip the earrings from Caroline's earlobes and the diamond ring from her finger.

"I wanted to lift Caroline into the bed," Mortimer stated. "Carrie said to let the bitch lay."

After unlocking the door, Carrie peeked outside. It was a busy Friday, and people were walking the street. Risking being spotted, they left the house, going up Washington to Stockton. On Stockton, they headed to Sacramento, taking Sacramento south to Kearny, then back to Washington. Passing city hall, they noticed three policemen: Lawrence Selinger, William S. Jones, and Daniel Coffey. In particular, Mortimer remembered Coffey well. After all, Coffey had arrested Mortimer in early 1871 for being caught with clothing stolen from a *Chronicle* printer before the newspaperman, despite the urging of the police, had championed Mortimer's innocence.[9]

Seeing the policemen gave Mortimer an idea.

"The thought struck me that we had better take the desperate chances of being arrested on some old score and go and have a talk with those detectives, and by so doing it would be an easy matter to prove an *alibi*—at any rate would help to do so," Mortimer explained.

In his memoir, Mortimer dished that he was worried someone might enter Caroline's unlocked door and, finding her unconscious, rob her house. Once the police got involved, there was a good chance they'd turn up a witness who observed him and Carrie entering the place earlier that night and pin the robbery on them.

"At this time the thought never came into my head that Caroline was dead," Mortimer admitted.

Reaching the corner of Kearny and Washington, Mortimer and Carrie crossed to where the detectives were standing in front of city hall. Mortimer spoke to Selinger, asking the detective why he hadn't arrested Dick Owens for the robbery on Broadway.

Selinger responded that he had been "looking for him, but could not find him."

Mortimer told him that "he and his woman were guilty of the robbery and the property could be got."

Selinger then asked for Mortimer's help in the matter, and Mortimer promised to do so. Of course, Mortimer had no intention of giving away Dick or Julia, but if the officers took them to city hall that night to grill them on what they knew about the Broadway robbery it would be harder to prove they were at 115 Waverly Place, robbing Caroline Prenel. The officers, however, didn't see the need to arrest Mortimer or Carrie.

After the Mortimers bade the policemen good night, they headed up Kearny to Sacramento, up Sacramento to Stockton, and along Stockton toward Washington. As they walked they argued about their course of action. Carrie wanted to return to Caroline's and rob her. Mortimer thought it too dangerous. Eventually, at about eleven o'clock Mortimer and Carrie sat down in a doorway a few rods beyond the northwest corner of Stockton and Washington. After about an hour of being at loggerheads, Carrie said she would return to Caroline's alone.[10]

Meanwhile, Minnie Lorch noticed Henri Bec returning to 115 Waverly, opening the door with his key. Late, he went straight to his own bed without checking in on Caroline (possibly so as not to see her entwined with one of her customers).[11]

Around the same time, a tenth of a mile northwest of Caroline's house, Mortimer had given up trying to persuade Carrie from returning. But he wasn't about to go with her, refusing to budge from the steps of the doorway.

After several false starts, where Carrie headed off then turned back—once to chastise Mortimer for drinking more whiskey, which he continued to do—Carrie eventually walked to Waverly Place. Mortimer shadowed her. When Carrie looked toward Stockton Street, Mortimer felt satisfied she wouldn't dare enter the house again. Retracing his steps, Mortimer settled himself back into the same doorway and pretended to be asleep. A few minutes later Carrie appeared, keeping quiet. This time Mortimer actually nodded off.

"I fell off to sleep; I don't know how long I slept," Mortimer reflected.

When Carrie woke him before dawn, she revealed someone had come close to them while he slept. Finally, she seemed ready to leave. Through thick fog, they reached the grocery at the corner of Greenwich and Taylor, which had just opened. There Mortimer had another swallow of whiskey, and the shopkeeper made Carrie a cocktail. Afterward, they finally returned to their Greenwich home. Having been out in the cold all night, Mortimer busied himself making a fire.[12]

Three-quarters of a mile southeast of Mortimer's house, Henri Bec woke around six in the morning from a nightmare. Unable to shake the feeling that something was wrong, he went downstairs to see if the morning paper had come. He also looked in on Caroline. To his horror, he found her as Mortimer and Carrie had left her. Caroline's head was on the floor, her feet were on the bed, there were bruises on her neck, and she wasn't breathing. Bec quickly notified Officer Abraham J. Houghtaling, who visited the premises. Finding her stiff and cold, Houghtaling verified Caroline Prenel was dead.[13]

Meanwhile, Mortimer went back to the grocery store. He purchased some groceries, walked farther along Greenwich to the butcher's, and bought some meat. Returning home, Mortimer found Carrie in mischievous spirits.

"What do you think of my jewelry?" Carrie teased.

"What jewelry?" Mortimer asked.

"Where is your eyes? Look at my ears."

Mortimer saw them now. "Where did you get them? Yes, I know, damned if you didn't take that woman's rings out of her ears."

"Yes, and the ring off of her finger. You call me dull and stupid, but I have an eye to business."

The old arguments between them resumed. Eventually, Mortimer left the house again, walking back to the grocery store to fetch beer for Carrie. While there he looked over the papers. Dazed by the news, Mortimer later recalled that he wasn't completely sure which newspaper it was he read. He thought it might have been the evening edition of the *San Francisco Bulletin*.[14] However, it was the morning edition of the *San Francisco Examiner* that first printed the news of Caroline Prenel's murder, an hour after Bec discovered the corpse. Under the headline "Another Mysterious Death," the paper read:

> At an early hour this morning a woman of the town named Caroline . . . was found dead in her room, at No. 115 Waverly place. The position in which the body was discovered and its appearance have led to the suspicion of foul play. The body was dressed in its nightclothes, the feet were on the side of the bed and the body on the floor. About the neck there were deep blue marks and scratches, not such as would be made by hands, but rather which might be produced by a cord or rope tightly drawn. . . . A Coroner's inquest will throw much light upon the subject.[15]

Throughout Mortimer's criminal career he'd committed hundreds of crimes. They ran the gamut from highway robbery, pickpocketing, grand larceny, destruction of property, aiding and abetting, desertion, burglary, vagrancy, possession of stolen goods, breaking and entering, escaping prison, horse theft, perjury, public lewdness, criminal trespass, resisting arrest, assault, and assault with a deadly weapon. Never before had they involved murder. But after reading about Caroline's death in the Saturday paper, the event which he titled in his memoir "PEACE OF MIND FOREVER GONE," Mortimer knew that he was now an accessory to a murder, and his ungovernable wife a murderess. With a heavy heart, Mortimer returned home.

Sharing with Carrie what he'd read in the paper, Carrie's reaction was jubilant.

"She said if she ever knew of me going with a woman, she would poison them," Mortimer recalled.

Mortimer might have worried about the small bottle of strychnine they had in the house, but at the moment he had bigger fish to fry. Insisting that they exercise caution, Mortimer instructed Carrie to throw Caroline's jewelry away.[16]

Carrie had other ideas.

The Fall Guy

Assigned the Prenel case, Detective John Coffey wasted little time.

From the start, it was a cinch the Frenchman had killed his paramour. First, there was Minnie Lorch's testimony that Bec had previously attempted to slash Prenel's throat, that earlier in the week she'd heard her call out that he was strangling her, that they lived together and were fighting about the money she'd hidden. Then there was the state of Prenel's rooms, with the bureau drawers pulled out and Prenel missing her jewelry, indicating that robbery as much as anger may have motivated the killer. Officer Patrick Slavin also claimed that a little after three in the morning on May 25 he'd heard angry French voices coming from 115 Waverly. Bec claimed he'd been having a nightmare, which might account for this, but it seemed thin. The only thing that didn't track was the information gleaned from Owen Gaffney's saloon. Witnesses claimed that shortly after Prenel left the saloon a heavy man with a dark, sandy beard had followed her. This was a poor match for Bec—but it could have been just a coincidence.[1]

Chief Henry H. Ellis certainly thought so. At 10 p.m. on May 28, Ellis and Coffey arrested Bec on Market Street for the murder of Caroline Prenel. To conduct his case, Bec engaged Reuben H. Lloyd, a sterling attorney who had successfully defended a dozen men accused of murder. Bec seemed earnest to the point of madness that he had not done the deed, but Lloyd was at a loss of what to do.

Reflected Lloyd, "That was my thirteenth murder case. . . . [W]hile I felt sure that Bec was innocent . . . it seemed to me that while none of the twelve I defended before him had reached the gallows, he would have to go there."[2]

While Bec suffered in jail and Lloyd puzzled over his client's lack of options, Mortimer and Carrie celebrated. On Saturday, June 1, they visited the circus. Pushing through the Jackson Street crowd, Mortimer's sticky fingers somehow lifted another man's watch and chain, separating it from the ring. The man immediately noticed its absence but did not know who had taken it. Unfortunately for Mortimer, surrounding the man were friends of his from the woolen mills. Mortimer was the only stranger. Catching hold of Mortimer, the man demanded to know if he had his watch. Mortimer feigned astonishment.[3]

"If you are a gentleman, you will not hesitate to satisfy me on this point," the man growled.

By this time Mortimer had dropped the watch. One of the man's friends found it. At that moment an officer arrived. Glancing at Mortimer and the ringless watch, he said it was a plain case and booked Mortimer for robbery. On Monday the case was brought before Judge Davis Louderback. When the clerk read the charge, which had been elevated to assault, Mortimer astounded everyone by pleading guilty.

With the robbed man present, the court decided to hear his testimony. He explained that his watch had been stolen from him and recovered. At no point did he say anything to suggest he was assaulted.

While the detectives stood with their mouths open, Louderback, after scratching his head, ordered Mortimer to appear the next morning for sentencing. Mortimer was escorted below to the Tanks. The next morning Carrie came to visit him. Mortimer could see two detectives following her, one of whom was William S. Jones, one of the three officers Mortimer and Carrie had spoken with in front of city hall on the night of the murder. Mortimer knew in a flash it was about the Uhrig watch case.

"What shall I do?" Carrie asked.

"Fall back on your dignity," Mortimer urged. "Look the man and officers straight in the eye. Tell them it is false. Don't get excited. Try to convince the man that he is mistaken in your person. If he persists that he is not, tell him and all who speak to you of the matter, that you are sure that you never saw him before in your lifetime."

Seeing Officer Jones approach, Mortimer continued, "They are coming. Do you understand? When they speak to you on the subject, appear as though you were surprised."

When Carrie left, Jones took her spot.

"Charley, do you see that man at the desk in black clothes?" Jones asked.

"Yes."

"He says Carrie beat him out of a watch about a month ago, and he is going to put a charge against her if he don't get it back. But if she will turn it up he will drop the matter. If she has pawned it he don't mind about paying $30 or $40 to get it."

"I don't know anything about the matter," Mortimer lied. "But if the watch is of any considerable value, and she had anything to do with it, I think she would have let me know something about it."

"Well, it's nothing to me. I was only telling you for her good. Go and advise with her in the matter."

"You go to her. State the case in full. You would be more likely to be successful that I would."

Jones took Mortimer's advice. About ten minutes later he returned.

"What does she say?" Mortimer asked.

"She says she has not had a watch of any kind for years. I told her to look at the man. She did, and said that she didn't know him, and never saw him before."

Uhrig and Carrie soon joined them.

"You stole my watch and chain," Uhrig accused Carrie. "If you don't give it back I send you to State Prison. You going to let me have it? Hey?"

"Sir!" Carrie replied. "What do you mean by talking in that way to me? I don't know anything about you or your watch, and I care less. I never saw you before."

"I send you to State Prison," Uhrig threatened.

"Even if she had it," Mortimer commented, "you go in a very poor way to have her return it."

Things went on like that for some time: Uhrig blustering, Mortimer insulting, Carrie lying, and Jones observing. Ultimately, Jones said to Carrie, "Carrie, I am sorry for you, but it can't be helped. Just turn the watch up and you can go. Come, I must lock you up."

As Carrie was escorted to her cell, still arguing, the police bell rang, summoning Mortimer to court. Mortimer went upstairs and took his seat. He noticed his lawyer, G. W. Tyler, animatedly speaking to Judge Louderback. While he did so, Louderback periodically flipped through a law book and looked inquiringly at Mortimer. Eventually, Louderback declared, "Charles Mortimer, you appear to-morrow morning for sentence."

While closeted with Tyler, his attorney informed him that while he and Carrie had been performing their act in front of Jones and Uhrig, Chief Crowley and half a dozen detectives had "buttonholed" Judge Louderback. The meat of it was that they wanted Mortimer back at the "ranch," San Quentin. After all, Mortimer had chloroformed Charley Wiggin and given hell to R. C. Gilchrist. He needed to pay for his crimes, whether he'd assaulted the man at the circus or no. Louderback didn't like it. In his book, the punishment needed to fit the crime, and nobody got railroaded, even a scoundrel like Mortimer.

The next morning, Mortimer appeared for sentencing. Louderback sentenced him to three months in prison. However, instead of San Quentin Mortimer would do his time in county jail. Mortimer accepted his sentence. Taken below, Tyler shared with him that Louderback would have annulled the sentence altogether but had no legal means to do so.[4]

Meanwhile, the Uhrig case made the papers. On June 6 the *Sacramento Bee* reported, "Carrie Mortimer, who waylaid C. A. Uhrig on the street and got fifty cents from him in charity and then robbed him of his gold watch and chain, as she embraced him in gratitude, was committed for trial on a charge of grand larceny." The next day the *San Francisco Examiner* noted that she was being held on a thousand-dollar bail.[5]

Jones allowed Carrie to speak to Mortimer, probably hoping he might convince

Carrie to return the watch, either resulting in Uhrig dropping the case or cementing a guilty plea. Mortimer reflected that he might have had the watch returned to Uhrig, but he had no faith the street superintendent would drop the case. Instead of Uhrig's watch, Mortimer spoke to her about something more pressing. Carrie would almost certainly be locked up in the new part of the prison, where Henri Bec had been incarcerated while awaiting trial.

"And here I am wearing that woman's ring," Carrie lamented. "If he should see it he might know it. For God's sake take it."

"Yes, and throw it away," Mortimer replied.

"No, don't do that. I can wear it anywhere else."

That evening Mortimer visited Carrie, who still wore Caroline's ring.

"Charlie, that man Bec is in the next cell to me, and I have been talking to him," Carrie whispered. "He is almost crazy. And only think of it, he said that he felt sure the guilty party would be found out some time. When he said that I thought I would drop—that I would faint. What do you think about it?"

"Let the matter drop for present. If they send you up to wait the action of the Grand Jury I'll try to get a chance to talk with you. I will then advise you on the matter. Your present trouble will come out all right for you in the end. All you have to do is continue to say what you have said."

"I do hope that I won't have to go to County Jail. I dread it."

"You should have thought of that when you was taking the watch.... Here comes Jones. I must go; keep up a good heart."

As Jones arrived, Carrie pleaded, "Don't go. Mr. Jones, do let him stay."

"Turn the watch up and I'll let you out altogether," Jones promised.

"I never had the watch, never. Good night, Charlie."

"Good night."

Returning to his own cell, Mortimer passed by the one housing Henri Bec. This was the first time he had seen the man. Taking a good look at him, Mortimer couldn't help pitying him. Mortimer hoped his trial went well. If there were something he could do to help exonerate him, he'd do it—but not if it cost him and Carrie their lives.

As Carrie's trial began—an ordeal that would take about six weeks—Mortimer was made a prison trusty. This allowed him opportunities to make Carrie more comfortable and for them to see each other. When visiting Carrie, he purposefully spoke to her ten feet away from the cell holding Bec, whose examination before the Police Court had commenced on June 10. Mortimer often engaged the Frenchman in idle chitchat. Casually moving the conversation toward Bec's case, Mortimer's twin purpose was to suss out if there were any developments linking Caroline to the Mortimers and to note the effect these conversations were having on his emotional wife. Although Bec's case seemed increasingly hopeless, Mortimer could tell Carrie was deathly afraid she would be found out.[6]

As it happened, Carrie was right to be afraid. Although Mortimer did not mention it in his memoir, probably because Bec did not know and couldn't confide it to the friendly prison trusty, Bec's attorney had come up with a plan. To wit, Reuben H. Lloyd pinned all his hopes on the most accomplished policeman in California: Captain of Detectives Isaiah W. Lees.

"One day Reuben H. Lloyd, whom Bec had engaged to conduct his case, came to me," Lees recalled to an *Examiner* reporter. "He said that he saw plainly that all the evidence found so far tended to show the guilt of his client, and, as a lawyer, he knew that the man would be found guilty unless the real criminal could be found."

Lees agreed with Reuben that the evidence against his client seemed damning. "To be sure, it was all circumstantial," Lees reflected, "but it was very direct, and it looked as though the poor Frenchman must hang."

Lloyd swore to Lees, "on his honor as a gentleman," that Bec was innocent of the crime. He just couldn't prove it.

"I had not given any personal attention to the case up to that time, but Mr. Lloyd begged me to take hold and see if I could not unravel the tangle and find the real criminal," Lees recollected. "I consented to do so."[7]

While Lees began studying the case from the outside, and Mortimer kept tabs on the fall guy from the inside, the grand jury reached a decision concerning Uhrig's stolen watch. They chose to ignore the charges against Carrie. Whether they believed in the innocence of Mrs. Mortimer, or grew to dislike Mr. Uhrig, went unreported. Either way, Carrie was freed from County Jail. Mortimer suggested she get a job in Hayes Valley, working for a mutual acquaintance, L. P. Redwine, as a nanny. Carrie thought this a swell idea.

One Saturday, August 10, Carrie came to visit Mortimer in jail. By chance Mortimer happened to spot Redwine through a front window, watching Carrie intently as she approached the jail. Once they were together, Mortimer told Carrie that Redwine was watching her. Carrie explained that he must have been lying in wait for her, for she had stolen some articles from him before moving out of Redwine's house and into the home of a Jewish family. He must have suspected she'd taken them and wanted them back.

"I advised her to return them and try and make it appear as though it were done through a mistake in her hurry," Mortimer recalled.

After she left the jail, Mortimer could see Carrie and Redwine conversing. Neither looked happy. Carrie abruptly left for the horse cars. Redwine followed her. The following day Carrie visited Mortimer again. Redwine, she explained, had followed her to her new lodgings, made a scene, and gotten her thrown out. Now she had nowhere to go.

"Carrie, go and get and give to him all that belongs to him," urged Mortimer, exasperated, "then get a good boarding place, and for pity sake keep quiet until my time expires. Don't be taking things from houses you are at on a visit.... Only think of it for a minute—the other day you went to a house to answer an advertisement, the girl showed you into the parlor and, before the lady came in, you took an opera glass from the table.... Nearly every house you go into you take some little thing that is no account to you. Do stop such things. Don't keep him waiting out there. Go and give him what belongs to him; then do as I ask you to do."

"Well, I'll go," Carrie replied, "but I hate to give him anything back, for causing me to lose my place yesterday. If I could have remained there for two or three weeks, I could have got the run of everything in the house."

"Then what would you have done?" Mortimer asked.

"I would have gone up and left."

Mortimer tried to convince her she'd have been quickly arrested. But Carrie was headstrong. At least she agreed to return Redwine his property. On Monday Mortimer expected a visit from her. But Carrie did not show. It was the same on Tuesday. On Wednesday he discovered the reason, as printed in the *San Francisco Chronicle*. Carrie had been arrested in Oakland.[8]

According to the papers, on July 30 Carrie and Redwine had been in Oakland, at Hugh Gaynor's saloon on the northwest corner of Fifth and Broadway. They took drinks in an adjoining room, near the storeroom. On Sunday, August 11, Carrie and Redwine returned with a friend, Rickey. Once again, they ordered drinks in the adjoining room. Gaynor sensed something was fishy. Leaving a young man tending bar, he located officers Albert Shorey and G. F. Blake. Returning with the policemen, Gaynor found three boxes of good cigars missing from the storeroom. The three men tracked Carrie, Redwine, and Rickey to Market Street Station, where they captured them and found the stolen cigars. Upon her arrest, Carrie gave her name as "Butler." Detective David H. Rand, however, noticed a similarity between her and a picture he had of Carrie Mortimer, who had gained notoriety as a pickpocket. Examining the picture, he determined the female cigar thief was, in fact, Mrs. Mortimer.[9]

Having no money for bail, Carrie languished in Oakland's station house while Mortimer waited out his sentence in San Francisco's county jail. Letters passed between them, in which Mortimer remembered Carrie complaining about "her hard lot."

Finally, September 5 arrived, and Mortimer was set free. Crossing into Oakland on the first boat, Mortimer learned the particulars of the case. The robbery had been Carrie's idea. That night Mortimer, his frustrations obviously mounting, got some whiskey, got in a fight, and got severely beaten.[10]

Another man in Mortimer's position might have woken up the next morning and decided to leave Carrie and California far behind. With Carrie in jail, and the police believing they had French Caroline's killer behind bars, Mortimer had the perfect opportunity to retrieve the Santa Cruz Treasury money he'd planted and vanish. But with Carrie, Mortimer had a sexual partner, a junior partner in crime, and a demoiselle in distress—all of which stroked his ego. He wasn't about to give her up.

On September 6 Mortimer paid Carrie's fine. Taking a boat back to San Francisco that night, they rented a room at 217 Broadway at the Welsh Harp Hotel, a half mile northeast of where Caroline Prenel had been murdered.

Caroline was on both their minds. When Mortimer concluded they needed to pawn some jewelry—his stash of cash hidden farther away than he wanted to travel, considering he was still smarting from the beating he'd endured—Carrie slipped off Caroline's diamond ring and gave it to Mortimer to sell.

"I did not object to it," Mortimer reflected. "I was only too glad to get it out of my sight. Oh, God! Every time I would look at that ring on Carrie's finger or the earrings in her ears, what a horrible sight would flash to my mind's eye. She wore that ring all the time, from the 5th of June to the 6th of September."

Carrie still wore Caroline's earrings, but Mortimer may have decided to quit while ahead. Walking almost three-quarters of a mile west to the corner of Dupont and Broadway, Mortimer entered L. Abraham's pawnshop. Giving his name as Walker, Mortimer sold the ring, a brooch, and a few other pieces of jewelry. He did keep a watch Uncle Bill had given him before dying, though. He'd promised Uncle Bill he'd see it returned to its owner.

Carrie wasn't as sentimental as her uncle. No sooner had Carrie relinquished one piece of jewelry than she wanted another; back in the hotel, the kleptomaniac stole a box from the landlady, which contained a cheap watch and chain. Mortimer was losing patience. He ordered her to put it back. Carrie refused.

"Well, then, that being the case, the sooner we get out of this house the better," Mortimer huffed. "I'll leave in fifteen minutes—come, get ready."

In less than fifteen minutes they were on the street. Soon after they were on a boat back to Oakland, bidding San Francisco goodbye. Mortimer did not know it at the time, but that was the last time he would step foot in the Bay City. They stayed one night in Oakland, Friday the 13, and the next day caught the morning train for Sacramento. They reached the capital at 2 p.m. on September 14, 1872, and headed to the three-story Mechanics Exchange Hotel, located at 116 I Street, about five hundred feet east of the Sacramento River.

Although the criminal element tended to make the waterfront their stomping ground, the Mechanics Exchange was considered relatively safe by the denizens of Sacramento, considering the heavy police presence. After all, the hotel was situated 250 feet east of Sacramento City Prison, at Front and I Street, and a half-mile west of the Sacramento Courthouse and Sacramento County Jail, between Sixth and Seventh on I Street.

"Time passed very pleasantly," Mortimer reflected, "until Thursday."[11]

CHAPTER 11

The Murder of Mary Gibson

On Saturday, September 14, Mortimer spied Officer Len Harris on the street with another policeman. Mortimer approached Harris, who at first did not recognize Mortimer. But it quickly came back to him. While Harris had been the acting turnkey in San Quentin State Prison in 1870, serving under R. C. Gilchrist, Mortimer had been incarcerated there. At one point, Mortimer had intimated to Harris that he could make trouble for Gilchrist if Gilchrist didn't play nice. That Mortimer was trouble with a capital T wasn't the sort of thing a good policeman forgot.

Harris attempted to introduce Mortimer to his partner, Enoch Dole. Mortimer wasn't in the mood. Instead, he forked over the watch Uncle Bill had given him and asked Harris to see it returned to its owner, a man named Stanton. Harris promised he would.

The next day Mortimer and Carrie were strolling down J Street when they spotted Harris, pointing them out to Dole. This was too much for Mortimer. He told Carrie they ought to leave town "at an early hour."[1]

Mortimer was right to worry. After Mortimer had made his presence known to them, Harris had looked through a police book he kept of dangerous California criminals. Mortimer's physical description and known criminal history since 1864 were in there, including the robbery of Wiggin, the knifing of Rose, his conviction of grand larceny in Siskiyou County under the alias George Foster, and the theft of a watch at a San Francisco circus. Recognizing Mortimer as one of the most notorious criminals in the state, Harris and Dole made it policy to shadow Mortimer during their working hours, from midnight to 9:00 a.m.

Although Mark Twain was then living in London, enjoying the financial success of *Roughing It*, other ambitious crime reporters were on hand. One of the most talented was E. B. Willis, the city editor of the *Sacramento Record*, who had been made a special deputy sheriff by Sacramento County Sheriff Mike Bryte. Sensing a story, Willis often tagged along with Harris and Dole. Pointing Mortimer out to Willis, Harris described Mortimer as "the worst man in the State." Before turning in, the policemen reported Mortimer's whereabouts to Officer George K. Rider, who took over the daylight duties of tracking the ne'er-do-well.[2]

Irrespective of the ominous police presence, Carrie wanted to stick around. The

State Fair was to open in a few days, and she wanted to see it. Mortimer relented. A day or two later, Mortimer spoke to a man on the street about what houses in Sacramento had money in them. Later, Mortimer discussed the man's answers with Carrie. In particular, from the balcony of their room, Mortimer pointed toward one that seemed promising, 250 feet away, on Jibboom Street.

On the day the State Fair opened—September 19, 1872, a Thursday—Carrie probably expected Mortimer to escort her to the grounds. Instead, Mortimer decided to hit the sauce. Certainly, Mortimer had a wide variety of saloons to choose from.

Commented Mark Twain, "Sacramento [is] the City of Saloons.... I have been in most of the saloons, and there are a good many of them. You can shut your eyes and march into the first door you come to and call for a drink, and the chances are you will get it."[3]

Demonstrating the truth of Twain's description of the capital, Mortimer left Carrie at the Mechanics Exchange Hotel, beginning an epic pub crawl. He visited the bar in the Union Hotel, on the west side of Second Street between J and K, the Bank Exchange Saloon, on 2nd and K, and finally the Colonade Saloon, underneath the Grand Hotel, on the corner of Front and K. At the Colonade he evidently ran out of money, borrowing five dollars from the proprietor, Mose Drew. Feeling the effects of the liquor, he stumbled on back to the hotel, reaching their room a little before four o'clock. Inside, Mortimer lay down on the bed.[4]

"What's the matter with you?" Carrie asked.

"I feel sick," Mortimer replied.

"You are full of whiskey."

"I know I am, and that's what makes me feel so ill. You see, I am willing to acknowledge my faults."

"Yes. Go off and leave me here in this house alone all day—shut here like a prisoner. You don't care, so long as you are with your friends drinking and enjoying yourself. Yes, and if the truth was known, I'll bet you've been down among those damned fancy women. Maybe to the house they call the 'Palace.'"

"For God's sake, don't talk to me about going around the 'free and easy' women. The last place of that kind I was at is enough to last me the balance of my life. There is not a time that I pass one of their houses—particularly if it is a small brick—but that affair flashes across my mind. It comes to me in all its horrors, and I know that it is making a bad matter worse, but I can't help it. I make a dive into the first place where whisky is sold and take a drink or more. O God! If I could—"

"Oh, I know you feel very bad about the old French bitch. If it had been me, you would not have given it a second thought. I'll follow you some time, and catch you going into some of those places, and you can bet your life I'll make it hot for them. I don't care how much you go into saloons that are kept by men. But you have no business in places kept by women, and you shan't go. By God, if you do, you'll be sorry. I mean what I say."

"You may depend that I will mind what you say about that matter. You need not caution me on that subject. I have had all the caution necessary. Now drop the subject and let me sleep."

"Yes, let you sleep, and me to sit here and look at you. Sit here like a knot on a log."

"I never object to you going where or when you please—never. Let me sleep."

"I want to know what women you have been to see to-day. You need not lie."

"If I have seen any I don't know it. Let me sleep."

"Yes, let you sleep. Anything to sleep."

At about four o'clock Mortimer recognized that sleep might have been impossible and went outside. Standing in front of the hotel, he knew he was still somewhat intoxicated and would have to return to their room. But while he stood there, reflecting on his position, Carrie appeared.

"Why don't you go on?" Carrie asked.

Mortimer replied he had nowhere to go. Carrie thought Mortimer was lying, that he'd been planning to visit a woman, but now wouldn't for fear she'd follow him. Giving up, Mortimer said they could go anywhere she wanted. Walking aimlessly, they turned the corner, heading toward Yolo Bridge and the Sacramento River. They were nearing the house Mortimer had heard about, where they could potentially make a good score. When Carrie asked how close it was, Mortimer pointed it out.

"Let us go in there and see what kind of a place it is," Carrie suggested.

The house, as it happened, was a one-story frame house, raised fifteen feet over a stretch of brackish water, commonly referred to as "the slough." Located immediately behind the Water Works building, the front of the house functioned as a grocery and a saloon. The back of it doubled as a house of ill repute. The owner was a madam going by the name Mary Gibson.[5]

"Well, you remain back for a while," Mortimer cautioned. "I will go in first."

Mortimer entered, promptly ordering drinks. Mary Gibson, who went by the name Shaw and had become a Sacramento fixture, poured them up.[6]

Born in Ireland but growing up in New Orleans, Mary was by some accounts as young as forty-two, by others as old as forty-seven. She had come to San Francisco in the early days with her husband, John Shaw, a fisherman. Two sisters also made Sacramento their home, and two brothers lived in San Francisco. In 1852 John Shaw drowned in Sutter Slough. Suddenly a widow, Mary bought three buildings on Jibboom Street. She also remarried, this time to John Gibson, a steamboat man. They soon separated but never divorced. Mary also faced an uphill battle against Charles Crocker and the Southern Pacific Railroad, who were laying tracks on Front Street and demanded her property. Mary fought them in the courts, but ultimately was forced to sell, netting thirteen thousand dollars. To avoid taxation, she had given some of that money to friends to hold for her.

Although her Jibboom house wasn't much bigger than a rookery, and by some accounts cleanliness wasn't one of Mary's virtues, she reveled in her independence and enjoyed showing off her earnings. On her right hand she wore a gold ring, on her left a diamond ring, and she possessed a dazzling array of expensive silk dresses. She was known to keep some money on her person, and it was said somewhere on the premises she possessed a calico bag containing $2,250 in silver half dollars. Along with making money through the grocery, saloon, property sales, and one-woman bordello, she also sold cases of liquor to American Indians (a crime that had gotten her into hot water with the law that summer) and even rented rooms to the Indians.[7]

While Mortimer sized-up Mary, Carrie entered. Laying on the charm, Mortimer told Carrie "she looked good enough to kiss," or something to that effect.

"Yes, give the man a kiss," Mary encouraged, likely foreseeing a ménage à trois scenario unfolding. "I think he looks good enough to kiss, and if you don't kiss him I will."

Before Mary could make good the promise, Carrie threw her arms around Mortimer and kissed him. Afterward, they made pleasant conversation and drank their beer. An old man, Henry George Jefferson, whom Mortimer described as "agreeable," and everyone called "Uncle Jeff," was present. More patrons entered, and Mortimer bought a round of drinks. In due course Mary asked Mortimer and Carrie if they would like to withdraw to the sitting room, which would afford them more privacy. They accepted the invitation, and while they adjourned there Mary brought the beer.[8]

Still intoxicated from earlier in the day, Mortimer happily let Carrie do most of the talking. From their manner, he got the impression Carrie was intimating to Mary that Mortimer had quite a lot of money—which wasn't a hard yarn to swallow. He had been spending money like water. Mary also stole Carrie away to show off her kitchen. On returning, Mary eventually confided that she had to get back to the bar, but that they could stay in the sitting room and "talk and make all the love" they wished.

As soon as she'd left, Mortimer told Carrie he didn't like the setup. He felt sick and sleepy, and he wished to go back to the hotel.

"See how filthy everything is? Look at her, how dirty she is," Mortimer said.

Carrie disagreed. In the kitchen Mary had told her the place might look shabby now but given a half hour she could be dressed in as fine a silk dress "as any lady in the city." Carrie also said she'd seen gold in Mary's pocket.

When Mary returned, Carrie told her she must help persuade her beau to stay a while longer. Mary thought perhaps if she and Carrie were wearing the right clothes it would put Mortimer more at ease. Certain winks were exchanged between the ladies. Mortimer felt divided. On the one hand, if they did end up robbing Mary, plenty of witnesses would recall them having gone into the sitting room. On the other hand, Mortimer rather enjoyed where this was heading. He felt confident that he would be able to stop Carrie from doing anything foolish, and in the meantime he saw no harm in playing out the string a little longer.

At about 5:30 p.m. Mortimer excused himself, telling them he would return momentarily. Instead, Mortimer left the establishment. Even though they now had the run of the place, things had gone too far. Mortimer's plan was to wait outside until Carrie went looking for him, whereupon he could talk her into returning to the hotel with him.

Wandering toward Yolo Bridge, where the track crossed Water Street, Mortimer ran into a man with whom he soon became acquainted. Mortimer invited him to have a drink at a saloon farther up the street, but the man insisted on visiting Gibson's.

"We went to Gibson's, drank, and he sang two or three songs," Mortimer recalled. "He then went out. I was also going; Mrs. Gibson told me to wait, that she wished to speak to me."

Mortimer tried to excuse himself for a few moments more, but Carrie and Mary took hold of him, guiding him down the hall and telling him that he should sleep there that night.

"Wait, I'll shut the door," Mary said, "then no one will come in and disturb us."

Mary closed the front door, but Mortimer could tell it wasn't locked. Mary returned and led them through the second door on the right. Near dusk, the house had grown dark. When Mary lit a candle, Mortimer could make out a couple bunks, a chest of drawers, and a bed. The candle Mary placed on one of the bunks. Mary and Carrie sat on the bed, talking pleasantly.

After winking at Carrie, Mortimer said, "You and Carrie just arrange things to please yourselves, and I will be satisfied."

"Very well," Mary said. "There is not much business, and I won't open the saloon to-night. We will get supper, and then pass the evening with ourselves."

Finding this agreeable, Mortimer said, "You ladies amuse yourself for a few minutes. I must step out."

Mortimer backtracked to the front door, finding he could not lock it without a key. Walking quickly but softly back to the hall, he got out his skeleton keys. Before he could lock the front door, however, he heard raised voices from inside the bedroom.

"What are you doing? That's your game!" Mary shouted.

"Charley!" Carrie cried.

Bursting into the room, Mortimer saw that Mary had hold of Carrie's left hand, and her other hand was in her hair, forcing her head down.

"You commenced quarreling soon," Mortimer said dryly.

"The damned bitch had her hand in my pocket," Mary said.

"Well, let her go. Let's talk the matter over," Mortimer said.

"No I won't," Mary swore. "I am going to find out who she is."

Mortimer had moved to one side of Mary and attempted to catch her around the throat. Mary was too quick for him. Letting go of Carrie, Mary made for Mortimer. As she did so Mortimer raised one of the beer glasses, smashing it against her forehead. As it broke, Mary fell against his chest, raking her hand against his cheeks.

"Murder!" Mary shouted.

So it was. Mortimer pushed her back toward the bed. She fell—but not before ripping out a good chunk of Mortimer's beard and leaving bloody scratches on his cheeks. Alive but stunned, Mary had fallen onto the bed in the opposite manner of Caroline Prenel. Her torso was on the bed, her feet on the floor.

"She has pulled my whiskers out, and I guess the flesh with them," Mortimer said. He then instructed Carrie to lock the front door. She did so. Coming back, Carrie picked up the broken beer glass and stabbed Mary two or three times. Mary groaned and slid off the bed, took a long, shuddering breath, and groaned again. Carrie determined she needed something more decisive. Taking out a small penknife from her pocket, she cut Mary's throat.

To Mortimer, Carrie asked, "Now, Charley, don't you think I got any nerve?"

Like she had with Caroline, Carrie stomped down on Mary's neck. But this wasn't enough for Carrie. She needed one more thing to make the murder complete.

"[She] told me to do likewise," Mortimer recalled. "I did so."[9]

After making sure Mary's heart was no longer beating, Carrie robbed the corpse of five hundred dollars, picked out all the jewelry from the drawers, and decided on which dresses she desired. Mortimer brought a trunk down from Mary's wardrobe. Upon discovering them filled with undergarments, Carrie decided she wanted these as well. Rolling up the dresses, Mortimer clutched them with one hand while using both to lift the heavy trunk. Carrie herself hoisted the hair and hat boxes, having found a curly wig of which she was especially fond. Outside, the nearly full moon was up, and people were out and about. Trying to stay inconspicuous as much as possible, twenty or thirty minutes later they reached Yolo Bridge.[10]

"Damn the trunk," Mortimer cursed, and heaved it into the slough. With luck they could retrieve it tomorrow. Without the heavy trunk to weigh them down, they quickly retraced their steps to the Mechanics Exchange. Spying two or three men in the barroom doorway, they headed into the alley around back, near the hotel's back gate. While they did so, two of these men walked around the corner and, for a moment, looked into the alley before disappearing.

"I wish these damned things were in hell," Mortimer cursed and threw the dresses into the weeds. Taking the hint, Carrie hid the boxes she'd been carrying behind a wagon across from the alley. When she returned, Mortimer tried to open the back gate to the hotel. It was locked. A dog began to bark. Discouraged, Mortimer suggested they abandon their plunder.

"No you shan't," Carrie said. "Those dresses are good and I want them, and that hair I know will match mine. It's worth $15 or $20 dollars."

Disgusted, Mortimer took off his bloody cuff, tossed it in the weeds next to the fence, and said, "Damned if I remain here any longer, and these things can go to hell. Are you coming?"

"You can go," Carrie replied. "I'll take care of these things."

Needing no more encouragement, Mortimer walked through the hotel's front door, through the barroom—noticing the bartender and two patrons—and up to his room. There he washed his hands and face. Afterward he used the water closet, walked downstairs, and left the Mechanics Exchange. The night was young, after all.[11]

Heading down Second, Mortimer returned to the Colonade Saloon beneath the Grand Hotel. There he paid Mose Drew the five dollars he owed him and spent about twenty minutes shooting dice. Around midnight he walked 400 feet east to the Gem Saloon on Second and K, opposite the Bank Exchange Saloon.[12]

"I was still very drunk, and I had become indifferent to everything," Mortimer recalled. "The whole thing was so horrible, so uncalled for, that I did not want to become sober and think the matter over in a serious manner."[13]

Still, Mortimer had business to attend to. Outside the Gem, he heard Mose Drew inside. Barging in, he "grossly insulted" Mose Drew, as the *Sacramento Bee* later reported, calling him a liar. Drew responded by smacking Mortimer, knocking him down, and kicking him in the face. At around two in the morning, Mortimer was noticed outside the Gem by Harris and Dole, the officers surprised to see Mortimer's face scratched and bleeding and shirt bosom bloody as well. Mortimer explained to the officers that he'd been in a fight at the Gem with Mose Drew and had lost his hat. Determining this to be true, Harris and Dole escorted Mortimer to his room at the Mechanics Exchange.[14]

All in all, it had been a hell of a bender. He'd hit up half a dozen saloons: the Mechanics Exchange bar, the Union Hotel bar, the Bank Exchange Saloon, the Colonade Saloon, Gibson's, and the Gem. He'd had his face scratched, a handful of whiskers torn off, killed a woman, robbed her, left the plunder lying all over town, got in a barfight, got kicked in the face, and had the cops see him home. Certainly, it hadn't been Mortimer's day.

At least he wasn't in jail.

Red-handed

*T*he next morning, September 20, Uncle Jeff stopped by Gibson's to buy his daily groceries. Finding the store not yet open, he tried the door. It was unlocked. Entering, he called for Mary to wake up. When she didn't answer, he began to suspect she may have been locked up. Between the charges against her for selling liquor to Indians and her "other" profession, it was a fair bet she was behind bars. After walking to the City Prison, Uncle Jeff asked Officer George Wentworth if Mary had been arrested last night.

"I told him she was not," Wentworth recollected.

At that moment F. D. Chamberlain—who, by chance, had been one of the three policemen to arrest Mortimer for vagrancy nine years ago—came in to relieve Wentworth. Finding Mary's absence suspicious, Wentworth left Chamberlain in charge of the jail while he and Uncle Jeff went back to the Jibboom house to investigate.

Entering Gibson's, which was quite dark, they looked around the front of the house. There was no sign of her. Suspecting foul play, Wentworth continued to search the front room while Uncle Jeff, lingering in the doorway, spotted Chris Weiderholt passing by. After being appraised of the situation, Weiderholt, who was married to Mary's cousin and was commonly called "Holt," went to a nearby shop for a candle and joined Wentworth inside.

"We lit a light and went into her room, and still could not find her," Wentworth recalled. "I went down under the house, while he remained upstairs."

Wentworth was examining the bed of the slough beneath the house when Holt called that he'd found her.[1]

As the *Sacramento Bee* reported later that day, "[Weiderholt] discovered the missing woman lying in an east to west direction near the wall, just opposite the door, with her head terribly mutilated, in a pool of blood, the left side of her neck terribly cut, severing the jugular vein, and drawn up. She was of course dead."[2]

Wentworth left immediately for 112 Seventh Street, the residence of the new chief of police, Matthew F. Karcher. Karcher accompanied Wentworth to Gibson's, secured the premises from intrusion, and sent for the coroner. Policemen from all over the city soon arrived, including Harris, Dole, and Special Deputy Sheriff Willis.[3]

"Mrs. Gibson lay on her right side, her head pointing to the east, the floor under her neck being covered with the blood that had flown from a terrible gash in the left side of the neck," Willis reported. "There were several very severe wounds on her face, one over the left eye, another across the bridge of the nose and two or three on the sides of her head. The floor is full of wide cracks and the blood had dripped through and formed a pool on the ground some fifteen feet below, the house being raised from the slough on scantlings. On the floor beside the body was found a broken bar glass covered with blood which had evidently been used to do the foul deed."[4]

On the windowsill was a smaller tumbler, filled with stale beer. Willis noticed a white substance at the bottom of the glass he thought suspicious.[5]

In due course, Dr. Cluness, the coroner, arrived, removing the body to the undertaking rooms of Conboie & Co. at 108 J. The beer glass was removed for examination as well. Some of the officers initially concluded that the rooms had been ransacked, but later determined, because Gibson kept a messy house, it was hard to tell what, if anything, was missing. Although the murderer had apparently missed the bag filled with $2,300 in silver half dollars, which the policemen found lying in plain sight on top of the bureau.[6]

"Chief of Police Matt Karcher had been active," Willis reported, "and had detailed the entire police force to work up the case."

The prevailing theory was that Mary Gibson had been murdered by the Indians that commonly dried fish and camped behind the back of the house. Some were even known to sleep in blankets in Mary Gibson's rear bedroom. When a switch boy came forward, claiming he'd seen "some Indians" leaving the house early in the morning and left aboard the six o'clock freight train, that seemed to settle it. Mary Gibson had been murdered by savages.[7]

Several Indians were detained for questioning and taken to police headquarters. Three who had left on the morning train were brought back as well. Whether one or all of them committed the foul murder would soon be determined.

At nine o'clock news from the coroner's office soon spoiled this theory. Discovered in Mary's death grip was a good handful of curly, reddish-brown hair, evidently torn from the murderer's beard during the struggle. Although this should have ruled out the American Indians, the police continued to keep the men in custody. But, with this foolproof clue, their focus shifted. Rather than looking for an Indian, they sought a white man with a reddish-brown beard, partially torn off at the right side, probably with scratches on at least one cheek. The coroner also reported that a cotton bag Mary wore under her skirts, used to hide money on her person, had been turned inside out and the contents stolen. They now knew the murderer was also a thief.[8]

The *Sacramento Bee* published the story of the murder and the results of the inquest shortly afterward. Moving quickly, Chief Karcher also had published that the police were looking for a man missing a patch of curly, brownish-red hair from his beard. Mortimer did not reveal in his memoir whether he read the *Sacramento Bee* or the police notice that morning. But he'd already put it together that evidence of his guilt was written all over his face. Initiating the barfight with Mose Drew at the Gem Saloon had helped to camouflage with fresh bruises the scratches Mary had given him. Now all he needed to do was shave his beard.

At 10:00 a.m. Mortimer entered Charles Borkman's barbershop at 7 K Street, across from the Grand Hotel. He took the first seat and asked for a shave. A youngster named John H. Malleis lathered and shaved him, leaving only his mustache. Borkman noticed Mortimer's appearance. Responding to the police notice, Borkman went to police headquarters and announced he believed the man they were looking for had just had a shave. Descending on the barbershop, the police found Mortimer gone but showed the boy the clump of hair found in Mary's hand. The boy recognized it, in color and constitution, as identical to the beard he had just shaved. By the man's physical description, the lawmen correctly fingered Charles Mortimer for the murder of Mary Gibson.[9]

According to Willis, this came as no surprise to Harris and Dole. In fact, they'd never bought the Indian angle, thinking it a red herring. Instead, they'd figured Mortimer as the culprit. From the amount of liquor in him last night, he'd evidently been spending money like a drunken sailor. Knowing Mortimer, odds were that money was stolen. Add that to the blood covering his face, his reddish-brown beard, and his history of crime, the policemen were convinced they had their man. All they needed to do was arrest him.

A little before two o'clock, Karcher, Harris, Dole, and Rider located Carrie at the Mechanics Exchange. Mortimer was out, but they were closing in. In Carrie's valise they discovered five of Mary Gibson's dresses. More treasures were soon unearthed.

"There was also a large quantity of jewelry of almost every description, including some which Mrs. Gibson had owned in her lifetime," Willis observed. "All of these circumstances pointed most clearly towards Carrie Spencer and Mortimer as the guilty persons. The cause of the murder was then, evidently, plunder."

Desperate to save herself, Carrie claimed that the dresses were gifts from Mortimer. Dispatching Harris and Dole to locate Mortimer, Karcher placed Carrie under arrest. At two o'clock, just after Karcher and Rider entered the station house with Carrie and Mary Gibson's stolen possessions, the Indians were finally cut loose. Searching Carrie, the police also found $127 in gold coins hidden up her sleeve and a handsome watch and chain.[10]

Less than an hour later, Harris and Dole spotted Mortimer on the northeast corner of Second and J Street. Mortimer had washed away the blood and had his whiskers shaved, leaving only a mustache, but the black eye and scratches stood out. Mortimer didn't resist when they placed him under arrest—and they didn't tell him what they were arresting him for. At 3 p.m. they brought him to City Prison.

Borkman quickly identified Mortimer as the barbershop patron Malleis had shaved. Mortimer was escorted to the southeast corner cell. According to Willis, when the police searched Mortimer they turned up a gold watch and chain, a few silver dollars, and a bottle of strychnine, all of which they confiscated.[11]

The next day, September 21, 1872, the *Sacramento Bee* celebrated that, less than twenty-four hours after the murder had been committed, they had captured the killer. No rest for the wicked, that same day Harris, Dole, Rider, and Willis placed Mortimer in a carriage and drove him to Conboi's undertaking rooms. There, with only the lawmen and the coroner present, they led him to an open coffin. Instructed to look at the body, Mortimer gazed at the corpse of Mary Gibson, then back at the officers, seemingly uncomprehending.

"Charley, do you know this woman?" Harris asked.

"Why, that is the woman who lived on Jibboom Street," Mortimer answered.

"Do you know her very well?"

"Not very well. I have seen her."

"I should not think you could recognize her in that condition unless you knew her pretty well."

"Well, I only know her the same as anybody else I have seen."

At that Harris raised up his hand, containing the clump of beard Mary had torn from his face, and said, "This is what tells the story, Charley."

"What is that?"

"That's your whiskers."

"Oh, my God! Len, don't say that. That's not my whiskers. So help me God, it ain't."

Mortimer's lips quivered as he looked back to the body of the murdered woman, and as he looked at the terrible gash in her neck he leapt back, as though in horror. The police weren't buying it. They hauled him back to City Prison and, inside Karcher's office, Harris grilled him over his actions on September 19 while Dole, Rider, and Willis looked on, Willis copying down the answers.

"He denied having committed doing the deed," Willis noted, "and said that he spent most of Thursday afternoon and night at Mose Drew's saloon. He said he bought the poison in San Francisco and used a little of it to poison rats. He said that on Wednesday night he had been at the circus.... He claimed to have little recollection of any thing that occurred on Thursday ... because he was so drunk. He said that he had shaved his whiskers off because some one told him that he would look better."

That day the report from the coroner's inquest was delivered. Unsurprisingly, Mary Gibson had died from blood loss after her carotid artery was severed. The police also discovered bloodstains at the bottom of a pair of Mortimer's pantaloons, and on one of his boots, partially disguised by blacking. Both were taken as evidence. Mortimer was returned to his cell, and Karcher had him fitted with double iron rivulets.

"They consisted of a shackle around each ankle, and about four feet of a log chain attached to each shackle," Mortimer recalled. "Their weight was about thirty pounds."[12]

Over the next several days Mortimer would sometimes communicate with an inmate whose name he recalled as Mary Watson. Imprisoned thirty or forty feet away, Mortimer sometimes spoke very loudly so she could hear him. On September 25 or 26, Mortimer was speaking loudly to Mary when another voice responded. It was Carrie. She'd been imprisoned fifty feet away.[13]

"We exchanged a few words, and I told her to keep awake and at a proper time I would call her. . . . At about midnight I coughed," Mortimer recorded, "and in a few moments Carrie answered me with another."

Mortimer asked her to stand atop a chair, whereby she could look out over the top of her cell door to see if the doors leading out of the office were closed. Even in the darkness, Mortimer knew that Carrie would be able to tell if they were open or closed, for at night the open doors were illuminated by gaslight.

"Yes, they are closed," Carrie said.

"When was you arrested?" Mortimer asked.

"Very soon after you went out on Thursday," Carrie replied. "When was you arrested?"

"About an hour after I left the room."

"Have they asked you any questions?" Carrie asked.

"Yes, they wished to know where I was on Thursday night," Mortimer answered. "I told them at Mose Drew's and other saloons."

"Say you and I were at the circus till half-past nine," Carrie urged. "You got sick, and we left for home. That's what I told them!"

"All right. I'll do so."

Mortimer also told Carrie to say he'd brought her the dresses and jewelry on Thursday, and that he'd bought them off some man. They agreed to speak again on it the next night at about the same time. The signal would be Mortimer rattling his chains. The next night Mortimer told her that if she followed his instructions, either the justice or grand jury would acquit her.

"Be guided by me and you will come out of your present trouble all right; listen to what others tell you, and you will be forever lost. Go to bed—I hear the watchmen coming. Goodbye."

"Goodbye, darling," Carrie said.

This was their last conversation for some time, for over the next few nights a number of loud drunks were given lodgings in the cells, and the policemen kept the office doors open. Still, Mortimer was pleased. He knew at the upcoming examination he and Carrie would tell the same story before the judge. Even if he didn't get off, there was a good chance she would, which would be better for him.

"I knew that if she got clear, she would be of great service to me," Mortimer scribbled.[14]

Even while he schemed and plotted to free himself, to the guards he appeared to grow increasingly more agitated and violent. At one point he cursed at a Chinese janitor cleaning out his cell. On the morning of September 29, Mortimer told Wentworth that he would not eat anything prepared in the jail, convinced that his captors meant to poison him. Wentworth responded by telling him things would go much better for him if he kept civil, and that he was free to starve if he liked. When his breakfast was brought, Mortimer ate it without complaint. From these incidents arose speculation that Mortimer was angling for the insanity plea.[15]

Meanwhile, Karcher summoned Mary's sisters, Elizabeth Champion and Anna Stafford, who verified the dresses found with Carrie were indeed Mary's. Other witnesses, who had seen Mortimer on September 19, were located. The examination before the Police Court for both Mortimer and Carrie was scheduled for October 3, but when Judge Thomas W. Gilmer—a native of Ireland with a notably irascible temper—came down sick, the examination was rescheduled for the following Thursday. Mortimer still got to speak on his behalf on October 3, but it was to Special Deputy Willis.[16]

To Willis, Mortimer declared he'd been badly treated, unable to prepare a defense. He asked the special deputy to copy down his testimony. Willis obliged.

"He then went on and gave a full account for himself on the day and night of the murder, which differed greatly from the statements made to the officers in Chief Karcher's office," Willis noted.

It turned out Mortimer had bought the dresses and jewelry from a man he remembered only as "George," which were left for him in a clump of bushes near Yolo Bridge that Thursday. Passing Mary's, he'd gone in and had a drink, and Carrie had joined him a little later, the both of them imbibing till six in the evening. They returned to the Mechanics Exchange, had supper, went to the circus, and around midnight Mortimer found Mose Drew in the Colonade Saloon and repaid him the five dollars he owed him. At about two o'clock, he'd gotten into a fight with Mose Drew at the Gem Saloon, whereupon Harris and Dole had seen him home. Possession of the dresses and jewelry, his presence at Mary's, and the blood and scratches on his clothing and person were all neatly explained.

"This statement I wrote out in full," Willis recorded, "and preserved it with the first one taken for future use."

Willis's first instinct was to publish both, demonstrating Mortimer as a liar, but Karcher talked him out of it. With both statements made public, the defense could argue no juror could claim impartiality, thus making a fair trial impossible. Mortimer may have considered that a possibility, but more than anything he was establishing that, independent of him having conversed with Carrie (as far as anyone knew), they both told the same story of what happened on the evening Mary was killed.

On October 10 Mortimer was brought to Police Court and examination before Judge Gilmer. To the surprise of the court, Mortimer stated he could manage the case without the help of counsel. The evidence against him appeared damning. Karcher, Harris, Dole, and Wentworth testified against him. William S. Tassey, a switchman who lived at the Mechanics Exchange, declared that he'd seen Mortimer near the railroad track on the night Mary Gibson was murdered. Michael Haggerty, who lived and worked at the United States Hotel at 53 Front Street, had seen Mortimer at the Jibboom house at 6 p.m. Uncle Jeff declared he had seen both Mortimer and Carrie there. Mary's sisters identified the clothing and jewelry found in Mortimer's room. Dr. J. F. Rudolph, a respected chemist, claimed that the beer was indeed laced with strychnine. Furthermore, three-eighths of a small bottle had been emptied into the beer glass; the bottle Mortimer had been arrested with contained five-eighths of a full bottle. John Clark also testified that at about a half hour before midnight Mortimer had repaid Mose Drews five dollars at the Colonade Saloon, arousing suspicion of where the money had come from.

In his defense, Mortimer called Harris and Dole to the stand. Despite questioning them closely, their version of that night held up. Mortimer next called for Carrie to testify.

"Carrie was called in and gave her testimony," Mortimer recorded. "While she was giving it I could not help but think of the contrast between it and the truth—a fearful meditation. She had made so good a showing, and done it with such cool deliberation that I could plainly see, that with a little more doctoring, that we could make a much better showing than the prosecution could."

Heartened, Mortimer repeated the same version of events. To hear Carrie and Mortimer tell it, he was as innocent as the day was long. None of this made a dent with Judge Gilmer. Mortimer would be held to answer to the charge of murder before a grand jury. He was then led outside and taken to 111 J Street where Henry S. Beals photographed him. Afterward, Mortimer was transferred from City Prison to County Jail.[17]

Along with trading living quarters, Mortimer now found himself under the jurisdiction of Sacramento County Sheriff Mike Bryte. About forty-four years old, Bryte was striking: mustached, goateed, mostly bald, and, at three hundred pounds, exuding a hulking presence. Mortimer didn't seem to mind Bryte, describing him as "a big giant with an open face, and high-hearted and confiding; he is not a detective, and is inexperienced at that business."[18]

Bill Shearer was a different matter. The chief jailor of Sacramento County Jail did not make things easy for the accused murderer, and Mortimer grew to resent him. Small wonder, for Cell No. 5—the six-by-six dungeon in which he was placed, referred to as a "tomb" in his memoir—was particularly miserable. "I had no way of knowing what was going on about my case—no friend, no attorney to see me or help me," Mortimer lamented. "My fellow prisoners were not allowed to talk to me. I was allowed to see few papers. I was buried alive." One high point was that Mortimer was given an ink bottle and paper.[19]

On October 15, 1872, the breadth and depth of the trouble Mortimer was in, coupled with his hellish internment, seemingly got the best of him. Cutting his undershirt into strips, he braided it into a rope. Before he could make use of it, his guards caught him in the act and removed the rope. Speculation around the prison was that Mortimer either intended to cheat the gallows by hanging himself, or wanted to give the impression that he was suicidal.[20]

Meanwhile, a hundred miles southwest of Sacramento, Captain Isaiah W. Lees was hot on the trail of Caroline Prenel's true killer. "[A]fter studying the case thoroughly," Lees related, "I made up my mind that the real clew to the murderer was the jewelry which was stolen from the murdered woman."[21]

First, Lees looked hard at Bec, tracing his movements, seeking to determine if the Frenchman had ever possessed Caroline's jewelry, and if he might have stashed them somewhere. Discovering nothing, Lees then made a systematic search of San Francisco's pawnshops. Lees knew it wasn't enough to look at the pawnbrokers' books, for though they would give a description of the jewelry, they wouldn't contain the minute detail necessary to determine if they had been Caroline's.

"Day after day I continued my search and had gone through several pawnshops in this way until I was thoroughly tired of my work," Lees reflected, "but I knew that not a single package in any shop in town could be slighted. Finally as I was at work on the safe of a man named Abrahams, who kept a place on Dupont street, I opened a package which contained a brooch and a ring. The moment my eyes fell on them I knew that my search had resulted in success and that I held in my hand the first point in the game."

Referencing Abrahams's books, Lees determined the brooch and diamond ring had been pawned by a fellow who'd given his name as "Walker." Although Abrahams had written down that name, he'd recognized it as an alias. To Lees, Abrahams dished that the large, stout, bearded man who sold him the jewelry wasn't "Walker" but Mortimer—Charles Mortimer.

"I knew Mortimer as a professional thief and criminal, a bold, unscrupulous man, who had often been in the hands of the police," Lees reflected, "and who had only a short time before been discharged from San Quentin."[22]

Lees also knew Mortimer and his moll, Carrie, had traded San Francisco for Sacramento shortly after Caroline's body had been discovered, and he was currently incarcerated in Sacramento County Jail for the murder of another woman of the town. With Henri Bec's life at stake, Lees devised a secret plan to exonerate the Frenchman and, if all went right, make certain that Mortimer finally answered for his crimes.

CHAPTER 13

Captain Lees's Secret Plan

While Mortimer languished in Sacramento County Jail, the wheels of justice quickened. On October 17 Judge Gilmer held Carrie as an accessory to murder. Transferred to the women's section of County Jail on October 19, she was kept far away from Mortimer. Shortly thereafter, Bill Shearer—on a tip from Captain Lees—thoroughly searched Carrie's cell. The result was the discovery of a pair of earrings that matched the description of the ones stolen from Caroline Prenel.

Four days later, on October 23, 1872, Henri Bec and his lawyer, R. H. Lloyd, appeared in San Francisco's Nineteenth District Court. There, to the satisfaction of a few and the surprise of many, Lloyd moved for a continuance on the grounds that if further time were given, he could produce evidence that would clear his client of the murder of his lover and indict the true murderer: Charles Mortimer.

Lloyd also read for the court the affidavit Bec had sworn his name to. In it, Lloyd reiterated their side of the story: that Bec had been aware Caroline was keeping company with a strange man on the night she was killed, that her earrings and diamond ring had been stolen from her, that despite only circumstantial evidence against him, Bec had been arrested for the crime and given a three thousand dollar bail, which he could not pay. All of this was known to the court—but the affidavit then deviated sharply from the expected narrative. A few days ago, Lloyd had been presented with new evidence that Charles Mortimer had been seen with Caroline Prenel earlier that night, and after Prenel had walked home, Mortimer had followed her. Furthermore, Caroline's missing jewelry had been linked to Mortimer. For the earrings, Lloyd was offering a one-hundred-dollar reward.

District Attorney Daniel Murphy naturally opposed the motion. He claimed the affidavit was the work of a "strong imagination," reiterating the evidence against Bec and deeming the defense's motion to delay a stall tactic, motivated by hopes that the witnesses for the prosecution might in the meantime move out of San Francisco. Although Judge Edward D. Wheeler stated that he hardly thought the affidavit strong enough to warrant a continuance, he decided to grant it, to give the defendant every chance to prove his innocence. The case would resume on December 9, 1872.[1]

Not long after, Bill Shearer visited Mortimer in his cell to read him Bec's affidavit. The whole world now knew Mortimer as a killer. Mortimer suspected saloonkeeper

Owen Gaffney, who had seen him and Caroline that night in his saloon, as the man on whose testimony the affidavit was based, writing as much in his memoir: "I knew Owen Gaffney's testimony was all that could be brought against me in the matter."[2]

On October 25 the *San Francisco Examiner* reported that the result of Mortimer's mounting troubles seemed to be loss of appetite, for he ate only a trifle daily, but that this may have been only for show. "Mortimer . . . appears anxious to create the impression he is insane," the reporter concluded.[3]

On October 26 Mortimer fashioned another noose out of his shirt, tied it, and hanged himself. The rope broke. Attempting it again, he was dangling from the noose when the jailor found him and cut him down. The next morning Mortimer was so horribly sick that a physician was brought in. It was revealed he had eaten plug tobacco and an onion, possibly with the notion that the two of them together would cause him death. When Mortimer was seized with fits, few observers believed them genuine. Some suggested it would be for the best for Mortimer to be shackled to the wall, though for the moment they gave him the run of the cell.[4]

Several days later, Mortimer tried it again. At 9:45, on the morning of Halloween, the jailors heard a crashing noise coming from Mortimer's cell. Rushing to it they discovered Mortimer had made another noose, this time from his drawers. Although the noose had broken under his weight, Mortimer had succeeded in badly cutting his neck, though not grievously enough to bleed out. The guards immediately implemented the policy of shackling Mortimer to the wall.[5]

For a fortnight this policy seemed to work well, Mortimer appearing docile and making little trouble. If they only knew. From a tin cup Mortimer removed a thick wire. After making a small needle from a piece of the wire, he secured the wire in the bottom of one trouser leg. Using his skills as a tailor, he tore strips from his blanket and sewed them together with smaller strips he tore from a sheet, thus making two ropes which he stashed in the mattress. He also pounded out sharp pieces of glass from the corner of his bottle of ink. One of these pieces he kept as a makeshift shiv. The others he placed inside a box of pills given to him, hidden inside bread that he had chewed into dough. Although a particularly painful way to die, by eating the glass he could conceivably perish from internal bleeding.

Early in the morning of November 15, when Shearer came to clean out the cell, he discovered Mortimer had once again attempted to take his own life. Lying chained on his mattress, which was soaked with blood that had pooled onto the floor, Mortimer had evidently cut himself in the upper arm and passed out. Waking up as Shearer and jailor Brown searched him, Mortimer put up a brief struggle before they found the glass in his trousers pocket. At about ten in the morning Shearer returned, finding that Mortimer had nearly finished the job by reopening the wound with a comb. After Shearer and Undersheriff Alfred S. Woods handcuffed Mortimer, they located and confiscated all the other implements of destruction.

"Mr. Shearer is doing all possible to prevent suicide," commented the *Sacramento Bee*, "but the wretched man appears resolved to outwit him."[6]

Three days later Mortimer and eleven other prisoners were taken to the County Courthouse where the grand jury examined the charges made against them. Probably for the sake of impartiality, Judge Robert C. Clark ordered Shearer to remove Mortimer's heavy cross irons. Clark should have known better. Carrie was also in attendance. This was Mortimer's first glimpse of her since he'd been moved to County Jail. When Mortimer passed her, he asked, "How do you do, Carrie?" For some reason she ignored him. But she'd be hard-pressed to ignore him on the way out.[7]

"When leaving the court room, I had to pass within two feet of her, and the temptation was so great that I could not resist," Mortimer stated in his memoir. "I stopped in front of her and said, 'Halloa, Carrie. You seem to be ill.' At this stage some half-dozen officers—Shearer and the Chief of Police among them—made desperate lunge at me, to prevent me from speaking to her; in doing so, they pushed me onto her and it somewhat frightened her and her to make a little outcry."

According to Mortimer, Chief Karcher caught him with one hand by the neck and, surrounded by his officers, rushed him out of the courtroom. As Karcher marched him out of there, every so often the German socked Mortimer in the head. Mortimer cried out for help, but the policemen did nothing to stop the chief.

The *Sacramento Bee* told it differently. Concerned that Mortimer might try something at the courthouse, Shearer had asked Chief Karcher if he could spare any of his policemen to see that everything went smoothly. The result was that Karcher, Harris, and Dole joined Shearer, Woods, Deputy A. J. Barnes, and Deputy P. L. Hickman, all paying particularly close attention to Mortimer. After concluding their business in the courthouse, the prisoners were marched out to be returned to jail.

Noted the *Sacramento Bee* reporter:

> Charles Mortimer was the last in line, and as he filed past Carrie Mortimer who was sitting near the door inside the bar, he made a leap like a wild beast at her and tried to catch her throat. There was instantly the intensest excitement in the large crowd of lawyers, jurors, and spectators. Chief Karcher and County Jailor Shearer caught Mortimer and carried him struggling into the hall, where he kicked so savagely and yelled murder so lustily as to soon empty all the offices of their inmates into the big hall.[8]

With Karcher and Shearer occupied with Mortimer, the eleven other prisoners made for the street. Unfortunately for them, Woods, Harris, Dole, Barnes, and Hickman were ready for them, positioned to prevent a break. As Karcher and Shearer overpowered Mortimer, the policemen and sheriffs corralled the prisoners and returned them to their cells.[9]

Although the accounts of the sensational scene in the courtroom differed wildly, there did exist a commonality. If Mortimer's account was the truth, that he had been knocked into Carrie, and after she'd cried out the lawmen had seized Mortimer to prevent him from harming her, it indicates that the police were concerned that Mortimer might attack Carrie. If the account printed in the *Sacramento Bee* was correct, that Mortimer had deliberately attempted to throttle Carrie, it begs the question of why Mortimer might have wanted to injure Carrie.

Whatever the case, the lawmen fitted Mortimer's legs with thirty- to forty-pound cross-chains and returned him to his cell. A few days later, Shearer—claiming Mortimer had behaved himself "pretty well"—asked him if he'd like to see Carrie.

"I should like to speak to Carrie," Mortimer replied, "and shall consider that you have done me a very great favor, for which you shall have my sincere thanks."

At the same time Mortimer knew Shearer must have some ulterior motive, but he didn't care. By the time Shearer returned, Mortimer was lying down on his blanket, the bloody mattress having been removed.

"Charley, here's Carrie come to talk with you," Shearer said.

Mortimer stood up. Chained with the bolt ring to the back of the cell, he could only move about two feet toward the cell door, which he did in anticipation.

"Carrie, I am overjoyed to see you," Mortimer announced. "Why have you not tried to come see me before? You don't look well. What seems to be wrong with your health? Won't Dr. White give you medicine that will build you up?"

"I am not well," Carrie admitted. "It is the same old complaint."

"I feel so sorry for you. You seemed to be improving so rapidly before we got into this horrible trouble."

"Why don't you come nearer . . . it's dark in your cell and I cannot see your face very well."

"Didn't you know I was chained on the back part of my cell? They chained me in this way so I can't reach out and knock out the brains of those who chance to pass my door."

"They have told me many times that it would not do for you to get close enough for you to reach me. If I did, you would be sure to hurt me. I would tell them that no matter how you felt towards others, I was sure that you would not hurt one hair on my head. I would like to look in there and see how you are," Carrie said, almost shyly.

"Well . . . Stand up close. I have a small piece of candle. I will light it, and then you can take observations."

Mortimer lit the candle, and Carrie approached. After a moment, she exclaimed, "Oh! Charlie, what is the matter? You look awful bad!"

"My health is quite good," Mortimer said, declining to tell her of the multiple suicide attempts. "My appetite is somewhat poor. Perhaps I fret a little."

"Let me see how those chains are fixed, and what kind they are. Oh, ain't that awful. And no bed, and that cold iron floor. I should think you would die."

"I often think that people are anxiously looking forward to something of that kind. I think I'll weather the storm. The hopes of a happy future encourages me on wonderfully."

Mortimer's happy future lay in Carrie repeating word for word on the witness stand what Mortimer wished. He gave her the script he'd written for her to memorize and asked her to keep it hidden. Carrie promised she would stash it in her mattress. When Mortimer asked about her legal difficulties, she said that Shearer and Bryte had told her that her case was thrown out, that she was "all right." Mortimer doubted it, but Carrie spoke confidently.[10]

For the next several weeks, Carrie was allowed to visit Mortimer daily, sometimes as many as four times a day. Afterward it began to slow down. Then came November 28, 1872. On that Thanksgiving Day, Carrie appeared, looking sad and ill. When asked the matter, Carrie all but broke down.

"I am not well, and there is something else that troubles me," Carrie admitted.

"Let me know what it is, and perhaps I can advise you on the matter," Mortimer urged, his anxiety raised. When she hesitated, he continued to press her.

"I ... want to tell you, but I'm afraid you will be angry with me."

Mortimer had to tease it out of her, but eventually Carrie told Mortimer of her present difficulties, the details of which Mortimer did not record.

"Carrie, I'll try to advise you," Mortimer said, "but I am going to ask you a question and either tell me the truth, or don't say anything."

"I always tell you the truth," Carrie said. "Who else would I have spoken to about that—outside of you?"

"That's true. I am a fool. I do believe that my mind is a little weak at times ... I hear little things, and imagine them mountains ... "

"What are you talking about?" Carrie asked. "What is it?"

"Well, the truth is," Mortimer said, "I sometimes imagine you are doing or trying to do something against me."

"Charley, you know in the first place, I would not do anything against you. In the next place, I wouldn't dare to. I don't want you to think such things of me, if you care for—"

"O, don't say anything more! Drop it! I'm a fool. Not another word on the subject," Mortimer said, and changed the topic. "I don't really know just how to advise you in regard to what we were first talking about. Let me hear your idea on the subject."[11]

Banishing any thoughts of Carrie betraying him to the dark recesses of his mind, Mortimer again listened to Carrie's troubles, and tried to help her through them. But as the week passed, Carrie grew more and more distant. Word was that Sheriff Bryte's wife, Elizabeth, was very sick, and that he wanted Carrie to attend her as a nursemaid.

At first she was gone a few days. About a month later, she was gone for about a week. Three weeks after that she disappeared for eight days. Each time she came back, it was the same story: "gone to Bryte's to assist Mrs. Bryte." Mortimer corroborated the story with the guards and had no reason to doubt it.[12]

On December 23 Mortimer was arraigned before Judge S. A. Booker of the Sixth District Court. According to Deputy Willis, "Mortimer . . . feigned insanity, and gave a wild and bitter speech. He was given another day to plead. On the following day he was brought up again, and asked further time to obtain counsel. The Court finally gave him until the 6th of January to plead the indictment."[13]

On January 6, 1873, at 2:30 p.m., Shearer and Hickman brought Mortimer before District Attorney David Starr and Judge Charles E. Lott for the arraignment. Those who knew Mortimer saw him very much changed. With his whiskers having grown out half an inch in length, his hair uncombed, and looking thin and haggard, he wasn't a pretty picture. But the most striking thing about him was the vacant stare in his blue eyes. But the mind behind those eyes was as bombastic as ever.

The fireworks began when Starr asked, "Is that your true name—Charles Mortimer?"

"I don't know that that's any of your business," Mortimer replied.

"What is your name?" Judge Lott asked.

"I tell you it's none of your business," Mortimer shot back.

When Lott asked him if he had retained counsel, Mortimer mentioned that he had spoken to G. W. Tyler of San Francisco and N. Greene Curtis, but neither had come round. Despite Mortimer's wishes, Lott eventually appointed as his attorney Samuel C. Denson, a former assemblyman from Ormsby County, Nevada. Told he had no choice in the matter, Denson gamely rose to the challenge, attempting to get the case thrown out. For some reason, Judge Lott didn't go for it. Ultimately, Denson entered a plea of "not guilty."

Concluding his business with Mortimer, Lott admitted, "It is almost impossible for me to tell whether this man is in a proper frame of mind for trial or not. To-morrow, if the counsel thinks that he is not in his right mind, I will have his case examined by the proper Commissioners. If, however, you think that this is a sham—that he is putting on or pretending insanity—I will fix the time for trial."[14]

Although Mortimer was subsequently deemed mentally fit to stand trial, it wasn't until January 22 that Judge Lewis Rampage fixed *The People v. Mortimer* trial to commence on February 10. If Mortimer thought he'd spend those two and a half weeks inside Sacramento County Jail prepping his defense, he was badly mistaken. On January 25, under heavy guard, Mortimer was placed inside a stagecoach and driven 150 miles south to Santa Cruz. Reaching the seaside city on the night of January 26, Mortimer was to be called as a material witness in the trial set to begin the next week: *The People v. Blakely*. Evidently someone had been talking.[15]

On the morning of January 31, the Santa Cruz Courthouse was packed with spectators. Small wonder, for the infamous Charles Mortimer was set to testify. The papers had it that he had already confessed in private to robbing the Santa Cruz Treasury. Now he would make that public.

When the words rang out, "Mr. Sheriff, call Charles Mortimer," all eyes turned toward the prisoner. "Mortimer was neatly dressed," observed Deputy Willis, "and looked nothing like the desperado he is. He took his seat calmly and without exhibiting any extraordinary insanity."[16]

First to question Mortimer was Blakely's defense attorney, N. Greene Curtis, coincidentally one of the men Mortimer had wanted to retain before Judge Lott appointed him Denson. When asked his name, Mortimer replied, "My name is the one I go by of Charles Mortimer. I know something about the charge against Blakely."

"I would like you to state what you know," Curtis urged.

Mortimer related that on the night of February 2 he arrived in Santa Cruz. After visiting three saloons, he met a companion, whom he declined to name, outside the very courthouse in which he was testifying. After everyone had left but Blakely, they stole inside. While his companion grabbed Blakely's arms from behind, Mortimer made use of his Colt revolver.

"I jammed a pistol against his head," Mortimer testified, "and cocked it so that the click might keep him quiet. Don't know if I would have used it."[17]

Mortimer also divulged some details he hadn't placed in his memoir. He wore the Colt revolver in a scabbard on his right hip. On his left hip he had his knife. The Sharps four-shooter he kept in his back pocket. The handkerchiefs with which he gagged Blakely were silk. Mortimer was dressed in the same coat as he presently wore, though his pants had been darker.

"We put Blakely in the vault," Mortimer continued, "bound and gagged him, and then left. Made some remark about 'weighty swag.'"

"That means plunder?" asked the prosecuting attorney, Alexander Campbell.

"Those in the business generally make use of it," Mortimer explained, clearly enjoying himself. "We held a consultation before putting the party in the vault. My partner thought the best thing would be to 'slough him up with the gopher.' I raised objections, and said bucking him in the room might cause him to 'crook.'"

Although the crowd was certainly getting their money's worth with Mortimer, it was the afternoon session, during cross-examination, which provided the most entertainment. Noted Willis the following day, "Mortimer ... is shrewd and not easily caught in a trap. His answers are as unique as they are original, and some of them in reply to Campbell's questioning, did not fail to affect the risibilities of the spectators. His dry manner of rendering everything added to its humor."

For his opening salvo, Campbell attempted to discredit Mortimer by asking him to share his history in California. Mortimer was game.

"I arrived at San Francisco about the year 1858. Have no business in particular. Do anything I can get to do. I have tried farming, carpentering, teaming, and a little tailoring... Lived in San Francisco for a year.... Went from there to Sacramento... Was from March 1862, to 1863 in Marin County, in Point San Quentin. I went from Siskiyou County, under the name of Foster, for grand larceny."

"You were the man, I believe, who went with Officer Rose to 'raise a plant,' and then cut his throat and left him for dead?" Campbell asked.

"No, sir. I am the man whom Officer Rose took to raise some stolen property, and he wanted it all. We had a scuffle, and the best man had the plunder... left San Francisco the Wednesday preceding the robbery... when coming over the mountains to Santa Cruz, went out of the way to meet a friend. It makes no difference who he is. He is an honest man."

"Are all men honest?" Campbell inquired.

"Yes, we are all honest till we are tried."

"How much did you pay him?"

"What I owed him."

"How did you get into the city from the depot?"

"How do you suppose? By a balloon? Rode in the horse cars part of the way, and walked the balance ... Returned on Monday to San Francisco. My name is none of your business. I decline to answer who my accomplice was. He is my friend, and I shall not give his name."

Pointing to John Melville, Campbell demanded, "Is this the man with you the night of the robbery?"

"I decline to answer," retorted Mortimer.

Campbell next produced the rope which had bound Blakely's hands, and two clean handkerchiefs. Campbell then dared Mortimer to gag Campbell as he had supposedly gagged Blakely. Willis described there being "considerable amusement" in the courtroom as Mortimer gagged Campbell, and that the "torture" could not have been pleasant for the prosecutor to endure. Through struggling, Campbell did manage to partially remove the gag, but to the onlookers Mortimer was the clear victor in the battle of wits.

Curtis also got a taste of Mortimer's cheek. When the defense attorney asked where Mortimer had deposited the money, Mortimer replied, "I decline to answer."

"Is it deposited in a bank?" Curtis pressed.

"Yes, it is one kind of a bank—a sandbank."

All in all, everyone agreed that between the witness and the two lawyers, Campbell got the worst of it. Somewhat humiliated, Campbell did his best over the course of the next several days to tangle Mortimer in his story. When that didn't work, the prosecutor sought to paint Mortimer as an inveterate liar whose testimony couldn't be believed—although, certainly with the handkerchiefs, seeing was believing.

With his back against the wall, perhaps it was partially out of spite that prompted Campbell to ask Mortimer a question that was more of a pronouncement: "Are you not the Charles Mortimer that is indicted for the murder of Caroline Prenel, and that gave Carrie Spencer a pair of earrings, and she gave them to an officer, and they have been identified as having belonged to the murdered woman?"[18]

Those words "sent a cold chill to my heart," Mortimer recalled. On the stand, Mortimer appeared to have played it off, for neither the newspapers nor Deputy Willis made particular note of it—though Mortimer certainly did. He now knew that it hadn't just been Owen Gaffney who had told Captain Lees that Mortimer had been with Caroline on the night she was murdered. Carrie had turned traitor.[19]

It hadn't happened immediately, as Captain Lees detailed. After Lees acquired the earrings Bill Shearer had discovered while searching Carrie's cell, Lees showed them to Minnie Lorch, who verified they were Caroline's. Between the testimony of Gaffney, Minnie, and Abrahams, Lees knew he had a solid case that Mortimer rather than Henri Bec had committed the murder at 115 Waverly Place. But the detective wasn't satisfied. He wanted a confession. Knowing he was doubtful to get one from Mortimer, Lees targeted Carrie.

"Having thoroughly identified the jewels, we then approached the Spencer woman," Lees recalled. "After some prevarication she finally acknowledged that they had been given to her by Mortimer early in June. She asked him where he got them, and although at first he told her it was none of her business, he finally said that he had beaten a woman out of them."[20]

According to Willis, by this time Carrie and Bill Shearer were already getting chummy, splitting the one-hundred-dollar reward R. H. Lloyd had offered for the earrings. Certainly, Carrie needed a protector. Other than Mortimer, only Carrie knew that she had killed Caroline Prenel, and that she as much as Mortimer had murdered Mary Gibson. With her own neck on the line, Carrie agreed to testify that Mortimer had told her he had killed both women. The decision spared her from being indicted.[21]

"During this time Carrie Spencer had been very active," Willis reflected.[22]

First, Carrie and Shearer traveled one hundred miles southwest to San Francisco, where in late October she testified that Mortimer had killed Caroline. Along with the other evidence, Carrie's testimony resulted in Bec's release. Whether or not Mortimer actually did attack Carrie in the Sacramento Courthouse on November 18, after his examination, as the police and press believed, or was pushed into her, as he claimed, the game of cat and mouse intensified. In his memoir, Mortimer admitted that he sometimes suspected Carrie was working against him. For his part, although Shearer claimed he kept Mortimer shackled to his cell wall to stop him from killing himself, in actuality it was just as much to keep him away from killing Carrie when she visited him outside his cell.[23]

Naturally, Carrie's purpose in visiting her former lover was not to comfort him, but to attain further information the police might use against him. When Mortimer gave her the script he'd written for her to repeat at his trial, hoping her testimony would exonerate him, rather than stashing it in her mattress she turned it over to Shearer. Furthermore, Carrie divulged that Mortimer had been behind the Santa Cruz Treasury robbery. The excuse everyone repeated—that Carrie periodically left Sacramento County Jail to help take care of Sheriff Mike Bryte's wife—was also a deception.

Playing ball with the police might save her from the gallows, but that wasn't her only ambition. According to Deputy Willis, Carrie desired to locate Mortimer's cache of money as well, and made a deal with Shearer to find it. For that purpose, in the closing days of 1872, Carrie and Shearer left Sacramento.

"I am unable to say from my own knowledge where they went," Willis admitted, "but Deputy Sheriff [George] Swain, of Antioch, a thorough detective, who has since died, 'shadowed' a man and woman who made a midnight visit to Marsh Creek, carrying with them a shovel, with which they dug for some time in the bed of the creek. Swain made up his mind that they were digging for a 'plant' . . . Swain said that the man was a Deputy Sheriff from Sacramento."[24]

Although *The Sacramento Bee* reported that Carrie and Shearer returned to Sacramento on the night of January 3, they did not report whether they carried with them any heavy bags. On January 27 Carrie was also taken by stagecoach to Santa Cruz. Unlike Mortimer, she was given the freedom of the town. By now *The Sacramento Bee* had a nickname for her: Carrie Mortimer, the Belle of Antioch. The next day *The San Francisco Chronicle* reported that Carrie Mortimer was a witness for the prosecution in the Gibson murder case and had informed Sheriff Bryte of several robberies Mortimer had perpetrated.[25]

The day after Campbell revealed to Mortimer that Carrie had testified against him in San Francisco for the murder of Caroline Prenel, Mortimer was allowed to speak to Carrie.

"I told her that was a damned nice thing I heard she had been playing on me," Mortimer recalled. "I told her I'd make her sick if it was true."

"Charley, it's a lie," Carrie claimed. "I never said any such thing. They want me to say so but I know it will not do. Don't believe them."[26]

Shortly thereafter, while locked in his lightless Santa Cruz cell, George W. Tyler stopped by to see him.

"Well, Charley, I am very sorry for you," the lawyer told him. "It is two very bad charges that are pending against you."

"Mr. Tyler, I wish you would have the kindness to explain matters to me—let me know what you have heard or know. I begin to suspect some villainous treachery."

"Why, don't you know all about what Carrie has been doing?"

"I have heard something, but don't believe it. I want to hear it from you."

"Carrie testified at the Bec trial that you gave her the finger and earrings the morning after the murder, that you was out all night, that you had done the murder, and that you could speak the French language."

"It can't be possible that she has done that."

"Yes, she did. I suppose you knew all about it. Can you speak French?"

"No, not a word. This is so foreign from the truth that I cannot believe she has done it."

"It is just as I tell you," Tyler repeated.[27]

On February 8 Mortimer rattled into Sacramento on the Saturday night train, in the custody of Sheriff R. Orton. Afterward, Mortimer was returned to his old cell. As he tried to blot out the inescapable truth about Carrie, that she had wholly betrayed him and was set to pin on him the murder of Mary Gibson, Mortimer must have despaired. His best possibility of escaping the gallows, beyond suicide, lay in convincing the jury he was innocent or insane.[28]

That, or a jailbreak.

CHAPTER 14

The Ides of March

*I*n February of 1873 *The Boston Globe* printed a story about "The Famous Criminal, Mortimer." Included in the article was a list of his known crimes, beginning with the attempted robbery in San Francisco that sent him to San Quentin in 1862, ending with his indictment for murder in Sacramento a decade later. Any reader of the *Globe* who knew Mortimer's true identity would be quick to realize the gravity of the situation.[1]

Back in California, reporters and policemen around the capital were ready for blood. On the morning of February 10, with the Mortimer trial about to begin, Sacramento's Sixth District Courtroom was packed. Those looking for a spectacle, however, would be disappointed. For one, Mortimer seemed passive and disinterested throughout the whole proceedings, a far cry from the "Mad" Mortimer they had seen last year, and the showman Mortimer they had heard about in Santa Cruz. For another, S. C. Denson moved for a continuance, declaring that since Mortimer had been in Santa Cruz, he had had no time to confer with him on the case. Denson also stated that Mortimer wished G. W. Tyler, who wouldn't become available for a week or two, to replace him as counsel. District Attorney Starr objected, claiming these facts insufficient for a continuance, but Denson dug in his heels. Under no circumstances would he accept the grave responsibility of defending an accused murderer without being allowed time to prepare.

The court split the baby. Denson would remain as counsel, but the continuance was granted. The defense attorney had until March 12 to prepare for trial.[2]

Mortimer had no intention of returning to the courtroom. Back in his cell, he waited until the guards had disappeared. Clutching a shard from a broken saucer in his right hand, Mortimer used it to slash open a vein in his left arm. By the time the jailors discovered him his heart still pumped blood. After stanching the bleeding, they searched the cell for anything else Mortimer could use to do himself in.[3]

On February 16 Sheriff Mike Bryte visited Mortimer in his cell.

"Charley, do you think Carrie is true to you?" Bryte asked.

"In what respect do you mean?" Mortimer questioned.

"Concerning the Gibson case."

"I know it stands her in hand to tell the truth in all matters or troubles pertaining to me."

"There's not a word she has to say concerning the Gibson murder but will be against you," the hulking sheriff confided.

Bryte also dished that every letter Mortimer had written Carrie while in County Jail had been delivered by Carrie to him or Shearer. Mortimer passed it off that she was playing a "double game," telling the police one thing but on the stand would testify on his behalf. Mortimer didn't fool Bryte, and if he fooled himself, it wasn't for long. On February 28 the *Sacramento Bee* reported that Mortimer's insane act had gone from calm to crazy. Although clearly an antic disposition, the change may have been partially affected by the realization of Carrie's duplicity.[4]

In the days leading up to the trial, reporters revealed Mortimer ate little and grew weaker. On March 12 he appeared before Judge Thomas B. Reardon in the Sixth District Court. Denson made a strong case for another continuance, but Reardon wasn't having it. Circumstances gave Denson one more day, however, for they could only empanel nine jurors that day. The following morning, March 13, three more jurors were empaneled, and the young lawyer, Cameron H. King, was appointed by the Court to assist Denson. As for the prosecution, their team would consist of District Attorney Anthony Starr and S. S. Holl, who in 1863 as a Police Judge had sentenced Mortimer to ninety days for violating the Vagrancy Act. This time Holl was seeking a much harsher punishment.[5]

Around 11:30 a.m. the jury was sworn in, and Starr began his opening statement. After reading the murder indictment, he spellbound the jury with the case he expected to prove: that on the afternoon of September 19, Charles Mortimer had been drinking at Mary Gibson's house; that after learning she had stashed some of the railroad money at her house, he'd returned around 9:00 or 10:00 p.m.; that, after poisoning her beer, he'd cut her throat, but not before she'd scratched his face and pulled out some of his whiskers; that he'd returned to his hotel room at the Mechanics Exchange with some of Mary's possessions; that he'd admitted to Carrie that he'd "killed the damned bitch"; that he'd told Carrie, if she didn't testify on his behalf, he'd "cut her damned throat."[6]

For his first witness, Starr called Chris Weiderholt. Weiderholt described his discovery of Mary's corpse and the evidence of the brutal murder. Next on the stand was George Wentworth, who verified Weiderholt's account. The policeman also stated that before the suspicious-looking beer glass and Mary's corpse were sent to the coroner's office, he believed he saw clutched in Mary's death grip strands of auburn hair.

At this, the eyes of nearly everyone in the courthouse naturally drifted toward the defendant. For his part, Mortimer glanced around from time to time, and occasionally whispered something to Denson, but, as the *Sacramento Bee* noted, "[T]he long sustained hardihood in his eyes had faded."

After an hour-long recess, the prosecution called eight more witnesses: Dr. Cluness, Mose Drew, Dr. Rudolph, William Tassey, Michael Haggerty, Uncle Jeff, Chief Karcher, and Officer Harris. The jurors, who seemed an intelligent lot, listened with interest to the seemingly damning eyewitness accounts they furnished of Mortimer's actions on the night in question.[7]

The next morning, March 14, 1873, the courthouse was packed. This was unsurprising, for the rumor mill dished that Carrie Spencer, as she was now being called, was set to testify. Through her association with Mortimer, her notoriety in the Bay Area as a pickpocket, and her "treasure-hunting expeditions," as the *Sacramento Bee* referred to them, her fame nearly rivaled Mortimer's. Everyone wanted a good look at the demoiselle.

Naturally, Carrie wasn't the opening act. At 9:00 a.m. Judge Reardon ordered the prisoner brought forth, and Deputy Hickman escorted Mortimer to the chair between his two attorneys. Once again given the floor, Starr recalled Officer Len Harris. In particular, Harris testified that a large gold ring, which was exhibited to the jury, was either Mary Gibson's or a close facsimile. Sensing that Harris had raised the specter of ambiguity with this use of "or facsimile," Denson pounced, objecting to Harris's testimony on the grounds that Starr was "impeaching his own witness." In other words, Denson was claiming Starr (though clearly inadvertently) was making his own witness seem incompetent. Although Reardon overruled the objection, on cross-examination Denson made the most of the opening, forcing Harris to admit that he could not swear the ring was actually Mary Gibson's.

Starr's next witnesses included Officer Enoch Dole, Elizabeth Champion, Coroner Wilson, and Annie Baldwin. Dole and Wilson fared better. As for Mary's sisters, by the time Denson finished with them on cross it was evident that they hadn't paid too much attention to Mary's possessions while she was alive, and, like Harris, now that she was dead couldn't positively swear the jewelry and dresses found in Mortimer's room were actually hers.

With the defense gaining momentum, Starr needed to turn the tables on Denson. Fortunately, the district attorney had just the ticket.

"Mr. Sheriff, call Carrie Spencer," Starr ordered.

A general rustle was heard throughout the courtroom, and every eye fixed upon the doorway. It opened to reveal a tall woman, tastefully dressed in black, with a black hat and plume, gloves, and a short veil partially masking her face. Holding up her hair was a crimson red velvet band. Around her neck was a string of pearls. A broad blue necktie completed the picture. Mortimer, for once looking interested in the proceedings, watched her as Sheriff Bryte escorted her to the witness box.

"What is your name?" Starr asked.

"I answer to the name of Carrie Spencer. I have known Charles Mortimer going on two years."

"Did you know Mrs. Gibson?"

"I was not personally acquainted with her. I have seen her. I remember the 19th of September last. On that afternoon I was at her house with Charles Mortimer. Mortimer and I were rooming at the Mechanic's Exchange, on I Street, between Front and Second."

Denson asked Carrie to clarify her relationship with the defendant.

"I and Mortimer were living together as husband and wife, and passing as such."

Denson had heard enough. "I object, Your Honor, to her testimony, because this woman was de facto Mortimer's wife, and that therefore her evidence is incompetent."

Judge Reardon allowed that a common law marriage and a lawful marriage were not the same thing, overruling Denson. Through Starr's careful questions, Carrie then proceeded to weave a remarkable tale. Carrie and Mortimer had been drinking at Mary Gibson's earlier that day. After returning to their room at the Mechanics Exchange, Mortimer had gone out again. He returned at 9:30, carrying a large bundle of clothing. Carrie could tell at once that something was dreadfully wrong. Mortimer's black, stiff-brimmed hat was pulled low, his collar turned up, and his overcoat buttoned. Worse, his face was all scratched and bleeding, and some of his whiskers appear to have been torn out.[8]

"During the examination [Mortimer] watched her closely," Willis commented, "and this was the only time during the trial that he appeared to be interested in what was going on."[9]

Carrie told the jurors that she had then given Mortimer a clean shirt and a handkerchief to wipe the blood from his face. Mortimer left briefly, returned, then around midnight went out again. When next she saw him he was in the company of Officers Dole and Harris, who had brought him back after he'd apparently gotten into a drunken barfight. The next morning, Mortimer counted out about $300 on the bed, giving Carrie $245. When Carrie asked where the money had come from, Mortimer said he'd "croaked the damned whore."

"Why, Charley, you didn't do that, did you?" Carrie cried.

"Yes," Mortimer admitted. "The goddamned old bitch, she shan't tell anything on me."

When Starr had the clothing and jewelry shown as evidence, Mortimer rose to get a drink of water. Bryte told him to sit down and instructed one of his deputies to fetch a glass. Unsurprisingly, even after the water was brought, Mortimer refused to sit.

Glaring at Bryte, Mortimer asked, "Do you want to make a scene in Court? Do you think that will help?"

Bryte wasn't budging, and Mortimer was finally compelled to sit. Afterward, looking haggard and agitated, with his fingers twitching nervously, Mortimer stared daggers at Carrie. Carrie refused to look at him. Instead, she went through the dresses and pronounced them to be the same ones Mortimer had brought to their room. Carrie also testified that on the morning of September 20 Mortimer had asked her to trim his whiskers. She'd tried, but he'd grown impatient. Theatrically, Starr took the opportunity to produce the scissors. Carrie verified those were the ones and related that Mortimer had begun hacking off his whiskers himself. When he asked how his whiskers looked, Carrie told him they looked horrible. Afterward, he decided to visit a barber.

As if this testimony wasn't damning enough, Carrie also explained that in City Prison, while visiting her cell, Mortimer had pulled from his boot a copy of the testimony he wished her to memorize.

"That's your evidence," Mortimer told her. "That's what you have to say. Read it. If you don't do as I tell you, I am gone, and if you don't swear to it I'll cut your damned throat from ear to ear."

"I tore that paper up and burned it," Carrie testified, stating that Mortimer later gave her a similar statement at County Jail, which she had handed over to Shearer. Starr produced the statement, and Carrie verified it was Mortimer's handwriting. Before being submitted as evidence, Denson was allowed to look it over. Perusing the six-page letter, Denson objected on the grounds that there was no signature to it, no date, seemingly no beginning and no end. Reardon, who may have been curious to its contents, admitted it as evidence.[10]

"My darling pet: This is all of your evidence," Starr read out. "You must not forget any of it. If you do you will make it bad, yes, very bad, for yourself and me. . . . You do not want to be sent to the State Prison for ten or twenty years, and have me hung for something that we are innocent of, do you? Then you must not forget anything. Oh, darling! Do think this over a hundred times. Think of it day and night."

Along with cautioning her not to trust Shearer or any officer, who would "sell us straight into hell for a song," declaring that he loved her "better than anything," and promising that they would have many more happy days together, Mortimer provided the details of what she needed to say. The script she was to follow was essentially the same story Mortimer had been repeating since October 3, with a few new details. Carrie was to testify that Mortimer had bought the dresses on the afternoon of September 19 from a man at Yolo Bridge. Furthermore, they had seen a man at Mary Gibson's that day who looked an awful lot like Mortimer, perhaps two or three inches taller, with a thick beard of the same color. The bottle of strychnine was three-quarters full. Along with getting kicked in the face by Mose Drew, Mortimer also had fallen out of bed, accounting for his bloody face.[11]

"Mr. Denson subjected her to a rigorous cross-examination, but she stuck to her story," Willis noted.[12]

By the time the court adjourned, things were looking grim for the defendant.

Picking up the next morning, coincidentally the Ides of March, Mortimer was led to his seat, and Special Deputy E. B. Willis was called to the stand. Willis explained that at first Mortimer told him that he'd been so drunk on September 19 he had very little recollection of what had happened, but on October 3 he'd changed his story. Suddenly, Mortimer claimed to know every little detail of where he was. Both statements were read as evidence. Last to testify was Bill Shearer. The head jailor revealed that Mortimer oftentimes asked the African American jailor, W. H. Knox, to take his bread to Carrie. Instead, Knox would take the bread to Shearer, who occasionally found inside the bread notes Mortimer had written, urging Carrie to be true.

With that, District Attorney Starr rested his case.[13]

Denson rose and explained to the jury that the wrong person was on trial. Mortimer was innocent of the crime. But a crime had been committed—by Carrie Spencer—who had perjured herself in falsely testifying against her lover. Denson, it seemed, had determined if he could undermine the credibility of Starr's chief witness, Mortimer might walk, despite the mountains of evidence against him.

First, Denson recalled Elizabeth Champion to the stand. Answering Denson's pointed questions, Mary's sister admitted that she had seen Carrie Spencer, wearing a pink dress, at Mary's house a few days before the murder, establishing that they had been acquainted. Next, the defense called Barney O'Neill. The rancher testified that in November 1871 he had hired Mortimer, under the name of Butler, as a lumberjack, and that he and Carrie had robbed him. Seeking to paint Carrie as a thief and a liar, Denson recalled Carrie. Under his withering questions, Carrie admitted to her part in robbing O'Neill. Cross-examining Carrie, Starr worked to repair the damage Denson had done.[14]

A little after midday, there was some discussion of adjourning until Monday, but Judge Reardon had plans and decided an evening session would take place. With no more witnesses left to call, closing arguments soon followed. Denson argued that he be allowed to speak last.

"The Court refused to allow this," Willis recorded. Instead, each of the four attorneys would be granted an opportunity to speak, in the order of prosecutor, defense attorney, defense attorney, prosecutor. At one o'clock in the afternoon S. S. Holl took the floor.

"Holl opened the argument for the prosecution in an able manner," Willis remarked. "He was followed by Col King, who made an excellent speech for the defense and was highly complimented thereon by the older members of the bar."

Both speeches were merely warmup acts for Denson's argument, which Willis described as "masterly." Taking center stage, Denson promised the jury that they would hear no flowery rhetoric from him, or pathetic appeals. He also stated that, working without a fee or reward "save that reward I hope to earn of the consciousness of duty performed of the best of my ability," he would speak without the zeal of a man paid to put on a performance. Denson then sought to convey upon the jury the solemnity in judging a man guilty of murder. He mentioned the horror of an innocent man being consigned to "the disgraceful gibbet" and "the fatal noose."

"Death, gentlemen of the jury, is a solemn thing at all times—an ignominious death a doubly solemn subject," Denson declared. "In view of the awful responsibility that now rests upon you; of the important results to come from a correct or an incorrect consideration of this case, I ask you to bear with me; to think calmly, coolly and deliberately with me about the facts and circumstances of this case as we rumble through them."

Before rumbling through them, Denson explained that there were two great weaknesses to the prosecution's case. First, their case was made up wholly of circumstantial evidence. Secondly, their lynchpin was the testimony of "this woman" whose testimony "I will for the present ignore." Considering the evidence brought against the defendant, Denson first discussed the matter of the scratches Harris and Dole noticed on Mortimer's face at around two in the morning on September 20.

"Mose Drew told you that he took that great paw of his and slapped this man of the side of the face," Denson reminded the jurors. "The man being very drunk at the time, fell upon the floor and skinned his face on the matting. Drew either kicked him in the face or stepped on his beard and tore some of it out by the roots."

Denson also asked the jury to consider the testimony of John Clark, who testified that on the night of September 19 he had stood opposite Mortimer, from across the bar, under the "flaming, brilliant bar-room lights" while Mortimer shot dice and noticed nothing unusual about Mortimer's face.

"Now, do you think it possible that twenty or thirty scratches could have existed on the side of his face, his beard pulled out and his face bleeding, the flesh torn out, without any of these witnesses noticing it? Impossible. Then comes Mose Drew; he saw him too, and did not notice this disfigurement."

The scratches on his face, the torn beard, the blood on his shirt and pants—all of that Denson laid at the feet of Mose Drew, "kicking him when he was down." His face had been scratched from the matting, his beard torn when Mose Drew stepped on it, the blood flowing from his face to his shirt, and dripping down to his pants as he walked home.

The defense attorney expressed exasperated disbelief at the prosecution's argument that Mortimer had stepped on Mary's neck after cutting her throat.

"It is ridiculous bosh," Denson scoffed. "Why, Dr. Cluness tells you there was a gash two or three inches deep; that the carotid artery was severed; and you know that when that artery was severed, the blood came from it as from a force pump or hydrant, his pants would have been soaked in blood, and that there would have been bloody tracks on the floor. There is no such evidence."

Denson heaped more derision on Chief Karcher's testimony that on one of Mortimer's boots he could "almost see blood upon it now." In other words, Karcher didn't know if there was blood on it. Dr. Cluness said he saw "something red upon it" but couldn't swear it was blood.

As for how Mortimer might have found the money to buy the dresses, hours after he had borrowed five dollars, Denson believed he had the answer: "The testimony shows that he was on a glorious, jolly, hilarious drunk—so drunk that he would stand and look away up into Mose Drew's face and call him a liar . . . he got one on his face that knocked him down and peeled his face. He was roystering around town, borrowed five dollars from Mose Drew, went out and bet on a faro game, and with drunken, fool luck, won a lot of money."

Toward Carrie, whom Denson sarcastically derided as "the elegant and refined Miss Jones, alias Carrie Mortimer, alias Spencer, alias Wardell" and a "critter," Denson expressed particular disdain:

> This woman comes up here bedizened with paint, befrilled with pearls, with the very stench and nauseous odor of the jail upon her; decked out in frills and furbelows—hat, cloak, vail . . . to walk from the lower story up here. Now, I have heard of theatrical acting in court on behalf of the defendant. I have heard of a poor weeping wife and seventeen or eighteen young children being rung upon . . . but never before in my life did I see a better illustration of a white sepulcher of Scripture. This miserable, low, contemptible, treacherous hussy; taken by this man from the slums of filth of Dupont street—from a Dupont street beer-jerker saloon—rigged up like a lady; supported, as she says herself, by him ever since. Now she turns traitor upon him, and is brought in here rigged up in this style to give effect to her testimony; to make her pleasing before the jury, to make her impress upon the jury that she is telling the truth. She is a lady?

Calling it an insult to the jury's common sense, Denson expressed indignation on behalf of the jurors that the lawmen thought by dressing her in such a manner they could pull the wool over their eyes. As for the clothes, he remarked that they were bought with the money the police paid her to testify in San Francisco that Mortimer had killed Caroline Prenel, clearing Bec. Doubtless Denson hoped that these arguments planted the seeds of doubt in the jurors' minds about the veracity of Carrie's statements, both in San Francisco and Sacramento, considering she may have been financially motivated to make them.

Building momentum, Denson described Carrie's history of theft, including larceny in Alameda and the robbery of Barney O'Neill. He also questioned why the police never found the bloody handkerchief Carrie had supposedly used to wipe the blood off Mortimer's face. "Did she throw it away?" Denson asked. "Where is it? She was arrested the next day and everything the officers could find was picked up. They did not produce it. That bloody handkerchief would be very strong evidence to corroborate her story. I do not see how else it could happen, that a man could cut her throat . . . and not get any blood upon him except the few drops. . . . It's too thin. It won't wash."

Circling the truth, Denson also pointed out that Michael Haggerty and Peter Matthews's testimony contradicted parts of Carrie's. Furthermore, Carrie had all of the dresses, money, and jewelry in her valise when the police entered their room, not Mortimer. In fact, Chief Karcher testified that Carrie had told him she had packed the valise herself.

"Is there not a motive to swear his neck into the halter and get hers out?" Denson asked. "I do not pretend to charge the crime on her. But . . . [t]here is more evidence here against her than against him—a great deal more."

Lastly, Denson raised his strongest argument for sparing Mortimer the death penalty, calling attention to his drunkenness and very subtly hinting toward insanity. Describing him as "beastly, boisterously drunk," Denson reminded the court's jurors to take into consideration whether or not they believed an accused man deliberately plotted a murder. To wit, this was the difference between first-degree and second-degree murder.

"Now, even if you believe this miserable woman's story, you cannot believe this man intended to murder that woman, and did it deliberately," Denson reasoned. "Why, it is preposterous. The man must have been drunk or crazy to go down there to a place he had been drinking, and talking, and singing . . . and brutally murder the occupant of the house."

Along with raising the absurdity of carrying plunder back to the hotel, under the noses of the policemen, Denson noted that men who deliberately plotted murder generally made an escape plan. In closing, Denson added, "If this man did commit the deed, it was done in a drunken brawl without premeditation, and your verdict can be nothing more than murder in the second degree. Gentlemen of the jury, I leave the case in your hands, and in the name of justice, in the name of all that is good, and noble, and true; in the name of humanity; in the name of mercy; in the name of God, do not take the life of this poor demented creature."[15]

Had the jury retired that moment, Denson's speech might have done the trick. Instead, Starr rose and, according to Willis, nimbly eviscerated Denson's "ingenious" arguments. Afterward, Judge Reardon prepared the charge, and at 10:35 the jury retired. Thirty-five minutes later, fifty minutes before midnight, they returned and announced their verdict: "We, the jury, find Charles Mortimer guilty of murder in the first degree."[16]

Judge Reardon ordered the sentencing to take place on March 29. Another man might have been depressed at the outcome, but not Mortimer. That night, while locked in his cell, the convicted murderer appeared to be in fine spirits, cheerfully singing songs. As a reporter for the *Sacramento Bee* noted, when Mortimer spotted Carrie washing up at the hydrant, he gallantly blew her a kiss.[17]

It was almost as if he had a plan.

CHAPTER 15

Scalawag

Shortly after being judged guilty of murder, Mortimer began composing a history of his life. To his partners in crime who might be arrested because of his memoir, he gave aliases. His family he never mentioned by name, nor exactly when and where he was born, likely to preserve his true identity and not bring hardship upon his relatives. Although he made it difficult to figure out his family history, it wasn't impossible.[1]

Charley's parents, John and Louisa, had what he called a "roaming disposition." Certainly this was the case for his father. Born in June of 1809 in Ireland, John Flinn had voyaged nearly three thousand miles to the United States. For Louisa Lydia Bates—born in Stoddard, New Hampshire, on January 17, 1806—the journey was less arduous. The couple married in 1828 in Plymouth, Massachusetts, before moving forty miles north to Boston. Their union proved fruitful, Louisa giving birth to two daughters. Afterward, the family traveled to the hamlet of Landgrove in Vermont's Green Mountains to move in with Louisa's parents, Edward and Polly Bates. In 1834, within the family home, Louisa gave birth to a blue-eyed, auburn-haired son. They called him Charley.[2]

Had his parents settled down in Vermont, Charley might have lived an entirely different sort of life. In particular, the hamlet of Landgrove and the surrounding villages, including the county seat of Bennington forty miles to the south, were famous for producing the Green Mountain Boys. These scions of the Green Mountain State became renowned in the Revolutionary War, capturing Fort Ticonderoga in 1775, invading Canada later that year, and in 1777 trouncing the British in the Battle of Bennington. Naturally, the Green Mountain Boys fought for the Union, and Charley, who would have been about twenty-seven when the war erupted, might have answered the call as well.[3]

Instead, while Charley was but an infant, John and Louisa Flinn moved 150 miles southeast to Boston. There they settled at 206 Ann Street. By 1835 Boston was a bustling center of commerce, boasting a population of 75,000. Tragedy struck the family, however, when the clothing of one of Charley's sisters caught fire from an old-fashioned fireplace. Before it could be helped, the girl burned to death. Mary Elizabeth Flinn, five years his senior, was now Charley's only sibling.[4]

"My mother's health was affected by this loss," Charley noted in his jailhouse memoir, "and my father receiving an advantageous offer, concluded on her account to leave Boston."

Traveling forty-five miles west to Worcester, the Flinns moved into the same household as John's employer, who himself had three daughters who delighted in Charley's company. At school, the three sisters would divide their lunch with him after he ate his own lunch for breakfast. For this conduct, Charley was called "glutton" and "hog" by the other students.

"This led me to deception," Charley reflected, "eating my lunch on the sly, and then showing my empty pail, as if the contents had been stolen." Of the sisters, Mary in particular aided Charley in this ploy.

On half-holidays, Charley enjoyed stealing large eggs from a barn with the sisters and getting "in mischief" at school. Charley completed many of his lessons imperfectly and was punished as a result. But one day it was the schoolmaster who made a mistake.[5]

"[T]he master in punishing me accidentally hit me with the strap in the eye. I made a great ado about it," Charley remembered. With the help of the sisters, especially Mary, Charley incited resentment toward their teacher. When Mary hinted that their teacher deserved a taste of his own medicine, half a dozen of them let him have it. "Shortly after the master was discharged, for allowing himself to be whipped, I suppose," Charley ruminated.

Before long the family moved northeast to Salem, which Charley described as "the ancient city of witchcraft." There, Charley adapted to being one of three hundred or so students, and having five or six different teachers. One day a flash of lightning struck the schoolhouse. Although Charley survived, it had a more devastating effect on some of the others, killing several pupils. Charley attributed his strong dislike of school to this incident.[6]

On December 24, 1839, John and Louisa gave birth to their second son, John William Flinn, whom everyone called William, or Will, probably so as not to confuse him with his father. Despite the joy the Christmas baby brought, Charley could tell that something was very wrong between his parents. Louisa was often in tears, and when Charley sought to determine what was the matter, she gave him kind but evasive answers. Eventually Charley got to the truth of it, eavesdropping on a conversation between his parents. John was drinking more and more, and as a result his tailoring business was suffering. Charley also noticed his father suffered violent mood swings when imbibing, ranging from "pleasant" to "cross."[7]

Things hit a violent crescendo when John, somewhat intoxicated, threw something at Louisa, which missed her and struck baby Will in the head. At first it appeared Will had been killed. Only after a long illness did Will return to health.

"From that time there was a marked change in my father," Charley related. "He abandoned the grog shops, and things began to prosper."

Between the years 1840 and 1842, ranging from when Charley was roughly between the ages of six and eight, his father caught him playing hooky.

"My father punished me severely when I disobeyed him," Charley reflected. "He had warned me about my leaving school and about certain habits. But I disobeyed him."

Hopping a southbound train, Charley reached Boston before nightfall. But when the sun set, Charley was at a loss of what to do. As he stood crying, a lady approached him. Arousing sympathy, Charley told her that his parents were dead, and that, after being homeless in the country, he'd gone to Boston to try to find his uncle. Kindly, the woman took him home, convincing her husband to take in the poor orphan.[8]

After two weeks, Charley grew restless. Joining in with some boys who were imitating a political torchlight procession, they stole some streetlamps from their boxes. While Charley was taking one down, a policeman caught him and returned him to the home of the couple. While the officer was talking with the lady, Charley got it into his head that the officer meant to punish him cruelly, overhearing the policeman tell the woman that Charley would have to be put in the "paper," though Charley at first thought he'd said "pepper." Visions of being soused in a box full of pepper filled his imagination. To escape, Charley took the pail and went outside for the pump.

"By taking the pail with me I supposed I had thrown the officer off his guard, and as soon as I closed the door I sat the pail down and made distance between him and I," Charley recalled.

Charley spent that night with a friend in South Boston before hoofing it six miles west to Watertown. Meanwhile, John and Louisa had marshalled their resources, looking for their boy inside and in the vicinity of the city. They also employed the town criers, police, and press. Soon the Salem and Boston papers advertised that Charley had run away and for any information on his whereabouts, or his safe return, a reward would be forthcoming.

Unaware that he was being hunted, Charley grew homesick and returned to Boston. While at the eastern depot, hoping to hop a train home, someone approached him. To Charley's utter relief it was his mother, Louisa. They both broke down crying.

"On arriving home there were no angry words—no lash waiting for my return," Charley reflected. "The feelings were those of joy. My father and mother showed me . . . the wickedness of the course I had taken. . . . I also displeased God, and caused sorrow among His angels."

In 1842 Edward Daniel Flinn was born. Because Charley's sister Mary was then living with their grandmother in the Green Mountains, and with Will only a toddler of three, many of the domestic duties were given to eight-year-old Charley. These Charley did not relish.[9]

Putting his wits to work, Charley conceived a plan. Instead of doing housework, he convinced his parents to let him take care of his younger brothers. It soon became Charley's habit to place little Edward in the carriage and take him along with him, meeting up with his fellows who were also skipping school.

"I have often looked back at those rambles, and wondered that no harm ever came to my brother," Charley ruminated. "I would often go three or four miles from home. I would go in the most wild and romantic regions, then known as the 'witchcraft,' of which that part of the country is noted for."

Charley owned a book that detailed all the places in Salem where "witches" and "robbers" had carried out their mysterious deeds. When he and his comrades gathered, Charley read them chapters. Afterward they hatched plans of their own.

"It seemed to be our most earnest desire to follow in the footsteps of those we had been reading of," Charley admitted.

To the vexation of their schoolmaster and parents, Charley and the boys began spending more and more time playing hooky. Then, almost inevitably, came a June day when the boys did not return home. Although the adults tore through the "witchcraft" of Salem and their various other haunts, looking for the unruly children, it did them no good. Small wonder, for the boys had traveled eight miles south to the peninsula of Nahant, with the intention of turning pirate.

After appropriating blankets, bedding, two tents, and a boat from the wharf, the would-be buccaneers made for Egg Rock, an island three-quarters of a mile northeast of Nahant. On this scrap of land, the young scalawags plotted their campaign of terror. "Our intention was to get a brig, arm her, and go privateering," Charley boasted.

To Charley's chagrin, they were quickly informed on by some of the schoolmates they had urged to join. The schoolmaster and some others promptly captured two of Charley's mates and the boat itself. However, the adults—having arrived during high tide—could not find a safe place to land.

"We laid down out of sight and would not respond to the calls, promises or threats made by those in the boat," Charley recorded.

In the evening the adults gave up, leaving Charley and the six others stranded on the small island. Charley and the six refugees determined that the adults would certainly row back in the morning and capture them. In hopes of procuring a boat, Charley took their one board, lunged into the Atlantic, and began paddling for Nahant.

"The water was nice and warm.... As my companions saw, after a hard struggle, I landed on Little Beach," Charley recollected.

Once ashore, Charley recaptured the boat and paddled back to Egg Rock. Wasting little time, the seven would-be pirates boarded the boat and cast off, seeking a new base of operations.

"We rounded the outer point of Nahant with the turn of the tide," Charley noted. "We pulled to Dungeon Rock, which is at the northwest end of Lynn, then fully three miles from any house. In the early days it was said to have been the resort of pirates and witches. There was a cave there known as the 'Pirate's Cave.'"[10]

Reaching Pirate's Cave, they made several raids into town. In doing so they ran into some of their old schoolmates and told them where they were headquartered. This proved a mistake. Soon the schoolmaster knew their secret location, and early one morning he and their fathers suddenly appeared and marched them back to Salem.

In the schoolhouse, the schoolmaster read to them a moral lecture. He closed by stating they would all be severely punished for their sins. Naturally, Charley was called out first.

"I was considered a bad boy, yet had many friends among the scholars. . . . I told the master he should not punish us because he was angry—that he had been threatening this punishment and he had better not do it," Charley reflected.

The schoolmaster certainly wasn't about to back down. He commanded Charley to extend his hand. Charley did so, but once the schoolmaster brought down the strap Charley pulled his hand away and tackled him around the legs. That was the moment the others had been waiting for. Rushing in, they overpowered their nemesis.

"[I]n a twinkling we had him down," Charley recalled.

In the process they tore off the schoolmaster's pants. In shock, the schoolmaster retreated to a private room, and the "pirate band," as Charley styled them, made for the street. Once home, Charley told the whole story to his mother. Louisa delivered a lecture, and Charley promised to reform.

At some point John and the schoolmaster had a conversation; shortly after John told Charley he no longer needed to attend school. Whether or not Charley had been expelled went unsaid, though certainly the schoolmaster must have been relieved that young Charley would no longer be around to terrorize the school.

Without a schoolmaster to instruct his willful child, it fell to John to set Charley on the proper path. John did his best. "He laid down a course he wished me to pursue," Charley recorded. "I followed for some months steady as a clock . . . my change was marked and I felt the benefit of it myself."[11]

As Charley grew to manhood he became enchanted with a young lady named Ada. She and Charley enjoyed picnicking and riding. They also engaged in more clandestine meetings. Unfortunately, their excursions cost more money than the family tailoring business could support, particularly with two new mouths to feed: Franklin "Frank" Michael Flinn born on October 26, 1844, and Thomas Henry Flinn born in 1848. When Ada told Charley she wanted to attend the upcoming picnic, Charley kept his lack of funds to himself. However, Charley did tell his troubles to a friend, referred to in his memoir as "Dick S—," and asked to borrow money.

"[J]ust then he had none, but told me he could get it if I would help him. I took till evening to reflect on the proposition. Meanwhile, I met Ada and some young people, and Ada said she and I were going. I had not the courage to tell her my true position."

Charley soon met Dick, who shared his plan. Dick had observed a shopkeeper, Mr. B—, put away a sack full of money in his store before locking up. Dick planned to gain entry to the shop that evening by removing a glass pane window. All Charley had to do was keep watch.

"It was a hard struggle for me to break away from the good path I had chosen and had come to love," Charley reflected, "to trample all my good resolutions under foot. While I still meditated, Ada's disappointment flashed across my mind, and then Dick asked me if I was afraid, and I told him no; 'go ahead.'"

As the young men approached Mr. B's store, they could hear the nearby church bells ringing for the evening services. Timing it right, Dick broke the pane of glass, using the ringing of the bells to drown out the sound. After Dick slipped in through the window, Charley closed it and kept watch. Presently, Dick appeared outside the back door, telling Charley he needed aid.

Inside, Charley quickly located the money in the tea chest. On splitting it, Charley cagily helped himself to the lion's share. With Dick ignorant of the value of sums of money, this was easy to pull off.[12]

Along with treating Ada to the picnic, the young couple decided to expand their adventuring from Massachusetts to Maine, traveling one hundred miles north to Portland. More excursions with Ada followed, all of which cost money. "All my good resolutions failed me, struggle as I would," Charley lamented. "The more money I had, the more I had call for it."

Charley and Dick soon pulled another job. More and more burglaries followed. Eventually a private watchman accused Charley of being part of a gang "doing mischief." Charley feigned outrage.

"He afterwards became convinced of his error," Charley recollected, "but this did not satisfy me, and I and others resolved to give him trouble. One night when he stepped into a saloon we broke glass and done damage to the property under his charge."

Charley should have covered his tracks better. The following day Charley was "fixed on as the offender" and convicted of the crime. The law officers attempted to induce Charley to "peach" on his friends, but Charley refused. He was then forced to choose between the House of Reform in Boston or the State Reform School in Westborough, fifty miles southwest of Salem. Despite his aversion to schoolhouses, Charley chose the State Reform School.[13]

Soon after entering, Charley and a fast friend planned to escape, rob a store of two hundred dollars, and disappear. After stealing some knitting needles, they fashioned them into skeleton keys and fitted them to the door. The outer doors needed to be fitted as well.

"While doing this, the Superintendent, W. R. Lincoln, caught us at it," Charley admitted, "and, after a good strapping, he locked us up in a dark cell where we remained two weeks on bread and water."

The punishment didn't end there. Detailing the sort of quintessentially puritanical punishment that Nathaniel Hawthorne wrote about in his 1850 masterpiece, *The Scarlet Letter*, Charley continued, "We were then put into the black line with half our hair cut off and a leather medal on the front of our jackets. While in this line for each misdemeanor we got a strapping, and one if we talked to each other, or to our playmates without permission."

Gradually, Charley and companion returned to their old standing. Once suspicion died down, they again made skeleton keys. Determined to escape, they unlocked three doors before reaching the courtyard. From there they climbed the bell rope to the roof, pulled up the rope, repositioned it, and used it to descend. Believing themselves safe, they took the road. Before noon, a buggy drove up, out of which sprang a man who captured them and returned them to the school, where they were made "prisoners" again. After being "severely punished," they were once more put in the black line.[14]

Solitary confinement, the bread and water diet, the beatings, and the leather medal eventually had the desired effect. Charley walked the straight and narrow, serving out his time. Returning to Salem, Charley indeed seemed like a new man. He'd lost interest in his roguish companions, and many families looked at him as a model of what the reform school could do.

Although Charley worried that Ada would give him the cold shoulder, she proved among the first to welcome him back. Charley reflected that she had never led him astray, being only "indirectly" the cause of his first important crime. Certainly, she was no Lady Macbeth.

"All my affection for Ada revived," Charley rejoiced.[15]

One day, Charley and a companion spied some young ladies they knew from school skinny-dipping in the pond. Demonstrating "the spirit of mischief," while the young ladies enjoyed themselves, Charley and his friend crept forward and stole their clothing. After the boys revealed themselves, the girls were shocked to find their clothing gone. Charley and his friend claimed it had been some other boys who must have taken their clothes. Eventually, the boys "found" their clothing.

Not long after, Charley, a friend, and these same young ladies were left alone in their classroom and ordered to sweep it. One thing led to another. When they were discovered, they were "partly disrobed." Given a few minutes to dress, Charley and the others made the most of it. Dressing hastily, they "sprang out a window and escaped, thus outgeneraling the master."

When the story of Charley's schoolhouse romp and expulsion got out, Ada decided this was the last straw. Without school or Ada to keep him grounded, Charley found other entertainments.

"I fell in with my old comrade, Dick, and I began to run wild," Charley recalled.[16]

Sticking around Salem, Charley made Sam Gardner's Gambling Saloon one of his favorite haunts. When not carousing, he worked as a tailor for Samuel Chamberlain at 29 Washington Street. Gainfully employed, Charley was able to afford a room at a nearby boardinghouse. But his luck turned when he took sick while working for Chamberlain. Fortunately, a young lady named Charlotte, also rooming at the board-inghouse, acted as a nursemaid to Charley. "She was a good kind woman and treated me like a Christian," Charley reflected.

While Charley convalesced, some "mischief-makers," as Charley dubbed them, began a rumor about Charlotte. Doubtless they didn't call her a witch, but another five-letter word beginning with a "w" might have passed their lips. Once well enough, Charley, feeling "red-hot" about the matter, went after everyone connected with the scandalous rumors. According to Charley, he soon made the mischief-makers "take water."[17]

Charley also took a new job as a tailor at Thomas Quinn's at 184 Essex. This was a two-minute walk to Old Town Hall, and a stone's throw away from the present-day Witch History Museum. It also put Charley a little closer to Sam Gardner's Saloon, where he liked to gamble. Hitting a hot streak, Charley embarked on a fifty-mile trip to Portsmouth, New Hampshire, rambled up to Augusta, Maine, and summered between Augusta and Portland. That fall, now in his mid-teens, Charley returned to Boston, reacquainting himself with some chums from the State Reform School.[18]

"Some of them had Boston down to a focus," Charley marveled. "Like myself, their short stay at the Reform School had not done them much good."

The leader of the pack was Jerry Aiken. About the same age as Charley, having been born around 1834, Jerry had been sent to the State Reform School for highway robbery. After his release, he'd quickly fallen back into old habits. Presently, Jerry had his eye on a rich clothing store on Ann Street, close to Oak Hall.[19]

Joining the gang, Charley, Jerry, and the other hoodlums broke in and stole coats, vests, silk handkerchiefs, and a little money. After selling their plunder to a man on Elm Street, Jerry revealed his plan to rob a house in Roxbury while its inhabitants slumbered. Although Charley worried that this was too bold a score, he quickly relented. Jerry next introduced Charley to many of the "free and easy" places in Boston, where the company of women could be purchased. One evening, while in one of these establishments, Charley witnessed policemen arrest a man for robbing the clothing store near Oak Hall, overhearing that they were looking for Jerry Aiken and another robber.

Locating Jerry, Charley shared the news. Jerry laid low for two days, then took ship to New York. Afraid he was the other suspect, Charley soon left too.[20]

"I often wished to go to the old Green Mountains to visit the town where I was born," Charley recollected. "I had a good supply of money and clothes, and all that was lacking was a supply of presents for my cousins.... I bought a ticket for Fitchburg, which was as far as the cars went at that time."[21]

Disembarking fifty miles northwest of Boston, Charley found Fitchburg so lively he decided to stick around. After taking a room at a house near the train station, Charley located a barroom. At that point in time Charley didn't drink or smoke. Instead he kept himself occupied by listening in on the conversation of a stock drover from New York. The man, Captain C., had made a bundle selling sheep and cattle in Brighton, a town just west of Boston. In due course the landlord, noting Charley's good clothing, introduced Charley to Captain C., and said he would put them both in the same room, vouching for the drover. Charley raised no objections.

"The Captain asked me to drink and smoke but I declined.... He was very talkative, and I encouraged it in him," Charley recalled.

In their room, Charley watched clandestinely as the drover placed his watch on the nightstand and placed his money in his vest, which he tucked under his pillow. When the drover fell asleep a little after midnight, Charley pocketed his watch and reached beneath the pillow. Charley could feel the man's wallet through the vest, but he could not pull it out without startling him. Eventually the man rolled over. This gave Charley the opportunity he sought.

Working with quiet efficiency, he slid the vest out from beneath the pillow. After securing the banknotes in his pants, he threw the wallet out the window, slipped out the door, and soundlessly broke the crystal of the watch, leaving the damaged watch and the vest lying on the floor. After using the key to unlock the door, Charley left the key on the floor, and scattered the contents of his own valise about the room. Satisfied, he went to sleep.

In the morning, the drover awoke and announced they had been robbed. Not so Charley. As it turned out, Charley had tucked his own wallet beneath the sheets of his bed, and it was still there.

"Why didn't I do that with mine?" Captain C. lamented.

Charley could only offer kind words as consolation. A few days later, Charley caught a stage thirty-seven miles northwest to Keene, New Hampshire, where he stayed about a month with his uncle, James Lovell Bates, and James's family.[22]

"I introduced myself to them, and my reception was all that I could desire," Charley reflected. "I remained there something like a month."

Becoming restless, Charley visited his sister Mary, who lived nearby with her husband, before returning to the Green Mountains.

"I visited ... finally the place where I was born, the old house of my dear mother. Here I found my grandmother, an aunt and a dozen cousins. They gave me hearty good cheer. I was greatly interested in all the old associations of which my mother had so often told me, and for a time was perfectly happy."[23]

Bidding goodbye to his grandmother, aunt, and cousins, Charley journeyed fifty miles southeast back to Keene. There Charley shared a carriage to Cheshire County with a couple young ladies, taking in the local fair. In particular Charley observed a man playing the roulette wheel. While everyone else watched the wheel spin, Charley kept his eyes on the prize, lifting the man's wallet. The next morning he rose early, paying the hostler with stolen money to drive him back. Once in Keene, he got his team of horses and started for Massachusetts.[24]

Passing by Mount Monadnock, likened to "a sapphire cloud against the sky" by Nathaniel Hawthorne and "the new Olympus" by Ralph Waldo Emerson, Charley reached Jeffrey, New Hampshire, seventeen miles from Keene. From there it was a straight shot of fifty miles to Concord, Massachusetts, where Charley stopped for a few days, walking the battlegrounds at Concord and Lexington and visiting the state prison. The sight of the convicts reminded him of his parent's counsel, and once again Charley vowed to keep to the sunny side of the street.[25]

Returning to Boston, he found employment as a tailor near the old South Church on Washington Street, whose congregation once included Samuel Adams and Benjamin Franklin. Making thirty dollars a month, Charley gave it his all for half a year. But his attention began to wander after he fell in with a burglar named George Pond. Pond kept company with Mary McIntosh, who had an honest job but also doubled as a woman of easy virtue. Intelligent, quick, and refined, with dark curly hair, bright eyes, and a pretty face, Charley quickly became enamored.

"I fell in love with her on sight," Charley recalled.

Although Pond suggested they rob Charley's employer, Charley refused, for the man had been kind to him. Pond did persuade Charley to spend money liberally, though what or *whom* he spent money on was never implicitly stated. After Pond was arrested for a robbery in Worcester, Charley traded Boston for Lowell, twenty-five miles northwest. There he found employment on Central, working for a man named Shattuck, boarding with his family.

"Lowell was just the place to make me worse," Charley lamented. "There were scores of young women there, many of them of a very lively turn. To keep up appearances I required more money than I was earning, so I singled out a dwelling in Dracut."[26]

While the family was at a prayer meeting, Charley used a skeleton key to enter the home. When the family returned, Charley snuck out with a fortune in plunder. For several weeks Charley continued his career as a burglar, stealing watches, chains, and jewelry. Traveling to Boston, he exchanged the bounty for cash and returned home to Salem high on the hog.

"I always managed to give a pretty good account for myself," Charley recollected. "My mother was a deep thinker and I know she suspected all was not right, from the way she would talk to me."

Returning to Boston, Charley acquired a set of burglar tools, using them to visit businesses and houses. Never one to gather moss, Charley rambled up to New Hampshire, working the small towns as he went. Outside Lebanon, New Hampshire, Charley made one of the most dramatic changes in his young life; he decided to join the United Society of Believers in Christ's Second Appearing, colloquially known as the Shakers.

"I had heard the Shakers were very wealthy, and determined to reach their treasure lore," Charley recalled. "My fancy pictured to me the possession of several thousand dollars, a fine house and plenty of land."[27]

As he approached the small village, Charley had an inexplicable change of heart. He began to think of settling down and redeeming his past by "doing good to the poor and needy." Professing his desire to join the Shakers, the trusting elders quickly accepted him into their fraternity. In short order, he was stripped of his clothing, had his hair cut short, and shaved of his first whiskers. Enthusiastically joining in the services, Charley sang, shouted, and prayed as lustily as the others. Two weeks later, however, his newfound religious fervor waned.

Sneaking away, Charley crossed the Connecticut River near White River Junction, heading into Vermont. Charley robbed a lawyer's house in Bradford, then traveled twenty-five miles south to Hanover, New Hampshire, "doing a very fair business." Afterward Charley cut a hundred-mile swath to Montpelier, Vermont, hitting Haverhill, Newbury, and St. Johnsbury along the way. Montpelier in particular he recalled as "very profitable."

"From there I went to a little village on Lake Champlain, and then returned to Montpelier, from when I went to Randolph, Vermont, Tunbridge, and Chelsea, leaving the last named place under very suspicious circumstances," Charley related.

Venturing next to Brattleboro, Vermont, Charley gained employment at William P. Cune and F. S. Brackett's four-story emporium, located at 5 Granite Street, which sold dry goods, groceries, and clothing. Once again, Charley was an honest-to-God tailor. It didn't last long.[28]

"In a month I left and went to Hinsdale, N. H., working there some three months," Charley related. "This long stay grew out of love."

While walking, Charley fell in with two young ladies. When they invited him into their cottage, Charley was quick to accept, and there met a third young lady. Hitting it off, one day soon they all traveled seven miles south to Northfield where Charley fell in with an old chum named Frank. For the next four months they worked the surrounding villages, becoming accustomed to stealing not only money and jewelry but property as well. Driving their team of horses to a distant depot, they shipped their goods to a fence on Sudbury Street in Boston, while in Greenfield they pretended to be upstanding young men, visiting with nice families and attending church. The deception didn't last.[29]

After one such burglary, Charley and Frank carted two trunks full of plunder to a train station. As the train rattled in, their horse became skittish. While Charley concentrated on keeping the horse calm, Frank recognized two Greenfield policemen stepping off the train. Frank jumped into the buggy, hollered for Charley to do the same, and grabbed the reins.

"I was not more than half in when Frank started the team," Charley recollected, "but we were a half minute behind time. One of the officers and a citizen sprang forward and caught the horse by the bit, and stood over us."

As the train departed for Fitchburg, the trunks were investigated. Charley and Frank pretended that they had no idea what was in the trunks. The policemen didn't buy it, taking Charley, Frank, and the stolen loot back to Greenfield.

For three months they lay in jail before being taken to court and pleading guilty. The judge sentenced them to one year in Massachusetts State Prison in Concord, including three days of solitary confinement. On a gloomy October day, they entered the guard room. Walking into a little room just beyond, they were stripped of their civilian clothing, weighed, had their heads shaved, and their markings recorded, including the color of their eyes and hair. Only then did the grim-looking superintendent speak to Charley.

"Open your mouth," the superintendent commanded.

Charley complied. After the examination was over, the superintendent asked, "Hain't used much tobacco?"

"No, sir," Charley answered.

"That's what you are to do as long as you remain here. 'Sir' to all that speak to you, except convicts. If you are known to speak to them once without permission, you will regret it. Do you understand?"

"Yes, sir."

Charley dressed in prison clothing and was taken to the left wing of the prison, built in 1804. After entering a solitary corner cell on the lower tier, the iron door was slammed shut.

"It was quite dark in the cell," Charley remembered. "It was stone over head, sides, ends—excepting only the door and floor, eight or ten feet high, eight feet long and four feet wide, a small iron bedstead on hinges and turned up against the wall. . . . And here I was left to put in my three days of solitary confinement. I was then put to work."[30]

Charley spent this terrible year in a state of despair. Released, he found himself outcast.

"[W]hen I went forth into the world I had determined to live down my shame and overcome the feeling of degradation that existed in my breast," Charley reflected. "But even after going to a strange place.... I soon discovered that I was talked of, was known as a discharged convict, and strange glances and avoidance constantly met me."[31]

Determined to leave New England behind, he traveled to New York, signing articles for five years' service in the US Navy. At about twenty-three years old, Charley Flinn—who as a boy had dreamed of turning pirate—became a US sailor. Neither the captain nor the crew knew what sort of man they were about to unleash on the high seas.

CHAPTER 16

The Far West

*A*fter a two weeks' stay in New York, Flinn boarded a gunboat bound for Brazil. The five-thousand-mile journey to Rio De Janeiro took six weeks. From there they made an excursion south, traveling along the Uruguay River, before returning to Rio.

Evidently, a sailor's life wasn't for him. While in Rio, Flinn deserted, hopping a brig to Kingston, Jamaica. From Kingston he traveled to Havana, Cuba, from Havana to Aspinwall, Panama, and from Aspinwall to Valparaiso, Chile. In Valparaiso he had a change of heart, once again signing articles under Uncle Sam's flag, this time pledging his service aboard the war steamer USS *Saranac*. By the time the *Saranac* docked in Panama, Flinn had developed a grudge against the sergeant of marines.

Flinn recalled, "When my liberty day ashore came, I had some forty dollars saved up and drew ten dollars more the purser. I went ashore with the sergeant of marines ... he was a mean, overbearing fellow."

By dark the sergeant was feeling his whiskey. While they crossed the plaza, Flinn hit him with a "jimmy," laid him out, and frisked him. With the sergeant's money swelling his purse, Flinn changed clothes and left for the depot. Instead of boarding a train, Flinn paid an elderly Black man for a bed, bribing him extra to keep his whereabouts under his hat. A few days later the man introduced Flinn to another refugee he was keeping hidden, Tom Edwards.[1]

Tom was a San Francisco criminal who'd been expelled from the Bay City by some hard cases. They weren't lawmen, exactly. Instead, they called themselves by a different name: vigilantes.

With San Francisco overrun by lawlessness, in 1851 a vigilance committee had arisen. During the three months of its existence, the seven-hundred-man San Francisco Vigilance Committee of 1851 hanged four men, deported fourteen more ruffians known as "Sydney Ducks" back to Australia, and scared the run-of-the-mill criminals into towing the line. In 1856 the vigilance committee reformed, hanged eight men, banished dozens, and after helping themselves to San Francisco land titles, disbanded. Tom Edwards was one such man they'd sent packing.[2]

Prone to violence, Tom had taken a wound while serving with William Walker and his filibuster army in Central America. Still suffering from the wound, Tom was after easier prey. He suggested they loot the establishment of Madam Myers, one of the locals. Flinn was game.

In the meantime, Flinn took an evening stroll, but from bad luck the *Saranac's* petty officer spotted Flinn and he tried to arrest him single-handedly. This proved too bold. After socking the officer in the ear and tripping him, Flinn fled. The attempted burglary of Madam Myers followed.

"Tom and I soon had all our plans ready," Flinn reflected. "We had some 'dagos' to stand guard at one side and plunder at will, while we tackled the safe. It was an old affair with an uneven key hole. The 'dagos' got whisky in 'em, cleaned out the show case and got to quarreling. They struck a light, and this the police saw through the shutters."

While the police entered, Flinn and Tom fled up to the ancient roof. As they tried to clamber atop it, a section of the roof gave way, and they plummeted into a ground floor room inhabited by two women. Without a word, they shot into the street and back to their room.[3]

The next day their elderly friend told Flinn and Tom that one of the women into whose room they'd crashed had given birth to a stillborn son. Public sentiment had it that the fright she'd suffered had caused the baby to die within her. "[T]he 'dagos' ... told all they could and a reward was offered for us," Flinn recalled. "The 'dagos' did not give a good description of me, and so I continued to visit the town and make a few dollars here and there."

One night Flinn robbed sixty dollars and a gold watch and chain off a man he had fallen in with. To Tom's woman, Flinn gave twenty dollars and the gold watch and chain to dispose of. Flinn always felt it was greed rather than jealousy that prompted Tom's response. Two nights later, Tom led Flinn to a lonely place where they could waylay travelers. "I had no reason to doubt him," Flinn reflected. "He got me out beside an old ruin and suddenly dealt me a heavy blow upon the forehead with a stick which he used as a cane."

Struck, Flinn whirled around and began to run, Tom hot on his trail. Flinn soon outdistanced Tom and melted into the shadows. When he felt he was safe, Flinn sat down, rubbed at the "horn" that had formed on his head, and mulled it over. He had all of fifteen dollars in his pocket, his partner in crime had tried to rob him, and there was a reward out for his arrest.[4]

Flinn still had his freedom, but he must have wondered how long that could last. Perhaps it was time to leave, trading the Caribbean for the Pacific. After all, the Far West promised a land of golden opportunity, where fortunes were made by day and lost overnight. Surely, Flinn could find honest employment there. And if he returned to his old ways in the alleys of Sacramento, the grog shops of San Francisco, and the highways in between, well . . . who would know? Resolved to "migrate at once," Flinn caught a Pacific mail steamer, offering to pay his way with work.[5]

On May 5, 1858, Charley Flinn reached the Golden Gate. Inhabited by roughly fifty thousand people, San Francisco wasn't as populous as Boston but was certainly more diverse. During the Gold Rush, thousands of Forty-Niners poured into California from all over the world. From Europe, scores of Italians, British, Irish, Scots, French, Dutch, Spaniards, Germans, Prussians, and Russians sailed to San Francisco. From China came thousands of Cantonese, carving out an area in the northeast section of the city soon to be called Chinatown. Speaking English, plenty of Australians turned argonaut as well. More traveled north, predominantly from Chile and Mexico, the Mexicans joining their brethren who remained after California had been ceded to the United States in 1848 at the conclusion of the Mexican American War. American Indians, free Blacks, Yankees, and Southerners who hungered for adventure journeyed by horse, ship, wagon, and even on foot. All hoped to make a fortune.[6]

Flinn spent only a few days in San Francisco before heading one hundred miles northwest to Sacramento whose population of about 12,500 made the capital dramatically less crowded and more rural than San Francisco. The day after his arrival, Flinn found employment at the ranch of Mr. Tibbett, located on the old Stockton Road. "I proved a poor hand and was twice sick there, but they were very kind to me," Flinn recalled. Moving on, Flinn found similar work at Cooper's, eight miles from the city, on the lower Stockton Road. Flinn dwelled there for a longer stretch, but his itinerant nature got the best of him and, without any particular destination in mind, began heading southeast to the mountains.

Along the way Flinn fell in with a tramp. It was evening when they reached the gold-mining town of Mokelumne Hill, whose populace was a dangerous mixture of Americans, Chinese, Chileans, Germans, Mexicans, and Frenchmen. Prior to 1851, the town had averaged one homicide a day, and the notorious Mexican bandit Joaquin Murrieta had frequently been seen at the gambling tables—before a vigilance committee had arisen in Mokelumne Hill and, through the threat of a hempen rope, persuaded the worst of the elements to move along.

Flinn and the man he'd "chummed in" with stored their bags in a saloon. Flinn left on an errand, and when he returned he discovered that the tramp had made off with all his goods. Despite this inauspicious start, Flinn stayed at Mokelumne Hill for a month before heading farther southeast to Jackson. It was in Jackson—the county seat of Amador County—that Flinn returned to his life of crime. The catalyst was meeting a woman whom he called "Mag Storey" in his memoir, an alias used to protect her identity. The woman was a gold digger, but not the sort that panned along Jackson Creek. Engaged to a man who owned a rich gold claim six miles from town, the femme fatale wished to somehow extract from her fiancé his money without going through with the marriage. Flinn thought he could help with that.[7]

Soon the wedding day was set, the man expecting a luxurious honeymoon in San Francisco. But his plans went awry one morning when, on a rainy January day in 1859, his bride-to-be inexplicably distracted him. Running late, he didn't arrive at his place of business until the afternoon and found himself riding to town that evening during a hard rain, loaded up with a purse and a buckskin bag filled with money meant for the San Francisco honeymoon.

The money would find its way to San Francisco, but by a different route.

Waiting for his quarry near the bank of a grade, Flinn was ready when the man and his horse came into view. Grabbing the reins, Flinn brought the horse to a stop and put a pistol to the man's head.

"Sit perfectly still!" Flinn commanded.

The man obeyed and Flinn took his weapons.

"[H]is purse and a buckskin bag [were] filled with gold coins," Flinn recalled. "I turned the horse about and made him drive another way."

Counting the money, Flinn found $2,000 in gold coins in the bag and a little over $100 in the purse. Flinn pocketed $1,000 and gave the remaining $1,100 to the woman, promising to meet her in Sacramento. Instead, Flinn traveled to San Francisco, planning to board a ship back home. Flinn's sudden change of heart raises several questions.[8]

Were Flinn and the femme fatale lovers? Flinn never suggests they were, but by obfuscating her name he does reveal a certain degree of feeling, or at least professional courtesy, for his confederate. Bolstering this argument is the fact that "Mag Storey," by Flinn's own admission, had played her fiancé for a fool. If she and Flinn were lovers, and Flinn had developed feelings for her, it may be that the lizard part of his brain recognized that if they rendezvoused in Sacramento, she might just continue her duplicitous pattern of manipulating and robbing the man who had fallen for her. There is also the question of the money: $1,000 for Flinn, $1,100 for the woman. Did Flinn fork over the extra hundred as a way to assuage his guilt over disappearing from her life?

Whatever his reasons, after splitting the money and splitting up, Flinn traveled 120 miles southwest to San Francisco, looking to board a ship. There he frittered away most of his ill-gotten gains. Lamented Flinn, "Before steamer day most of my money was gone—the 'tiger' had proved too much for me."

In Old West slang, the "tiger" stood for gambling with professionals and dependence on alcohol. Knowing Flinn, both cards and saloons may have emptied his pockets. Flinn may have also been referring to a "tiger claw"—a sophisticated device made of springs that grifters clandestinely secreted up their sleeves, capable of slipping a card into their hand—indicating he dropped his wad playing faro or poker.[9]

His money gone, Flinn returned to Sacramento rather than taking ship to Boston. He found legitimate work at a carpentry shop on the southwest corner of Second Street and Q, box making part time for William Nichols, also from Massachusetts. While in Sacramento, he again saw "Mag Storey." Like Queen Elizabeth, the honey-pot had put off the marriage time and again before finally breaking the engagement. Evidently, the man they'd fleeced never put together her involvement in the highway robbery.[10]

Never one to grow roots, in 1860 Flinn traveled to San Francisco, making boxes for Caleb Hobbs and George Gilmore at the San Francisco Planing Mill and Box Factory on South Market Street. In the fall of 1860 Flinn journeyed seventy-five miles north to Napa Valley, sewing sacks for a Mr. Edgerton. He next moved to Napa City, where he was engaged to drive a team of oxen hauling a wagonload of lumber across a thirty-mile stretch to a sawmill six miles north of St. Helena. Flinn proved abominable at his newest vocation. On his second trip driving the team to St. Helena, Flinn nearly lost his life when, as he recalled, "[W]agon, lumber and oxen rolled down a mountain side. I unyoked such of the creatures that could move, put them on the road to the mill and myself took the stage road, got to Napa, and from there to San Francisco."

Flinn wasn't in the Bay City long, journeying again to Stockton where he fell in with a family of transplanted Southerners, the Wambles. Flinn and the eldest Wamble son spent some time working in the country, but Flinn gave this up after a month. Back in Stockton, he raised a stake gambling and drifted to Sacramento. Around the summer of 1861, while on K Street, Flinn ran into his old chum who'd robbed his baggage in Mokelumne Hill. The man pretended it was a case of mistaken identity. Flinn saw through the charade. Noting his bedraggled appearance, Flinn told him there were no hard feelings, gave him some money, and wished him well. Not long after, Flinn left for San Francisco.

"I vacillated between Sacramento and San Francisco," Flinn admitted. Taking after his old man, Flinn also began hitting the bottle harder and harder. "I had become habituated to the use of liquor, and it often threw me out of work. I tried hard to stop from drinking, but never fully succeeded, nor from keeping away from old associates."[11]

In explaining away his lost year, Flinn also made a comment that speaks volumes: "Nothing of note now happened till the fall of 1861." This may have been true for Charley Flinn, whose rambles between Sacramento and San Francisco became lost in an alcoholic haze. But for the country as a whole—particularly his brothers Will and Frank, who were about to join the Civil War on the side of the Union—the events that took place between the fall of 1860 and the fall of 1861 were as unforgettable as they were consequential.[12]

Flinn, however, ignored these events in his memoir, and seems to have largely ignored the Civil War. But as the rains began in the fall of 1861, Flinn sobered up in a hurry.

When the storms hit the West Coast in November 1861, it was the American Indians who first recognized the danger. The Nevada City *Democrat* reported that the Indians, leaving for the safety of the Sierra Nevada foothills, warned the white men that "the water would be higher than it has been for 30 years, and pointed high up on the trees and houses where it would come."[13]

The fifteen atmospheric rivers that followed proved the Indians correct. Between November 1861 and January 1862, Washington Territory, Oregon, and California saw more rain than anyone could ever remember. Worst hit was Sacramento, built perilously close to the American and Sacramento Rivers. On January 10 newly elected governor Leland Stanford was forced to take a rowboat to the Governor's Mansion, where he climbed in through a second-story window. The residents of Sacramento largely fled the city. On January 22 the legislature did as well, for the next eighteen months making San Francisco the unofficial capital.[14]

To most Californians, the Great Western Flood was a nightmare of Noachian proportions. But where others saw ruin, Charley Flinn sensed opportunity. "When the big flood set in, I did well boating," Flinn recalled. "I made money and took a pride in assisting those in distress. I look back with pleasure to many charitable acts I then did." Utilizing the skills he'd learned on the Massachusetts coast as a would-be Captain Kidd, this may have been the happiest time of Flinn's life. For most of the flood, Flinn "headquartered" himself in the Stanford House on K Street between Twelfth and Thirteenth.

To the man and woman who kept the house, Flinn was effusive with his praise: "The lady and gentleman who kept this house during the flood should be known to all the world, they opened their doors to all and it was packed with women and children."[15]

While engaged as a boatsman Flinn met the future governor of California, Newton Booth. Born in Salem, Indiana, in 1841, Booth had earned a law degree before journeying to Sacramento where he made such a fortune as a saloonkeeper that in 1861 he purchased Governor Stanford's grocery store. Employing Flinn to remove his baggage from his flooded residence on Seventh Street, between G and I, and deposit it at the steamboat landing, Booth couldn't have suspected that a dozen years later he would have the power to pardon this transplanted New Englander for murder.[16]

When the rains abated in January, Flinn traveled back to San Francisco. There he learned from a friend that his father had died in September. This time Flinn was determined to board the next steamer for Massachusetts, even going so far as to stash two hundred dollars so he could not access it on a drunken ramble. But fate, in the form of a sack full of money, intervened.

One rainy, windy evening in February 1862, Flinn was lounging in a saloon on the corner of Kearny and Washington when he noticed two Germans enter and begin conversing with the saloonkeeper, Conrad Phister. Flinn was especially attentive when he saw the Germans hand Phister a sack of white cloth. Looking around, Flinn noticed two other men had seen the transaction. When the Germans left, Flinn and the others found reason to convene. After sounding each other out, Flinn learned the bag contained nearly a thousand dollars, and the Germans had given it to Phister for safekeeping. The trio waited around until night fell. After closing the place down, Flinn just happened to be walking in the same direction as Phister, toward Dupont Street.[17]

Flinn started up a lively conversation on a subject he knew interested Phister: women of easy virtue. Engaged in loose talk, Phister did not see Flinn's fast friends trailing behind them. None of them noticed San Francisco police officer Ben Bohen, who lived nearby at 411 Dupont Street, sheltering from the rain in a Dupont Street doorway.

"My confederates were a rod or two behind us," Flinn recollected. "They were to act on impulse of the moment, as we had no preconcerted plan of action."

As Flinn and Phister conversed, Flinn walked on his left and felt the bag in Phister's pocket. It was at that point that he "slipped the roll," pulling the sack from the saloonkeeper's pockets while simultaneously making as though he had tripped and fallen against him. But Phister hadn't been fooled.

"Give me that!" Phister cried out. "Give me my money!"

By this time Flinn's chums had arrived.

"Gentlemen," Flinn said boldly, "this drunken wretch has been trying to rob me; hold him while I call an officer."

"No!" cried Phister. "He has got my money!"

Flinn's confederates evidently weren't looking for a tussle, running "like wild deer." Flinn now knew he was in a fight and, using the sack as a bludgeoning weapon, struck Phister in the face. Phister threw his arm around Flinn, but that didn't stop Flinn from pummeling him with the sack of money. Flinn might have stopped when the man dropped to the ground, but his blood was up. With a loud shout, Flinn struck at Phister again and again.

Naturally, this brought Bohen running. About the same age as Flinn, Bohen was a rookie, having joined the police force in 1861. But what Bohen lacked in experience he made up for in raw strength. Bohen had little trouble pulling Flinn and Phister apart.[18]

While bleeding from his head, Phister grabbed Bohen's wrist and declared he'd been robbed. Flinn stuck to his story, saying that he'd been the one being robbed, and had justly defended himself. By then a crowd had gathered. Flinn attempted to subtly "hint" to Bohen that they could split the money, but—having been on the job for only three months—the officer was slow on the uptake. After the $980 in the sack was exposed to the crowd, Bohen muttered, "Damned fool that I am."[19]

Bohen marched both Flinn and Phister to the station house. Bohen later reported to a *San Francisco Chronicle* reporter that "I . . . saw that he was a man of fine physique, and was surprised that he had not given me a hard fight instead of yielding so gracefully. He was about twenty-seven years of age, stood about five feet eight inches in his stockings. His face was shaven clean, with the exception of a heavy, dark brown mustache, which gave his appearance an unpleasant look."[20]

While awaiting trial, Flinn became friendly with one of the jailors, whom Flinn initially thought kind. "He would do anything for me," Flinn recalled thinking. After some time, Flinn told him about the two hundred dollars he had stashed. Flinn wanted the jailor to locate the money and give it to a trusted friend, whom Flinn referred to in his memoir as "Captain Mc————," with instructions for the captain to send the money to Flinn's mother in Massachusetts. The jailor promised he would help.[21]

The next month, in March 1862, Flinn was formally tried in County Court of Sessions, the Honorable Maurice Blake presiding. If Flinn and his attorney, Nathan Porter, held out any hope for a self-defense plea, it was dashed the moment prosecutor Daniel Murphy sprang his trap. When Flinn's chums were called to speak, they double-crossed Flinn once again, testifying that Phister was the victim, not the villain.

Unsurprisingly, Judge Blake found Flinn guilty. Before the sentencing, Flinn addressed the court, pleading that the crime had been borne out of "inability to get work" and "starvation." Flinn also claimed that this was his "first offense."

Bohen observed that the man had "in a simple, manly way said that he had lost everything he owned at Sacramento, that he was starving here, and not knowing the man was carrying money he had attacked him in the hope of getting provisions. The Judge swallowed this fairy tale."[22]

Porter also urged the judge to show some leniency. Apparently having bought the story hook, line, and sinker, Judge Blake sentenced Flinn to only one year in prison. Reflecting on the short sentence, crime reporter Mark Twain groused, "For the same offence, in the interior of the state, he would have got ten years at least."[23]

Flinn had his mugshot taken, was given the number 2323, and entered San Quentin State Prison on March 7, 1862. But not as Charley Flinn. Without any identifying papers, Flinn had found it prudent to give a different name during the arrest and trial, one that would soon become infamous throughout California. Charles Mortimer had been born.[24]

Thicker Than Water

*A*lthough Mortimer did his best to leave his family and accomplices out of his memoir, with his enemies he pulled no punches. Unfortunately for Carrie, she now topped this list. On March 16, 1873—the day after the sentencing—Sheriff Mike Bryte asked Mortimer what he thought of what Carrie had done.

"I wouldn't do her any harm if I could," Mortimer answered, "but I will do as the Quaker did with the dog."

"How was that?" Bryte asked.

"Why, the dog snapped at the Quaker and the Quaker said, 'I won't kill you, but I'll give you a bad name,' and he called, 'Mad dog! Mad dog!' and the dog was killed before he could run a block."[1]

On March 22 Mortimer learned that Carrie's trouble in Alameda had come back to bite her. Although she'd served her time, and Mortimer had paid the fine, that had been for the charge of larceny. The greater charge of burglary was still pending. The following day, Mortimer wrote a letter to Police Captain F. B. Tarbett of Oakland, concerning the cigar case:

> Dear Sir. I suppose you read the result of my trial. That result was arrived
> at principally through Carrie's perjury of the most damnable nature; and
> it has broken my heart. Oh! when I think of what I have done for her, and
> then for her to treat me so! I have every reason to believe that matters will
> take a more favorable turn soon—that is, for me.... She tells all here that
> if that charge is for those cigars she will beat the case easy by putting it
> onto Redwine. Poor Red, I think, has suffered enough on her account.[2]

On March 25, ten days after the grand jury had found Mortimer guilty of murder, Sheriff Bryte visited his cell, explaining that Carrie would be sent to Alameda later that day.

"Do you want to see her?" Bryte asked.

"Certainly," Mortimer replied.

Before long Deputy Sheriff Manuel L. Cross knocked on the cell door. A former assayer from Truckee, it was probably nepotism that landed the thirty year old the position of night watchman at Sacramento County Jail, for Cross and Shearer were brothers-in-law.

"Charley!" Cross called. "Carrie is here and wishes to speak to you."

Mortimer went to the door. For a minute or so, they stood looking at each other, as silent as the grave. Eventually Carrie broke the silence.

"I am going away," Carrie said.

"Do you intend going very far?"

"I have to go to Alameda, to answer that charge."

"It would be well for you, if that charge was the only one that you will have to answer to."

Carrie shook her head and gave a look to indicate she was worried about Cross eavesdropping. Mortimer asked Cross to give them some privacy, convincing him that Sheriff Bryte had given them permission. Cross obliged.

"I hear that you are telling everything you know against me," Carrie accused.

"Not everything, but before long I intend to do so," Mortimer pledged. "Oh, Carrie! How could you have the heart to perjure yourself against me. I now must have the true facts brought to light."

"Then what will become of me? I could not help swearing in that way. If I didn't, there would charges put against me and I would be sent to State Prison."

"That is a poor excuse.... You can plainly see that the public believe that you have lied. The officers ... want me to assist them in arriving at the truth, and this I am going to do."

"No, Charley. Don't. Don't," Carrie begged, crying. "They will hang me or send me to State Prison for life."

"I did not think you were so selfish. You know I have done all that lay in my power to save you, and ... you were doing all you could to hang me. I know of no case of ingratitude to equal yours."

"If I had got clear I would have helped you."

"Impossible ... I truly pity you," Mortimer said, "but I must try now to help myself, even if you should hang."

"Oh, don't talk that way! I can beat the case in Alameda and then I'll go where I can't be found."

Mortimer didn't let her rest on this fantasy, telling her that even if she beat the Alameda case, she'd be arrested for something else. If he was bluffing, it fooled Carrie. In a last, desperate attempt to curry favor, to get out of Mortimer what knowledge he might have on her, and to prevent him from speaking about her to the police and revealing her crimes in his memoir, she offered to bring him some sugar and coffee.

"You can please yourself," Mortimer said.

"I'll get it."

Fifteen minutes later she returned. Through the wicket Carrie handed him sugar, coffee, and a cup of milk. Mortimer might have grabbed her at that moment. But he had a sweeter revenge in mind.

With tears in her eyes, Carrie said, "They say I must go today. Oh, Charlie! Goodbye."

Mortimer reached his hand through the wicket. Reflexively, she took it.

"Oh, what made you shake hands for?" Carrie asked. "Bryte and Shearer are looking down here. I wanted to pretend I was afraid to shake hands with you."

"That is all right. They know better than that. Goodbye."[3]

At 11:00 a.m. on March 29, four days after having said goodbye to Carrie for the last time, Mortimer was brought up to the Sixth District Court. Denson and King made a motion for a new trial. Judge Reardon deemed the one trial had been sufficient and delivered the pronouncement.[4]

"I was sentenced to be hanged until I was dead," Mortimer recalled.[5]

The execution date was set for May 15, 1873. Seemingly in a stupor, Mortimer listened to Judge Reardon's sentencing without expressing any emotion, the entire time looking the judge in the eyes.[6]

"It is very seldom that a lawyer can be heard to pray, and particularly in public," Mortimer reflected. "But upon this occasion the Hon. Judge Reardon did appeal to the Almighty Judge to have mercy on my soul. His Honor had so little sympathy for my body that I fear that his prayer was not that of a 'faithful, fervent man,' and will 'avail' but little."[7]

With only forty-seven days to finish his memoir, Mortimer devoted himself to it. He also wrote a letter to his younger brother William J. Flinn. In it, Mortimer stated that he was in great trouble and asked Will if he or any of the younger brothers— Ed, Frank, or Thomas—could come to Sacramento. Mortimer placed the letter in the hands of a prison trusty, who did as Mortimer asked. Receiving the letter, Will responded with actions rather than words.[8]

On April 7, 1873—with only thirty-eight days remaining on Mortimer's sentence—Will arrived in Sacramento. The train car registry had him as J. W. Williams of Jersey City, but this was an alias. Like his older brother, Will was up to no good.[9]

Of medium height and build, thirty-two-year-old Will sported a dark brown mustache, a beard, and muttonchops. The joint of the middle finger of his right hand was bent over, a subtle scar could be made out on his forehead—the result of Charley throwing a rock at him while playing as children—and he bore a shrapnel wound in his right ankle, courtesy of taking part in the Siege of Port Hudson, a hundred miles northwest of New Orleans. A cowboy hat could have covered Will's bald head, though working as a tailor in the shop he co-owned with his younger brother Frank, he had little need of one.[10]

Three days after arriving in Sacramento, Will registered as J. W. Williams of Jersey City at the City Hotel at 70 K Street, situated between the Bank Exchange Saloon and the Colonade Saloon, a half-mile southwest of Sacramento County Jail. He was given Room 42, which he shared with some acquaintances from his train car. Although back home in Lynn he was an upstanding member of the Massachusetts Lodge of Sons of Temperance, in Sacramento he hit the bottle, seen lifting elbows at several of Sacramento's watering holes. In this respect, too, Will took after his older brother.[11]

Will's wayward brother was certainly on his mind, for he hadn't traveled three thousand miles just to check out the Sacramento waterfront. Will meant to force a new trial, even if he had to resort to bribery. Locating Mike Haggerty, Will asked him about the facts of the trial. If any money changed hands, Haggerty kept that tidbit to himself. P. L. Hickman was more forthright. When Will offered the deputy sheriff money to change his testimony, Hickman refused the offer, asking if he and Mortimer were friends.

"Yes, more than a friend," Will replied.

Immediately afterward, Hickman tipped Shearer to the news that Mortimer's brother might be in town. Unsurprisingly, not long afterward, S. Perry—a Sacramento County Jail watchmen—noticed a man beyond the outer gate of the jail, who looked extraordinarily similar to Mortimer. As the stranger rang the bell, Perry said to Deputy Sheriff Cross that he "must be Mortimer's brother."

Opening the door, Cross found the visitor well-dressed and respectable looking. He called himself "Williams." When Will requested to be shown around the jail, Cross obliged him—though he did not show him to Mortimer's cell.

"Well, there's no use beating around the bush," Will said at last. "I want to see that man Mortimer."

When Cross told him that would not be possible, Will departed.[12]

Will's next move was to visit the offices of S. C. Denson, introducing himself as J. W. Williams. When asked where he was from, Will replied, "Well, call it New Orleans."[13]

When Will asked if there was any legal hope for Mortimer, Denson told him they were appealing to the California Supreme Court to have a new trial, on the grounds that the prosecutor should not have been able to be the first to make an opening statement and the last to make closing arguments. Seeking his assistance to visit Mortimer, Denson obliged. On Saturday, April 12, Will returned to the jail in company of Mortimer's young attorney, Cameron H. King. This time Shearer was on duty. When King asked that they be allowed to visit the condemned man, Shearer replied that, as his attorney, King could visit him alone, but all others could only visit the prisoner in the company of an officer. Will agreed to this, and the three of them went to Cell No. 5 to visit the condemned man.

Reaching the cell, King introduced Will to Mortimer, calling him "Mr. Williams."

Although it had been sixteen years since the Flinn brothers had last seen each other, Shearer caught the look of recognition pass between the two men. He was so certain of it that, while King and Mortimer continued their conversation, he led Will away.

"Shearer remarked that he thought he was an old convict," Willis recalled, "and that he meant no good by his visits, and at the same time instructed Cross not to admit him in the future."[14]

Shearer was right on the money. With his brother's case nearly hopeless, Will determined he'd spring him the old-fashioned way. Visiting a barbershop, Will asked for his chin whiskers to be shaved off, leaving the mustache and muttonchops. To the barber, Will commented that he might be shaving a man as famous as the president of the United States and not know it and that he would be more famous after he left Sacramento than when he arrived.[15]

At 1:30 p.m. on April 14, Shearer was overseeing the jail when the African American cook came in from the yard, bursting with news. He'd spotted a man on the second story of the jail, near the water closets, nearly on top of Mortimer's cell. The man had called out, "Mortimer, recollect what I told you."

Listening hard, Shearer heard in the distance the name "Mortimer." Rushing out, Shearer looked around the corner of the building, catching sight of a figure dodging past the lattice work. Shearer ran up the stairs but found the man had disappeared.[16]

The next day, on Tuesday, April 15, Will's three acquaintances he'd met on the train left the City Hotel, and Will transferred rooms to No. 85. That night Will visited Joseph Davis & Co.'s pawnshop. Clerking that night was Max Marcuse, who had in the way of firearms a five-barreled Colt revolver, No. 7,287, with the initials "S. W. H." on the metal butt. When it was discovered the revolver only contained four bullets, Will allowed that that was plenty and instructed Marcuse to leave it so that the first time the revolver was triggered, the hammer would fall on the empty chamber.

Later that night, Will stole a twenty-two-foot ladder from Richard S. Jones's carpentry shop on I Street. Willis noted that the ladder was so heavy one man could barely carry it, prompting theories that Will may have had help. Whatever the case, shortly after midnight, the ladder was propped up against the jail yard wall on I Street. Climbing the ladder in the moonlight, Will scurried across the rooftops and hopped into the jail yard.

Will was prepared for several outcomes. The Colt revolver in his hand, the scabbarded five-inch, pearl-handled dagger on his hip, and the hand-drawn map of the jail in his pocket signaled that he was willing to shoot and stab his way in and out, if needs be, in order to affect the rescue. The white handkerchief covering the bottom portion of his face expressed his desire to remain incognito, so long as he could.

The twenty-five dollars and loose silver in his pocket could be used if they needed to make a quick getaway, though he also had his room key at the City Hotel on him if all went well. If everything went to hell, he carried papers related to the Mortimer trial on which he'd written "W. J. Flinn," and wore a Grand Army of the Republic badge and a ring, both of which bore his given name: "J. W. Flinn." Once these clues were deciphered, word of what happened could be sent back to Louisa.[17]

After violently yanking on the bell pull, Will ducked out of sight. When Cross appeared, he looked around and, like the thirty-year-old assayer he was, began searching for the intruder in the wrong direction. With the deputy's back turned, Will could have shot him. He'd trained for this, after all. Month after month had been spent at drill, in Massachusetts, Maryland, Virginia, and Louisiana, before Will and Frank first experienced combat at Fort Bisland in April of 1863. Two months later, during the bloody Siege of Port Hudson, he'd been on the front lines when a piece of a shell had caught him in the right ankle. He was no mere tailor but a soldier.[18]

Evidently, he wasn't a killer. As Cross spotted him, instead of shooting, Will said something, which the handkerchief muffled. Seeing Cross begin to wheel, Will still had time to trigger the empty chamber, possibly a live round as well. Instead, he froze, apparently unable to commit cold-blooded murder—even with his life on the line.

Cross's first bullet caught Will in the chest. The next smashed into his teeth. Outside the jail, the sound of running feet filled the air. Inside the jail, Mortimer leapt to his feet, his boots already on. Will dropped the revolver, but he hadn't given up the rescue attempt. Leaking blood, he lurched inside, making terrible choking noises as he headed for his brother's cell.[19]

Outside, Cross realized to his horror that his gun had jammed. Nor had he seen Will drop the revolver. Desperately, Cross called for Perry, who usually slept in the treasurer's office. According to Deputy Willis, "Perry, who had heard the firing, came in just as the desperate and dying man made a final rush along the back passage way and fell head first against the wall direct in front of Mortimer's cell."

Even with the intruder shot in the chest and face, Cross and Perry were taking no chances. After opening the cell door of the imprisoned soldier, John R. Powers—who had been confined for assaulting a "Chinaman"—the sheriffs instructed Powers to see if the fallen man was playing possum. Dragging the body down the hall to where Cross and Perry waited, making a bloody mess of the floor, Powers determined he was dead.[20]

Little sleep was had that night by Sacramento's lawmen, undertakers, and night owl reporters. Searching the body, the City Hotel room key was uncovered, as were the papers on the Mortimer trial with the name W. J. Flinn on one of them. With the coroner ill, messengers summoned undertakers R. K. Wick and Jerome F. Clark, who removed the body to the morgue. Bill Shearer also located Will's boots, hat, and a coil of rope in a water closet that used to be part of Mose Drew's previous saloon on I Street, near the south wall of the jail.[21]

Checking in on Cell No. 5, Mortimer was undressed. He appeared to have just woken from a deep sleep and claimed to have no idea who had died just outside his cell. Few jailors, if any, believed Mortimer, trusting instead the word of Henry Earl, imprisoned nearby, who swore he'd heard Mortimer leap out of bed with his boots on after the first shot rang out. Shearer also took the opportunity to rattle Mortimer's cage, telling the condemned man that he'd suspected the stranger intended to spring him from jail and that for the last five days he and others had been watching him.

"I was watching his moves up to half-past nine last night," Shearer gloated, "and if I had thought that he would have made the attempt, or attempt anything, last night I would have been here to receive him."

"Bill Shearer, whether that man is a relative of mine or not, God will hold you responsible for his death," Mortimer retorted. "Your own words prove that if you knew what his intentions were, you [should] have informed him what you had heard and warned him or had him arrested."[22]

Meanwhile, lawmen entered Room 85 in the City Hotel, finding in Will's valise an army blanket, clothing, a bottle of liniment, and an advertisement for a tailor and clothes-cleaning shop in Lynn, Massachusetts, located on 5 Tremont Street, owned by William J. Flinn and Frank M. Flinn. The tailor shop advertisement was of particular interest to the press and police. Suddenly, Mortimer's tattoos on his left arm—an anchor, C. Flinn, and C. J. F.—were beginning to make sense. If J. W. Williams, who had looked so much like Mortimer, was actually William Flinn or Frank Flinn, could the true name of Charles Mortimer be Charles J. Flinn?[23]

Tracing Will's movements a couple doors down from the City Hotel to Louis Strauss's saloon on 68 K, a girl mentioned that the drunken stranger had admitted to her that he was Mortimer's brother. Special Deputy Willis and some others also visited the offices of Denson and King. Mortimer's attorneys could only tell them that "Williams," as he had called himself, had unconvincingly claimed he was from New Orleans and that he'd been somewhat inebriated every time they'd met.[24]

Shortly afterward, Mortimer and G. W. Tyler confirmed the theory. Mortimer told Tyler that he would like to see the dead man, to see if he really was his brother. Tyler asked Mortimer if there were any marks on his brother with which he could be identified. Mortimer told him that his brother had a finger that could be bent over and a scar on the outer side of his right leg, between his knee and ankle. Visiting the morgue, Tyler found the body had the same markings as Mortimer had described. The dead man was indeed John W. Flinn III, better known as Will.[25]

At 3:30 on the afternoon of April 17, Mortimer—accompanied by Karcher, Bryte, and Shearer—was driven in handcuffs to the morgue.

"I had not seen or heard from my brother for nearly sixteen years," Mortimer claimed. "And the room in which I first viewed the remains was dark and I could not see clearly."

To accommodate Mortimer, Will's coffin was taken to a room where there was more light. Studying the body, Mortimer looked for the scar on Will's forehead he had caused twenty-five years ago, when he had thrown a stone at him while at play. Instead, there was a bruise made when Will had fallen dead in front of his cell. Underneath the bruise, Mortimer noticed the scar. Finding the end of Will's middle finger bent over erased any doubt from his mind.

"There lay my brother cold in death," Mortimer wrote later that day. "His devoted brotherly affection had not cooled after an absence of sixteen years. He had sacrificed his life in trying to liberate me."[26]

Mortimer asked that he have one of the advertisements from Will's valise and a lock of his hair. The police complied with both requests. Afterward, Wick and Clark transported the body to Sacramento City Cemetery where Will was buried in plot thirty-nine in tier twenty-nine, colloquially known as Potter's Field. Meanwhile, Mortimer was transported back to County Jail, where he allowed himself to be interviewed.[27]

"From the marks on W. J. Flinn, I recognize him to be my brother. I had not seen him for sixteen years.... He came to the cell door.... He gazed fixedly at me for some moments but did not speak. Many come here in a like manner, and look at me like I were some caged wild beast ... and I supposed that he, like some others, was attracted here out of pure curiosity."

The newspapers didn't buy it.

"Mortimer ... expresses the utmost amazement at the daring attempt," a reporter for the *Bee* reported, "yet he was beyond question perfectly cognizant of the whole plot."

The reporter also noted that Mortimer was anxious that word of his brother's death didn't spread East. But, like so many things, he was powerless to prevent it. One thing Mortimer could control was his memoir.[28]

Finishing it, Mortimer dedicated the book to S. C. Denson, as proof of his gratitude for doing his best during the trial. On the dedication page, Mortimer also admitted that had he "properly reflected, I would have served the Ruler of all good and perfect gifts, instead of the King of Evil." Throughout the book, he detailed hundreds of crimes, many of which could be corroborated through newspaper accounts. The most egregious crimes, of course, occurred in May and September of 1872. The murder of Caroline Prenel he laid at Carrie's feet, though he allowed he had been in the room at the time and that the robbery was his idea. He confessed to murdering Mary Gibson with Carrie's help, whom he admitted to still loving, despite her betrayals. He concluded the book with a warning that "a life of criminal acts won't prosper" and prayed for the souls of his dead brother, his "dear mother," and his father. The last lines he saved for his siblings: "My dear sister and brothers, I beseech of you to lead lives of obedience to God's holy will. Let us all exert ourselves to hold out to the end in faith. Let nothing separate us from the love of God, which is our Blessed Redeemer, and then we will be sure to meet in that blessed realm above."[29]

The Shakers of Lebanon, New Hampshire, with whom Mortimer had briefly joined, might have been proud had they not been appalled. Afterward, Mortimer presented the book to Denson, to be published after the execution. What did not make it into the memoir were the results of the trial held in Oakland—*The People vs. Carrie Mortimer*—printed on April 21.

"Carrie Jones Wardell Smith Butler Plantagenet Mortimer," as a wit for the *Sacramento Bee* had facetiously dubbed her (after Carrie had earlier in April unsuccessfully lobbied to get paid seventy dollars for testifying against Mortimer), had been found not guilty. The jury, it seems, were not convinced that the theft of the cigars had been premeditated. Elated, Carrie declared she would like to make the capital her home.[30]

"Carrie Mortimer will honor Sacramento by making it her place of residence," quipped the *San Francisco Chronicle*.[31]

The following day, on April 22, John Smith—a constable in the Massachusetts State Police who had enlisted in 1862 with Will and Frank, joining E Company of the Massachusetts Thirty-Eighth—sent Deputy Sheriff Manuel Cross a telegram. In particular, he wanted sent to him all the information available on the man he had shot and killed. Cross did so. The next day Chief Matt Karcher and Sheriff Mike Bryte sent word to Lynn of Will's death and Charley's incarceration. Photos were sent as well. Additionally, Karcher notified his counterpart in Boston, Chief of Police Edward S. Savage. On April 26 S. C. Denson wrote to the family.[32]

Louisa virtually fell to pieces on hearing the news that her eldest boy, Charley, whom she had given up for dead long ago, was sentenced to hang for murder, and that her third eldest boy, Will, had been shot to death while attempting a rescue. Detailing how the twin blows nearly drove her mad, Smith wrote to Denson on April 27, commenting that Louisa was "almost distracted in consequence of the sad affair."

That same day, Thomas H. Flinn and Ed D. Flinn sent Denson letters. Praising Denson for being a steadfast friend to his brother, Thomas asked that he share the enclosed photos with "my dear brother Charles."

Ed saved his praise for Will, describing him to Denson as "the bravest of the brave," recounting his war record, particularly his actions on the front lines during the Siege of Port Hudson, and having been a strong member of the Massachusetts Lodge of the Sons of Temperance. Ed also sought information on Carrie, asking if because of her testimony in San Francisco, Charley would be tried for murder again even if he beat the rap in Sacramento.

Referring to Carrie as a "harlot," Ed opined, "Why, the general opinion of all that have read his trial here, even lawyers, say she was the one who committed the deed, and think she got some one to pound and kick him to clear her skirts. Does she hold all of her ill-gotten wealth and then boast of being the one who convicted him? If she had the heart of stone she could not do that."

Smith also wrote Sheriff Bryte, praising Will's war record. As for Frank M. Flinn, no record exists of him sending a letter from Massachusetts to California, but that does not mean he was idle. After all, along with being brothers, Frank and Will had been comrades in arms during the war and partners at their tailor shop. He owed it to Will to do something, and if the circumstances surrounding Charley's trial were as fishy as Ed believed—that Charley's woman was actually the guilty party—maybe, just maybe, he could set that right too.[33]

In the first week of May 1873, Frank M. Flinn boarded a train for California.[34]

CHAPTER 18

Hanging Charley Flinn

On May 8, 1873—one week before the scheduled execution—the California Supreme Court affirmed the decision rendered by the Sixth District Court. No new trial would be granted Charles Mortimer. Denson and King telegraphed the melancholy news to Mortimer's family in Lynn, Massachusetts. They also visited Sacramento County Jail.

Escorted by Bryte, Shearer, and several others, the attorneys were startled by his appearance. According to the *Sacramento Bee*, "Mortimer was seen sitting therein with only his underclothing on, facing one corner of the room, and apparently engaged in conversation with some imaginary person. The sheriff called him by name, but Charley paid no attention to the call."

Mortimer also kept a bouquet of old flowers on the mattress, in the middle of which was the lock of Will's hair. With vacant eyes, Mortimer looked upon it. Failing to induce Mortimer to recognize them or put on clothing, Bryte and Shearer eventually took up the task, dressing the docile prisoner. Afterward, they guided Mortimer to the jail yard where he was placed in a chair. Denson and King again attempted to have Mortimer give some sign he recognized them, but Mortimer seemed almost catatonic. Eventually they asked Bryte to break the news.

"Charley, Mr. Denson has come to tell you that the Supreme Court has decided your case," Bryte said. "They have affirmed the judgment, denied you a new trial and you have to be hung on the 15th day of this month."

Not even that roused any emotion in Mortimer. Willis noted that many of the onlookers believed him truly insane, while others reasoned he was still angling to be placed in an asylum. Whether Denson or King truly believed Mortimer insane or not was immaterial; they saw a glimmer of hope and sought to capitalize on it. With Bryte's consent, they wrote a letter to Dr. George A. Shurtleff of the Insane Asylum in Stockton, requesting the doctor examine the condemned man.[1]

Two days later, on the afternoon of May 10, Frank M. Flinn rattled into Sacramento. Like Will, he registered at the City Hotel. Wasting little time, Frank met with Denson, King, another lawyer, J. N. Young, and Reverend Charles Schelling. Together, the five of them headed to Sacramento County Jail. What the lawyers and reverend made of this third Flinn brother went unrecorded, but it was a cinch they sized him up, wondering if he, too, would try to spring his older brother from jail.[2]

166

Frank certainly seemed the respectable sort. At twenty-eight years old, he was good looking, had a full head of black hair, sported a mustache, was a touch under the medium height, and was a married man, having tied the knot in Lynn with Catherine F. Hyde on July 7, 1867. Frank was also father to Flora Maud Flinn, born in February 1873.[3]

At the same time, Frank was the most experienced of the Flinn brothers at firearms. Joining the war at seventeen, Frank was made part of the Thirty-Eighth Massachusetts E Company. During the Battle of Fort Bisland, Frank recalled fighting through the "constant roar of artillery and musketry, grape, ball, and shell" in their efforts to seize the Confederate fort. Two months later, on June 14, 1863, Frank served on the front lines during the ill-conceived assault on Port Hudson. Unlike Will, Frank survived the bloody battle unscathed, though he'd remain haunted by "the most terrific cannonading . . . that ever stunned mortal ears."[4]

While Will was transferred to the Veteran Reserve Corps after his injury, Frank remained in the thick of it, serving in the ill-fated Red River Campaign and under Sheridan in the Shenandoah Valley, seeing action at the Third Battle of Winchester, the Battle of Fisher's Hill, and the Battle of Cedar Creek. After the war, he'd returned home to a hero's welcome. Liking the bottle as much as Charley and Will—a trait passed down from their alcoholic father—Frank nevertheless made a success of himself, partnering with Will at their tailor shop in Lynn.

As the jailors led the lawyers, the reverend, and this new Flinn brother to Cell No. 5, everyone was curious to see if Mortimer would recognize Frank. At first, Mortimer did not seem to see or hear him, engaged in rocking back and forth, wringing his hands, and concentrating on the spot on his mattress where he seemed to believe the ghost of Will sat. When Frank sat down on the mattress between Mortimer and that sacred spot, Mortimer roughly flung Frank away. In this manner, Frank may have helped Mortimer's case that he had lost his mind, for pushing aside one brother to converse with a dead one did seem a might peculiar.

The following day, May 11, Dr. Shurtleff arrived from Stockton. By this time, being summoned to Sacramento on business was old hat to Shurtleff. Elected president of the Medical Society of the State of California in 1872, in April 1873 he had delivered an address on criminals seeking to pass as insane.[5]

"The frequency with which the plea of insanity has of late been resorted to, with undeserved success, to avoid responsibility for crime—the irregular, unscientific, and generally unfair manner in which such trials are conducted with regard to medical testimony . . . all seem to call for reform in the law relating to the trial of criminal cases in which the mental condition of the accused is involved," Shurtleff lectured.[6]

With Mortimer, Shurtleff planned to be as regular, scientific, and fair as possible. To that end the jailors brought Mortimer out into the light, where the good doctor bade the prisoner open his mouth. This was a necessary part of the procedure to test for mental illness, for Shurtleff knew that such illnesses resulted from the nervous centers of the cerebral hemispheres of the brain becoming diseased, resulting in hallucination and insanity; because Shurtleff could not open up Mortimer's skull to look at the brain without killing him, he planned to examine Mortimer's tongue to see if deposits of the diseased conductive medullary fibers were in evidence. It was all very scientific sounding.[7]

Mortimer, however, kept his mouth clamped shut, and Shurtleff was unable to pry open his jaws. The next morning, May 12, at half past ten, Shurtleff tried it again. This time he managed to get a good look at Mortimer's tongue.

"It was full and exhaustive of all the methods known to science of fixing a man's condition of mind," the *Sacramento Bee* reported.

The *Bee* also announced the results. With Mortimer's attorneys and jailors as an audience, Shurtleff declared Mortimer quite sane. Instead of delivering Mortimer the news himself, Shurtleff sent Reverend Revilio F. Parshall to do so. Parshall, who later that year would be forced to resign from the church for taking liberties with young female members of his flock, informed Mortimer there was no longer any hope in his latest ruse to set himself free. At hearing this, Mortimer grew somewhat excited and pale, but did not speak. His only chance now of walking away a free man lay in Governor Booth issuing him a pardon. To prevent this, Shurtleff called upon the governor and informed him of the results of the test. Preparations were also made for the hanging, scheduled three days later.[8]

The next day, May 13, Mortimer was moved from Cell No. 5 to Cell No. 18. Several visitors passed by Mortimer's cell, seeking to catch sight of the infamous criminal while he still breathed. Denson, too, spoke to Mortimer, though Mortimer continued to act as though the only voice he could hear was that of his dead brother. Frank called at the jail as well but couldn't bring himself to visit his brother again—though he did catch sight of the gallows being constructed in the jail yard.[9]

As to Mortimer's mental state, the *Bee* noted that there was a great difference of opinion between Shurtleff and Mortimer, Shurtleff declaring Mortimer sane and Mortimer persisting in "remaining as insane as he knows how." The following day, May 14, Mortimer was moved to Cell No. 19. He ate a small portion of his breakfast and was observed rocking back and forth while sitting cross-legged on the floor, his hair uncombed and beard unkempt. In one hand he held a dirty towel, which he would strike angrily at the cell wall from time to time.

That day the *Sacramento Bee* published the dedication page of *The Life of Charles Mortimer* and the prisoner's reasons for writing the book. A certain passage may have been of particular interest to the friends and family of Mary Gibson: "Oh, Carrie, you have brought all this trouble on me. You are as guilty as I."[10]

With nothing to lose, on the evening of May 14 Denson and King asked Sheriff

Bryte to summon a jury to determine whether Mortimer was sane or not. King also wrote Bryte a formal letter, citing Section 1221 of the California Penal Code: "If after judgment of death there is good reason to suppose that the defendant has become insane, the Sheriff of the county ... may summon a jury of 12 persons to inquire into the supposed insanity."

King then presented Bryte his best argument for such a diagnosis: "The circumstances attending his case are surely enough to drive an ordinary man insane. The severe shock which the death of his brother must have given him, the ... treachery of the accomplices whom he had trusted, the ... pangs of conscience ... in contemplating his past life, his long incarceration in jail, would all conspire to overturn his mind and dethrone his reason."[11]

Of the opinion that Shurtleff's diagnosis was enough, and doubtless not wishing to see Mortimer institutionalized, Bryte declined to summon a second jury. Governor Booth also saw through Mortimer's charade, expressing hope he would drop it. To Parshall, Booth intimated that if Mortimer stopped his mad act, he would grant the condemned man a brief reprieve so that he could speak to Frank and a reverend.

On the morning of the hanging, May 15, 1873, Parshall hinted to Mortimer that the governor was willing to give him such a reprieve if he stopped the insanity dodge. Mortimer didn't take the hint or chose to ignore it. Meanwhile, outside the jail Frank grumbled bitterly to a *San Francisco Chronicle* reporter that Bryte was having his brother "officially murdered for the benefit of officers whom his living testimony would ruin," and were the truth revealed about his brother's accomplices on the police force, "it would create an entire revolution in the criminal history of California." Frank had also perused Charley's memoir and verified that the portions that took place in New England appeared true.[12]

At 8:45 a.m. the gallows were finally completed. Built of stout timbers, the entire apparatus was twelve feet square. With the cut of a cord, the trapdoors beneath the noose—the same rope which hanged John J. Murphy the previous month for killing his brother-in-law, Patrick Murray—would open, the prisoner would fall, and if all went right, his neck would snap. Making sure everything was in order, Sheriff Bryte tested the mechanism with a sack of potatoes and was satisfied with the results.[13]

At 11:25 Bryte instructed Cross, Barnes, and Hickman to deliver Mortimer a clean linen shirt, a hat, and a plain black suit. The deputies found Mortimer rocking to and fro and slapping at imaginary flies. Paying no attention to their order to stand, Mortimer gazed dully about the cell, and the deputies had to take on the duty of dressing him. They had gotten him to his feet when, all at once, the old Mortimer reappeared. Gathering his strength, Mortimer made a break for it. The muscular deputies prevented this sudden escape attempt, but when Cross saw him eyeing his revolver, he prudently passed it to someone outside the cell. Shortly afterward, Mortimer broke down sobbing.

"You had better make your peace with God, Charley," Barnes told him, "instead of struggling with us. You had better think where you are going to and make preparations for taking a flight into the other world."

At 12:15, when Mortimer was finally dressed, Shearer gave it a try. "Charley, you have been here a long time with me," the chief jailor said. "You know I am not to be deceived. Your brother begs to see you. He will not come till you send for him. This is the last time I shall ever speak to you. Shall I tell him you want him? Oh, Charley, I beg of you, call him in; think of home and mother and brothers, and see the one who has come so far."[14]

Shearer's plea fell on deaf ears.

Reverend David Deal also attempted to cajole Mortimer to drop the act. "Charles, you have a mother that feels for you," Deal implored. "Speak and have your brother called here and talk to him. This is no time to feign insanity. Have you no message to send to your mother? You have but a very few moments before you are ushered into eternity."

Affected by the reverend's appeal, King spoke next to Mortimer. "Charley, do you know me?" the attorney asked. "We have done all we can for you. You must place your trust in God; there is no hope." Mortimer gave no sign he understood either man.

At 12:25 Mortimer made another attempt at freedom before Cross, Barnes, and Hickman overpowered him. Mortimer grew pale. Reverend Parshall, Sheriff Bryte, and Bryte's guest from Alameda, Sheriff Harry N. Morse, joined them. As the clock rang out half past twelve, Sheriff Bryte said, "Charley, the time is about up. Have you anything to say before you are led out to your execution?"

Mortimer did not.

"Barnes, put on the straps," Bryte commanded.

Gamely, Barnes endeavored to lock Mortimer's elbows and bind his wrists to his thighs, but Mortimer put up a struggle. It took the combined efforts of all the deputies and both sheriffs to bind him. For Morse this was all part of the job. As the most celebrated sheriff in California, he'd done just about everything, including two years earlier shooting it out in Sunol Valley with the notorious bandido Juan Soto, later nicknamed "The Human Wildcat," killing Soto with a shot from his 1866 Winchester.[15]

Afterward, Parshall whispered to Bryte, "Don't let him drop until I say 'Amen.'"

"All right," Bryte replied, then turned to Mortimer. "Now, Charles Mortimer, we are about to start for the place of execution. Have you anything to say before we start?"

Mortimer kept quiet.

Watching the sheriffs and deputies escort Mortimer into the jail yard were Undersheriff Al Woods, Bill Shearer, and the men that Bryte had invited to view the execution. From within Sacramento came Chief of Police Matt Karcher, Captain

E. M. Stevens, Special Deputy E. B. Willis, a handful of other reporters, Reverend Charles Schelling, and Reverend Revilio Parshall. Also in attendance were sheriffs and deputies from the California counties of Solano, El Dorado, Placer, San Joaquin, Yolo, Amador, Nevada, Salinas, and Napa. Everyone wanted to see Mortimer get his just deserts.

Carrie, however, was not in attendance, and although she had made it clear she wanted to call Sacramento home, she hadn't graced the papers since late April. Nor was Frank in the crowd, apparently sticking to his decision to not see his older brother unless Charley asked for him.

As Mortimer entered the jail yard he glanced for a moment at the bright sky. Afterward, he looked toward the courthouse, its windows crowded with spectators. Shifting his gaze back to the scaffold, he marched there without trembling, and stood in the center of the trap. He looked up at the sky again and listlessly at the people. They looked back at him: a thirty-nine-year-old convicted killer.

Mortimer's body slightly swayed, and his lips moved as if he were repeating something to himself, but no one could make it out. At that point, Undersheriff Woods read out the death warrant, beginning with the verdict rendered by the jury in the Sixth District Court for the murder of Mary Gibson, ending with Mortimer ordered to stay imprisoned "until the 15th day of May, 1873, and that on said day the said Sheriff take him from the jail to the place of execution in said county, and there hung by the neck until he be dead."[16]

Sheriff Bryte asked Mortimer for the last time if he had anything to say. Mortimer ignored the question. Next a cord was strapped around his ankles, his hat was replaced with a cap covering his face, and the noose adjusted around his neck. Afterward, Schelling read some of the Parable of the Prodigal Son and from the Book of John. Parshall gave a prayer, preaching, "Because sentence against an evil work is not executed speedily, therefore the hearts of the children of men are fully set in them to do evil."

In other words, Parshall wanted to get on with it. Parshall concluded, "God grant that this scene, so full of gloom and sadness, may be sanctified to the good of the living. This grant, in the name of the Lord Jesus Christ. Amen."

As soon as that word left the reverend's lips—at 12:45 p.m.—Barnes cut the cord. All at once the bolts flew back, the trapdoors opened, and the weight tightened around the noose. Mortimer plunged six feet toward the ground before the noose caught him, breaking his neck with a snap. His head lolled forward. For thirteen minutes the crowd watched the body dangle before someone felt for a pulse. There was none.

Charles Mortimer was dead.[17]

"Rather Have a Rattlesnake"

*F*ollowing the hanging, Mortimer's corpse was delivered to Reave's undertaking rooms, and into the care of R. K. Wick. The physicians removed the black cap and ascertained that the execution couldn't have gone more smoothly. His neck had broken instantly, shocking his nervous system and completely separating the cervical vertebrae. Afterward, not a muscle in Mortimer's body had moved. Crowds gathered to view the body, including a French fortuneteller. From the lifeline on Mortimer's palm, the mademoiselle deduced that women had been Mortimer's downfall.[1]

Later that evening Sheriff Bryte invited the officers present and members of the press to dinner at the Capitol Hotel at the southwest corner of Seventh and K, just down the street from Sacramento County Jail. There it was almost unanimously agreed upon that Mortimer had been feigning insanity in a last-ditch attempt of receiving a pardon or being sent to an asylum. It was one of the most bizarre executions anyone could recall, but justice had been done. As for Denson and King, it was admirable how hard they had fought for Mortimer's release, particularly considering that they weren't paid a dime. At the same time, more than a few believed the attorneys had taken it too far by sending Bryte the letter wherein the California Penal Code was cited, imploring Bryte to call for a jury to determine Mortimer's sanity.[2]

Seeing it through to the very end, Denson and King were present at Mortimer's funeral the next morning, held at eleven o'clock at Wick & Clark's. Of the others that attended, Frank was the most conspicuous. Frank had already paid R. K. Wick to remove the body to City Cemetery, after all. Mortimer was buried in tier 29, plot 28 1/2. This was near where Will had been buried, in tier 29, plot 39, before Frank had Will dug up, sent to Lynn, and buried in the family graveyard.[3]

Mortimer's final resting place can no longer be found. After the Great War, family members were given notice that if they wanted the remains of their loved ones moved, this could be done. Otherwise, their headstones would be buried beneath eight feet of dirt, and the coffins of the WWI veterans placed atop them. Once done, Potter's Field was transformed into the "Veteran's Area."

Considering Mortimer had spent his whole life seeking anonymity, that his grave is unknown is fitting.

Beyond the mystery of just where Mortimer's grave is located, another mystery centers around just what happened to Carrie. At first her whereabouts were tracked by newspapermen and lawmen. On May 3, 1873, having beaten the case in Alameda, Carrie arrived by stagecoach in Sacramento. She didn't stay long. Four days later she was in San Francisco and was in the act of robbing a man from the rural districts, John Johnson, of twenty dollars when he caught her. The next morning, May 8, she was brought to Police Court, but as Johnson did not show, she was released. On May 30 it was reported in the *Sacramento Record* that she had returned to Livermore Valley "dead broke" and was living once more with J. R. Wardell.

On June 5, 1873—three weeks after Mortimer's hanging—Carrie was back in the Sacramento Courthouse, brought up on a charge of perjury. Carrie had previously claimed that while locked in a cell, Harris had searched her, found a quantity of money, pocketed some of it, and given the rest for Dole to put in the safe. Harris and Dole both claimed that they had found the money in a shoe under the mattress, and without pocketing any of it, Harris gave it to Dole to put in the safe. While they testified before Judge Gilmer, Carrie wept into a white handkerchief.

If Carrie served any time for accusing Harris of robbing her, it was very little. On June 17 she boarded the steamer *Amador*, deciding this time to "honor" San Francisco with her presence. Grandly dressed, she caught the eye of a successful pugilist, Thomas McAlpine, nicknamed "Soap," who had just defeated two opponents. The *San Francisco Chronicle* noted that Carrie and the boxer were quickly engaged in "amorous conversation" and that Soap seemed "deeply enchanted." After a satisfactory private conversation, Soap went to the bar for a little liquid courage when a gentleman, who had recognized Carrie, told the man who she was: "the infamous Carrie Mortimer."

"He declared that he would rather have a rattlesnake in tow than Carrie Mortimer," reported the newspaperman.

A few weeks later, Carrie resurfaced in Sacramento. There she was arrested for luring a girl into her house with the intention of turning her into a prostitute. At least that was the charge; if Mortimer's memoir was to be believed, it could have gone much worse for the girl. Whatever the case, Carrie was acquitted on September 13.

Lying low for a year, Carrie once again popped up in San Francisco. On September 19, 1874—the one-year anniversary of the murder of Mary Gibson—a Sonoma man named Richard Oskins accused night watchman John Pygorge of robbing him of seventy dollars in gold and silver. Pygorge told it differently and pointed out that on that evening Oskins had been seen in the company of Carrie Mortimer, claiming that if Oskins had lost any money it was assuredly Carrie who had stolen it. The argument was solid, and the charges against the night watchman were dropped.[4]

Carrie next crossed paths with James Willis, a Barbary Coast ruffian who fell for her charms. When Willis was arrested on January 27, 1876, for knocking down and kicking an African American woman who refused to drink drugged beer, newspapermen noted that Willis was Carrie's lover and protector.[5]

After that, Carrie disappeared from history. It could have been innocent enough. If her family allowed her to share their roof, Carrie may have returned home to Healdsburg, convinced to give up her wicked ways and live quietly. Another prospect is that, using her charms, she met a rich stranger and sailed with him overseas. Likelier, Carrie could have left California under an alias and worked the towns and cities where she wasn't so well-known. Another eventuality is that the lingering ailment about which she had confided to Mortimer finally did her in.

Whatever the case, after 1876 Carrie was rarely if ever mentioned in the newspapers, histories, and articles except in conjunction with Mortimer. As for Mortimer, his name continued to be spoken of in San Francisco, Sacramento, Virginia City, Siskiyou County, and in all his old stomping grounds for years after his death. Particularly in Santa Cruz, his memory had an effect, helping to clear S. W. Blakely of robbing the Santa Cruz Treasury.[6]

Various stories also circulated that Mortimer's wraith had been "poking around his old quarters" at Sacramento City Prison. For years, prisoners, guards, and visitors claimed the cell was haunted. The noose with which Mortimer had been hanged also became quite the attraction. On March 19, 1875, it was used to hang Mortimer's old comrade in San Quentin State Prison, Tiburcio Vasquez. Afterward, the rope was taken by the enterprising officer F. D. Chamberlain, who added it to his collection of macabre artifacts. These included Mary Gibson's broken beer glass, the hair found clutched in her death grip, and portraits of Mortimer and Carrie, all of which were placed in a box painted blue on the outside, red on the edges, and black on the interior. Glass topped the box, so the viewer could see at a glance the contents of the collection.[7]

Copies of Mortimer's autobiography also made for entertaining reading. By riding shotgun with Mortimer, readers were able to plunder their way through the one-horse towns, thriving cities, and treacherous highways of the Far West. Although it didn't ruin the careers of any lawmen, it did prove somewhat embarrassing to some, George W. Rose in particular. Even in Salt Lake City, where the disgraced former police detective ended up working as a private detective, the story of how he'd lost his finger to Mortimer ate at him. Suggesting Rose may well have been as corrupt as Mortimer and the San Francisco papers alleged, in October of 1876 Rose was arrested for his part in robbing the Wells Fargo & Co. express car on the Utah Central Railroad the month before.[8]

Most criminals who thumbed through Mortimer's memoir breathed a sigh of relief, however. Because of Mortimer's reticence against "turning traitor" and his playful use of aliases, Carrie was the only accomplice whose crimes were brought to light. In later years, the book became a collectors' item. At an auction in 2020, nearly 150 years after its first publication, a copy of Mortimer's autobiography kept by a resident of Sacramento sold for $998. The book can also be found in academic libraries: the Huntington Research Library in San Marino, the University of California's Bancroft Library in Berkeley, the University of Michigan's William Clements Library in Ann Arbor, the New York Historical Society Library, and the Library of Congress. For historians seeking information on the Old West, particularly those interested in criminal slang, post–gold rush California, and the shadowy inner workings of San Quentin State Prison, Mortimer's account proved indispensable.

Mortimer's memoir proved fifteen years too early for modern psychologists, however, for the term "psychopathological"—first called *psychopastiche* by German psychiatrist J. L. A. Koch—wasn't used until 1888. Yet Mortimer displayed the characteristics of the archetypical psychopath: charming, cunning, bereft of almost all genuine empathy, predisposed toward criminal enterprises, and possessing a grandiose sense of self-worth. Another aspect of his psychopathy, Mortimer proved a masterful liar, artfully fabricating stories to gain an advantage over his victims, to cover his tracks, and for the sense of superiority he felt in hoodwinking those around him.[9]

As for Mortimer's final summation of his life story, that crime doesn't pay, the adage rings true but fails to capture the broader picture. Taken as a whole, Mortimer's violent career and fitting climax demonstrates a universal truth: just as a land of opportunity attracts industrious pioneers, it also attracts vicious predators. And as roguishly charismatic as Mortimer could sometimes be—playfully sardonic and occasionally generous to his victims—Mortimer was as opportunistic as a hungry wolf. The true heroes of the Mortimer story are the lawyers and lawmen who sought to uphold the statutes of society, even in the great Wild West.[10]

Decades after the book's first publication, newspapermen continued to keep Mortimer's memory alive through interviews with key policemen, in particular Ben Bohen, Abraham Houghtailing, and Isaiah W. Lees. Thomas S. Duke also included the murder of Mary Gibson in his 1910 history, *Celebrated Criminal Cases in America*, under the title "The Criminal Career of Charles Mortimer—A Remarkable Case of Circumstantial Evidence."[11]

As much as the Flinn family wanted to forget about Charley, it proved a difficult task. Frank, in particular, was haunted by the events in April and May of 1873. Initially, Frank took to the bottle, attempting to drown his sorrow. Despite his predilection for drinking, Frank continued to run the tailor shop, and in 1875 Catherine gave birth to a healthy baby boy. Frank named him John William Flinn, after his father and brother. About three years later, Frank managed to kick the drinking habit—but he didn't stop there.

After conquering his own alcoholism, Frank sought to help others with their addiction. To this end he became the superintendent of the Massachusetts Inebriates Home in Lynn. Frank also organized and became president of the Reform Club, helping convicts and inebriates reenter society. Noted the *Boston Globe*, "It was his practice to visit the police station and aid men by encouraging and helping them with money. In this and like ways he appealed to their better nature, and in the end induced many to respect themselves and become useful and respected members of society. In this way he has saved a vast army of drunkards."[12]

Doubtless, by helping convicts and alcoholics reform, Frank sought to change the course of their lives so that they didn't follow the same path as his brother Charley. In this manner, Frank helped restore the family name. Frank also tried his hand at writing. After all, if Charley could do it, so could he. With the encouragement of Charles H. Taylor, Frank's friend from the Thirty-Eighth Massachusetts and the editor of the *Boston Globe*, Frank wrote down his Civil War stories, publishing in 1889 *Campaigning with Banks in Louisiana '63 and '64 And with Sheridan in the Shenandoah Valley '64 and 65*. He ended the preface:

> Yours truly,
> In Fraternity, Charity, Loyalty, and Sobriety,
> F. M. Flinn,
> Lynn, Mass.[13]

Frank died the following year, on December 7, 1890, of an intestinal tumor. He was only forty-six, but he had still outlived his brothers Charley and Will. At Frank's funeral, members of Post Five, Grand Army of the Republic, served as his pallbearers. C. H. Taylor sent a wreath of flowers. Frank was buried near Will's grave in Lynn's Pine Grove Cemetery.[14]

Sacramento City Cemetery is more of a draw. Along with searching for Mortimer's grave, sightseers can marvel at the graves of Governor Newton Booth, who declined to pardon Mortimer, and John Sutter, on whose land was discovered gold, initiating the California gold rush.

And while in Sacramento, should that sightseer find themselves in a crowd of people, and their fingers happen to become tangled with another man's wallet, which innocently enough falls into their possession—well, never mind.

Glossary of Criminal Slang

The terms and phrases used below were commonly used by Old West criminals. Some of them faded out of use, while others became staples of ordinary English.

BUCK: Toss

BURST: Financially ruined

CONS: Convicts

COPS: Constables of the Peace

COLLARED: Arrested

COAST CLEAR: No one is watching

CHUM IN or STAND IN: Partner

CLEAR HER SKIRTS: Clear her name

CROOK: Die

CROSS-MAN: A man having served time in prison

FREE AND EASY PLACES: An establishment where drinking, smoking, and carousing is encouraged, oftentimes a brothel or bordello

FREE AND EASY WOMEN: Prostitutes

FROLIC: Merry-making

GOOD INDIAN or GOOD INJEN: Easy mark

GUTTERSNIPE: A scruffy and badly behaved outcast

HANG HIM UP or THROW OUT THE WING: Garrot or strangle

KNUCK: Thief

KNUCKING: Stealing

LAMPS PEELED: Eyes peeled; eyes open and alert

LIMBS OF THE LAW: Lawmen

THE OFFICE: A hint or signal, sometimes in the form of a cough

ON THE DIP: Out pickpocketing

PASSED IN HIS CHECKS or CASHED IN HIS CHIPS: Killed

PLANT: Buried plunder

PUSH: A large crowd

THE RANCH: San Quentin State Prison

RINGERS: Watches separated from their ring and chain

SCRUGING: Dying

SENT ACROSS: Sent to San Quentin State Prison

SLOUGH HIM UP WITH THE GOPHER: Lock him up in the vault

STAGER: Experienced person; old hand

STOOL PIGEON or **STOOLIE:** A criminal who informs on other criminals

THE TIGER: 1) A "tiger claw" or claw attachment, secreted up a sleeve, used to cheat at cards; 2) Gambling with professionals; 3) Dependence on alcohol

TRUSTY: A trusted prisoner, given more freedom in the prison

TURN UP THE PLANT: Uncover buried treasure

WEIGHTY SWAG: Plunder

WHACKED UP or **WHACKED IT:** Divided

Notes

PROLOGUE

1. *Sacramento Daily Record*, 17 April 1873.
2. *San Francisco Examiner*, 17 April 1873.
3. *San Francisco Examiner*, 17 April 1873.
4. *Sacramento Daily Record*, 17 April 1873.

CHAPTER 1

1. Charles J. Mortimer, *Life of Charles Mortimer* (Sacramento: Record Steam Book and Job Printing House, 1873), 54. At some of the nicer San Francisco hotels in 1863, where tenants paid five dollars for a week's rent, individual meals cost fifty cents. Cheaper hotels charged fifty cents a night, and nearby grocers sold a quart of beans for pennies. With only $1.50 in his pocket, Mortimer knew the money wouldn't last.
2. Mortimer, *Life*, 54–55.
3. Mortimer, *Life*, 55.
4. *San Francisco Daily Morning Call*, 13 August 1863; *San Francisco Daily Morning Call*, 23 July 1863.
5. Mortimer, *Life*, 55; *The Deseret News*, 13 August 1862.
6. Mortimer, *Life*, 54, 55.
7. Mark Twain, *Roughing It* (New York: Penguin Putnam Inc., 1962), 271.
8. Mortimer, *Life*, 55–56.
9. *San Francisco Chronicle*, 19 March 1876; Mortimer, *Life*, 56.
10. *Daily Bee*, 6 December 1862; *Gold Hill Daily News*, 5 December 1865; Mortimer, *Life*, 56.
11. *San Francisco Chronicle*, 19 March 1876.
12. *Daily National Democrat* (Marysville, CA), 5 February 1861; Mortimer, *Life*, 56. In and out of California jails, one of George "Cockey" Wright's more notable convictions had taken place on May 2, 1857, in Sacramento after Officer Frank Hardy had arrested him for drugging and robbing a miner named McCullen. Wright unsuccessfully tried to hide the stolen money in his mouth.
13. *Sacramento Bee*, 26 May 1857. William B. Secrest, *California Desperadoes: Stories of Early California Outlaws in Their Own Words*, (Clovis, NM: Word Dancer Press, 2000), 93; *San Francisco Daily Morning Call*, 6 October 1864.
14. Mortimer, *Life*, 56.

15. *Virginia City Evening Bulletin*, 25 August 1863.

16. *San Francisco Daily Morning Call*, 3 September 1863.

17. Mortimer, *Life*, 56.

18. Mortimer, *Life*, 56–57.

19. Mortimer, *Life*, 57.

CHAPTER 2

1. *Sacramento Bee*, 23 September 1863; *Sacramento Bee*, 26 September 1863; *Sacramento Bee*, 3 October 1863.

2. Mortimer, *Life*, 57; *Sacramento Bee*, 15 May 1873; *Sacramento Bee*, 26 August 1861; Leonard Mears, *Sacramento Directory for the Years 1863–1864* (Sacramento: A Badlam, 1863), 57; *Sacramento Bee*, 21 July 1861; *Sacramento Bee*, 2 October 1860; *Sacramento Bee*, 15 October 1862. The Sacramento policemen who arrested Mortimer in September 1863 were used to hard cases. Fred T. Burke was a veteran of the Sacramento police force and bore the scars to prove it. On August 25, 1861, he'd attempted to arrest a Spaniard called Francisco for severely beating J. McCoy with a stick of firewood. Drawing a knife, Francisco had slashed two fingers on Burke's right hand before Burke pistol-whipped Francisco to the sidewalk and made good the arrest. Fred D. Chamberlain doubled as a saloonkeeper, owning a watering hole on Third Street between J and K, proving capable of mixing with the roughest elements in the city. Special Officer Samuel Deal, though not a full-fledged police officer, successfully petitioned to become a special officer in late 1862, and was granted as his beat a half-mile-by-half-mile square just east of the Sacramento River: Fourth and J to Eighth and L. None of them wanted the likes of Mortimer anywhere near the waterfront.

3. Mortimer, *Life*, 57.

4. Mortimer, *Life*, 57.

5. *Sacramento Bee*, 4 November 1864.

6. Mortimer, *Life*, 58.

7. *Sacramento Bee*, 2 November 1864; *Sacramento Bee*, 3 November 1864; *Sacramento Bee*, 4 November 1864; *Sacramento Bee*, 15 May 1873.

8. *Sacramento Bee*, 12 January 1864; Mortimer, *Life*, 53–54; James B. Hume and John N. Thacker, *Wells, Fargo & Co.: Stagecoach and Train Robberies, 1870—1884, The Corporate Report of 1885 with Additional Facts about the Crimes and Their Perpetrators*, ed. R. Michael Wilson (London: McFarland and Company, 2007), 211; *Placer Herald*, 28 February 1857; John Boessenecker, *Badge and Buckshot: Lawlessness in Old California* (Norman: University of Oklahoma Press, 1988), 19. Mortimer first met Ike McCullum during his first stretch in San Quentin, the both of them locked in Room No. 3. In the aftermath of slaying watchman Parker

McDonnell, Mortimer related McCullum had been shot by a comrade and sent up to San Quentin. "What I did not know already of criminal life I could easily learn here," Mortimer recalled. "There were some ten or fifteen of the most notorious highwaymen on the coast, all in consultation."

9. Henry G. Langley, *The San Francisco Directory for the Year 1863* (San Francisco: Commercial Steam Presses, 1863), lii, 66.

10. Benjamin E. Lloyd, *Lights and Shades in San Francisco* (San Francisco: A. L. Bancroft, 1876), 79. Although Mortimer's friend Rufe Anderson went by "Johnny Callahan," he was known to the police as John Anderson.

11. Mortimer, *Life*, 57. There were no twenty-dollar bills printed in 1864, but the first American twenties had been printed in 1861, whose backs were printed green and were thereafter referred to as "greenbacks." They were again issued in 1862 and 1863. Today, a twenty-dollar bill from the 1860s fetches over two thousand dollars.

12. Mike Campbell, "Belmont History," *San Mateo County Times*, 2021; Alfred Doten, *The Journals of Alfred Doten: Book 15* (Reno: University of Nevada Press), 358.

13. Mortimer, *Life*, 58.

14. Mortimer, *Life*, 58–59.

15. William B. Secrest, *Dark and Tangled Threads of Crime: San Francisco's Famous Police Detective, Isaiah W. Lees*. Sanger (CA: Quill Driver Books/Word Dancer Press, Inc., 2004), 25; US Census, 1860.

16. Bernstein, "The Shadow," *Wild West* 32, no. 6 (April 2020): 62–67.

17. *San Francisco Morning Call*, 3 July 1864; *San Francisco Examiner*, 17 October 1865.

18. Mortimer, *Life*, 57.

19. *San Francisco Morning Call*, 7 July 1864; Henry G. Langley, *The San Francisco Directory for the Year 1864* (San Francisco: Commercial Steam Presses, 1864). Mark Twain and his friend from the Comstock, Steve Gillis, actually changed their dwelling house four times and their hotel twice in the first four months of living in San Francisco. By September 1864 Twain returned to that same street, settling in at 44 Minna Street.

20. *San Francisco Morning Call*, 7 July 1864.

21. Mortimer, *Life*, 57.

22. *San Francisco Morning Call*, 7 July 1864.

23. *San Francisco Morning Call*, 7 July 1864; Mortimer, *Life*, 57.

24. Mortimer, *Life*, 57.

25. Mortimer, *Life*, 57.

26. *San Francisco Morning Call*, 11 September 1864. As a former Mississippi River steamboat captain, Mark Twain uses some of his own vernacular when describing Mortimer being "put ashore." Doubtless Twain saw many scalawags put ashore

on the Mississippi River, and there can be no doubt Twain's sympathies were with train conductor Nolan and not with Mortimer.

27. *San Francisco Morning Call*, 6 October 1864; Mortimer, *Life*, 60, 109. George Sibley, who turned traitor against Mortimer in 1864, bore a bad reputation. Born in Philadelphia, Sibley had worked as an engraver before turning to crime. After his 1861–1862 imprisonment in San Quentin for unlawful entry, he worked as a cook at a ranch in Napa Valley. One Sunday, while everyone else was at church, Sibley cut a hole through a trunk and lifted $2,300, but in his haste left $7,700 behind. From there he went to San Francisco and, according to Mortimer, "made his way to the 'free and easy girls' on Pike and Dupont streets, and in six weeks or less he did not have a dollar in money or value. At one time he could have been seen on the Cliff House road in company with six or eight of these girls, all on horseback, and all more or less drunk, and they were all on the lark at his expense."

28. Mortimer, *Life*, 60.

29. Frederic Hall, *The History of San José and Surroundings: with Biographical Sketches of Early Settlers* (San Francisco: A. L. Bancroft and Co., 1871), 287; Mortimer, *Life*, 60.

30. Mortimer, *Life*, 60.

31. William Dean Howells, *My Mark Twain: Reminiscence and Criticisms* (New York: Harper & Brothers Publishers, 1910), 29.

32. *San Francisco Morning Call*, 18 August 1864.

33. *San Francisco Morning Call*, 18 August 1864.

34. *San Francisco Morning Call*, 18 September 1864; *Sacramento Bee*, 18 August 1864; Mortimer, *Life*, 60. The attack on Henry Myers contained some of Mortimer's hallmarks: strangulation, beating, and the possession of a blade. On the other hand, Mortimer preferred committing armed robbery at the dead of night rather than during the busiest time of day. Despite Mortimer not claiming the Myers pawnshop robbery as his handiwork, it may still be that Mortimer did the deed, or knew who did, for his knowledge of it is revealing. For one, although the reporters made the mistake of calling it the "Meyers" pawnshop, with an "e" between the "M" and "y," Mortimer spelled it correctly in his memoir, as it is spelled in the census and in the *San Francisco Directory*: Myers. This suggests at least some level of intimacy with the establishment. Mortimer also stated that the robbery was kicked off when a "man stepped in on pretense of contracting business." It may be Mortimer intuited that the robber pretended to be doing business with Henry before assaulting him. Or perhaps Mortimer knew intimate details of the Myers robbery because he was the robber and kept that from his memoir for his own reasons.

35. *San Francisco Morning Call*, 18 August 1864.

36. Mortimer, *Life*, 58; *Gold Hill Daily News*, 22 August 1864; *Sacramento Bee*, 29 August 1864; *Gold Hill Daily News*, 31 August 1864; *Sacramento Bee*, 31 August 1864; *Gold Hill Daily News*, 1 September 1864; *Sacramento Bee*, 2 September 1864. Did Mortimer know Sam Wells? It may be that because both Wells and Mortimer had lived in Boston and frequented Virginia City and San Francisco they were acquainted, and Mortimer was at the dock to pay his respects. Or, more than likely, Mortimer knew the chaos a dark and crowded waterfront could bring and was looking to take advantage.

37. Mortimer, *Life*, 58.

CHAPTER 3

1. *Oakland Tribune*, 21 March 1896; *San Francisco Chronicle*, 17 December 1868; Henry G. Langley, *The San Francisco Directory for the Year 1861* (San Francisco: Commercial Steam Presses, 1861); Henry G. Langley, *The San Francisco Directory for the Year 1862* (San Francisco: Commercial Steam Presses, 1862); Langley, *The San Francisco Directory for the Year 1863*; Langley, *The San Francisco Directory for the Year 1864*.

2. *San Francisco Chronicle*, 13 October 1870.

3. Mortimer, *Life*, 59.

4. Mortimer, *Life*, 59; *San Francisco Chronicle*, 13 October 1870.

5. Mortimer, *Life*, 59–60.

6. Mortimer, *Life*, 59–60.

7. *Sacramento Bee*, 8 September 1864.

8. Mortimer, *Life*, 60.

9. Thomas S. Duke, *Celebrated Criminal Cases of America* (San Francisco: The James H. Barry Company, 1910), 240–43

10. *Sacramento Bee*, 8 September 1864.

11. *San Francisco Call*, 6 May 1900.

12. *San Francisco Call*, 6 May 1900.

13. *San Francisco Morning Call*, 11 September 1864; Mortimer, *Life*, 60.

14. Mortimer, *Life*, 60; *Santa Cruz Weekly Sentinel*, 17 September 1864.

15. Mortimer, *Life*, 60–61.

16. *San Francisco Morning Call*, 11 September 1864.

17. *San Francisco Morning Call*, 11 September 1864.

18. *Santa Cruz Weekly Sentinel*, 17 September 1864.

19. *San Francisco Chronicle*, 13 October 1870.

20. *San Francisco Morning Call*, 11 September 1864; *Santa Cruz Weekly Sentinel*, 17 September 1864

21. *San Francisco Morning Call*, 11 September 1864; *Santa Cruz Weekly Sentinel*, 17 September 1864.

22. *San Francisco Morning Call*, 11 September 1864; *Santa Cruz Weekly Sentinel*, 17 September 1864; *San Francisco Chronicle*, 13 October 1870; *San Francisco Call*, 6 May 1900; Bernstein, "The Shadow," 64.

23. *San Francisco Morning Call*, 11 September 1864.

24. *San Francisco Call*, 6 May 1900.

25. *San Francisco Call*, 6 May 1900. Later in life Mortimer and Officer Bohen discussed how Mortimer slipped away from the posse in Belmont. Spotting the posse, Mortimer said to his pal Hamilton, "There's every detective from San Francisco who's worth a rap, so I'm going back to San Francisco. There are too many of them to shoot, and, besides, Ben Bohen's dressed to the queen's taste, and I'd hate to spoil his pretty clothes!"

26. *San Francisco Morning Call*, 16 September 1864.

27. *San Francisco Morning Call*, 14 September 1864.

28. Mortimer, *Life*, 61–62.

29. *Sacramento Bee*, 5 November 1863; *San Francisco Morning Call*, 25 September 1864.

30. Mark Twain, *Complete Letters of Mark Twain* (Boston: IndyPublish.com, 2002), 65; *San Francisco Daily Morning Call*, 25 September 1864.

31. *Santa Cruz Weekly Sentinel*, 17 September 1864; *San Francisco Morning Call*, 25 September 1864; Secrest, *Tangled*, 182; *Sacramento Bee*, 24 September 1864.

32. Twain, *Complete Letters*, 65–66.

33. *San Francisco Morning Call*, 29 September 1864.

CHAPTER 4

1. Mortimer, *Life*, 62; John Boessenecker, *Shotguns and Stagecoaches: The Brave Men Who Rode for Wells Fargo in the Wild West* (New York: Thomas Dunne Books, 2018), 77–78. Born in New York, George Shanks traveled to California in the mid-1850s, working intermittently as a cook, a waiter, and a ranch hand before joining the Fourth California Infantry in 1861. Quickly deserting, he found employment in 1863 as a cook for the Barton brothers in Nevada City. Furious at being fired, Shanks returned that same night, shooting and wounding William Barton through an open window. To the frustration of law officers, Shanks had since disappeared.

2. Mortimer, *Life*, 62; *San Francisco Chronicle*, 13 October 1870.

3. *History of Siskiyou County* (Oakland: D. J. Stewart and Co., 1881), 169.

4. Mortimer, *Life*, 62.

5. *History of Siskiyou County*, 171; Mortimer, *Life*, 62.

6. Mortimer, *Life*, 62; *The Bay of San Francisco*, Vol. 1 (Chicago: Lewis Publishing Co., 1892), 543–44; Bernstein, "The Shadow."

7. *San Francisco Chronicle*, 8 June 1873.

8. *San Francisco Chronicle*, 8 June 1873.

9. Mortimer, *Life*, 63; William B. Secrest, *Lawmen & Desperadoes: A Compendium of Noted, Early California Peace Officers, Badmen and Outlaws, 1850–1900* (Spokane: The Arthur H. Clark Company, 1994), 236; *San Francisco Chronicle*, 8 June 1873.

10. *History of Siskiyou County*.

11. Mortimer, *Life*, 63. Unsurprisingly, the California Supreme Court upheld the ruling against the murderer Thomas King. On June 23, 1865, after Sheriff Crooks erected a gallows in the jail yard, the prisoner was brought to the scaffold. Shortly after 2 p.m. King was hanged.

12. *San Francisco Chronicle*, 8 June 1873; Mortimer, *Life*, 63.

13. Mortimer, *Life*, 63; *Gold Hill Daily New*, 18 March 1865.

CHAPTER 5

1. Mortimer, *Life*, 63; *San Francisco Examiner*, 12 November 1900; Langley, *The San Francisco Directory for the Year 1861*.

2. Mortimer, *Life*, 63.

3. Mortimer, *Life*, 63; *Evening Bee* (Sacramento), 12 April 1893; *Sacramento Bee*, 21 September 1872.

4. Mortimer, *Life*, 65, 84; *Sacramento Bee*, 17 March 1873.

5. Mortimer, *Life*, 65; *Petaluma Weekly Argus*, 25 January 1866.

6. *San Francisco Chronicle*, 31 March 1869; Mortimer, *Life*, 65–66.

7. Mortimer, *Life*, 65–66.

8. *San Francisco Chronicle*, 31 March 1869; Mortimer, *Life*, 65–66.

9. *San Francisco Chronicle*, 31 March 1869; Mortimer, *Life*, 65–66.

10. *San Francisco Chronicle*, 31 March 1869; Mortimer, *Life*, 65–66; *Sacramento Bee*, 29 December 1863; *Sacramento Bee*, 3 October 1864; Mears, *Mears' Sacramento Directory for the Years 1863–1864*, 11; *Sacramento Bee*, 26 October 1864; *Daily Alta California*, 20 November 1864.

11. Mortimer, *Life*, 65–66. During his first stretch at San Quentin between 1862 and 1863, Mortimer had been tied to the Ladder. According to Mortimer, prisoners Charles Hammond and Mike Brannigan planted yards of valuable burlap, which were soon discovered beneath Mortimer's workbench. Their actions were in response to the animosity brewing between Mortimer and the two convicts, for Mortimer considered Hammond a traitor for turning state's evidence against Jack Edwards and hated Brannigan for raping the actress Edith Mitchell. "I got twenty lashes there with a four foot rawhide in the hands of a powerful man, [Edward] Vanderslip, who seemed to delight in how deep he could sink the lash into a man's quivering flesh," Mortimer lamented. "Every blow laid open my flesh from six to fifteen inches."

12. *San Francisco Chronicle*, 31 March 1869.
13. Mortimer, *Life*, 66.
14. *San Francisco Chronicle*, 31 March 1869.
15. *Daily California Express* (Marysville), 11 October 1862; Mortimer, *Life*, 65–66. Mortimer noted in his memoir that several convicts turned traitor after the mush break. One was a gambler named Snell, who in 1862 had been shot in the arm outside a saloon in Marysville while resisting arrest. Snell was pardoned six months after the mush break. Another convict who sought a pardon shortly afterward was Patterson, who Mortimer noted had been with "Old" Jim Smith during the Escapade in 1862, one of the ten men who overpowered the gatekeeper and initiated the breakout. Patterson received a pardon a few months after the mush break. As for "Old" Jim Smith, although the Prussian sought a pardon at the same time Snell and Patterson did, he was serving fourteen years for his crimes—too long a stretch to immediately be granted his freedom. The highway-man-turned-traitor served out six more years before being pardoned.
16. Mortimer, *Life*, 53, 65–67; Boessenecker, *Badge and Buckshot*, 19–21; Secrest, *Lawmen & Desperadoes*, 35; *Sacramento Bee*, 25 May 1864; *Sacramento Bee*, 15 May 1873. The Rattlesnake Dick gang included George Taylor, Jim Driscoll, Aleck Wright, and Richard A. Barter, whose colorful moniker was "Rattlesnake Dick," himself a surviving member of the Tom Bell gang (Bell having been lynched in 1856). In 1858 Taylor was tossed into San Quentin on a murder rap. Both Taylor and Driscoll were languishing in Room No. 3 of San Quentin in 1862 when Mortimer was first incarcerated in the state prison. Though Driscoll escaped, Taylor finished out his sentence. But when on November 17, 1863, the Fiddletown stage was robbed between Fiddletown and Drytown—about fifty miles east of Sacramento—the driver swore it was Taylor who blew the safe and robbed it of two bags valued at a thousand dollars each in Wells Fargo & Co. gold dust.

    Arrested in Stockton, Taylor was brought to Jackson, where a grand jury found him guilty and sentenced him to seven years in San Quentin. The controversy occurred when in May 1864, Taylor's old partner Jim Driscoll—having been arrested in Stockton for burglary—swore before a judge that it was he, not Taylor, who had robbed the Fiddletown stage. "Taylor was convicted of doing what I did," Driscoll declared, "and here I stand, before this Court, a self convicted criminal, because it is my wish to do justice to an innocent man." Driscoll's stay in San Quentin proved a short one. In 1867, amid rumors that he was going to turn state's evidence on a different killing, one of the prisoner's dropped an iron bar on Driscoll's head. It took Driscoll some time before dying.
17. Mortimer, *Life*, 63; *Stockton Daily Evening Herald*, 11 December 1866; *Sacramento Bee*, 12 December 1866.

18. Mortimer, *Life*, 65, 67.
19. Secrest, *Tangled*, 142; *San Francisco Call*, 6 May 1900.
20. Mortimer, *Life*, 68.
21. *Sacramento Bee*, 17 December 1868; *San Francisco Chronicle*, 21 January 1869; *San Francisco Examiner*, 22 January 1869; *Santa Cruz Weekly Sentinel*, 23 January 1869; *Santa Cruz Weekly Sentinel*, 30 January 1869.
22. *Santa Cruz Weekly Sentinel*, 30 January 1869.
23. *Santa Cruz Weekly Sentinel*, 30 January 1869; *Salt Lake Tribune*, 24 October 1876.
24. Mortimer, *Life*, 67.
25. *San Francisco Examiner*, 11 December 1868.
26. Mortimer, *Life*, 67.
27. *San Francisco Chronicle*, 31 March 1869.
28. *Santa Cruz Weekly Sentinel*, 11 September 1869; Mortimer, *Life*, 67.
29. Mortimer, *Life*, 67; *Santa Cruz Weekly Sentinel*, 8 January 1870.
30. Mortimer, *Life*, 67.
31. *San Francisco Chronicle*, 13 October 1870.
32. Mortimer, *Life*, 67.
33. Mortimer, *Life*, 67.
34. Mortimer, *Life*, 68; *San Francisco Chronicle*, 21 September 1871.
35. Mortimer, *Life*, 68.
36. Mortimer, *Life*, 68; William Shakespeare, *Henry VI, Part I: The Complete Works of Shakespeare* (New York: Longman, 1997).
37. Mortimer, *Life*, 68.
38. Mortimer, *Life*, 68–69.
39. Mortimer, *Life*, 69.

CHAPTER 6

1. Mortimer, *Life*, 70; *San Francisco Examiner*, 5 August 1872; *San Francisco Examiner*, 13 December 1870; *San Francisco Examiner*, 13 December 1871. Operating her saloon on Kearny Street between Broadway and Pacific, Kate Dunn was a madam and a heavy drinker. Her fortunes did not improve when her husband, John, a petty thief, was shot in the arm by Deputy Sheriff Nathaniel L. Jehu while resisting arrest.
2. Mortimer, *Life*, 70.
3. Mortimer, *Life*, 70.
4. Holly Hoods, "Local Girl Makes Bad: Carrie Spencer and Charles Mortimer (Flynn) Murder Trial," *Russian River Recorder* (Winter 2007), 12–13.
5. Mortimer, *Life*, 71.
6. *San Francisco Call*, 6 February 1873.

7. Mortimer, *Life*, 71.

8. Secrest, *Tangled*, 134, 137; Mortimer, *Life*, 71.

9. Mortimer, *Life*, 71.

10. *San Francisco Chronicle*, 21 September 1871.

11. Mears, *Mears' Sacramento Directory for the Years 1863–1864*, 28; McKenney, L. M. *McKenney's Sacramento Directory for the Year 1870* (Sacramento: Russell & Winterburn, Steam Book and Job Printers, 1870), 16.

12. Twain, *Roughing It*, 308–9.

13. Mortimer, *Life*, 71.

14. *Sacramento Bee*, 6 June 1873; *Cultural Resources Report: Morrison Creek Mining Reach, Downstream (South) of Jackson Highway* (San Francisco: Garcia and Associates, 1995), 6.

15. *Sacramento Bee*, 15 March 1873.

16. Mortimer, *Life*, 71; *Sacramento Bee*, 6 June 1873; *San Francisco Chronicle*, 16 March 1873.

17. Mortimer, *Life*, 71.

18. *Sacramento Bee*, 6 June 1873.

19. Mortimer, *Life*, 71.

20. Mortimer, *Life*, 72; *Russian River Flag*, 20 March 1873; *Russian River Flag*, 28 May 1874.

21. Mortimer, *Life*, 72.

22. Mortimer, *Life*, 72.

23. Mark Twain, *Mark Twain: San Francisco Correspondent, Selections From His Letters To The Territorial Enterprise: 1865–1866* (San Francisco: The Book Club of California, 1857), 92–94.

24. Mortimer, *Life*, 72.

25. *San Francisco Chronicle*, 27 January 1873.

26. Mortimer, *Life*, 72–73, 102.

CHAPTER 7

1. Mortimer, *Life*, 73, 101–2.

2. Mortimer, *Life*, 73; *Santa Cruz Sentinel*, 20 June 1867; John Leighton Chase, *The Sidewalk Companion to Santa Cruz*, 3rd ed., ed. Judith Steen (Santa Cruz: The Museum of Art & History, 2005), 174.

3. Mortimer, *Life*, 73, 103.

4. *San Francisco Examiner*, 1 Feb. 1873.

5. Mortimer, *Life*, 73, 103.

6. *Santa Cruz Weekly Sentinel*, 10 February 1872; Mortimer, *Life*, 74, 102.

7. Mortimer, *Life*, 74, 103. In his memoir Mortimer claims that the lawyer he visited

was A. B. Towne, not G. W. Tyler. Along with no one by that name living in San Francisco at the time, newspaper articles and Tyler's own admission make it clear that it was Tyler, not Towne, whom Mortimer visited.

8. *Santa Cruz Weekly Sentinel*, 10 February 1872.
9. Mortimer, *Life*, 74; *San Francisco Examiner*, 15 February 1873.
10. Mortimer, *Life*, 74–75.

CHAPTER 8

1. Mortimer, *Life*, 75.
2. *San Francisco Chronicle*, 4 August 1871; *Oakland Daily Transcript*, 15 August 1871. Although in his memoir Mortimer referred to L. P. Redwine as "L. P. Blackwine," this was an alias. During the early 1870s Louis P. Redwine, not Blackwine—who in August 1871 had been arrested for beating his wife—owned a tailor shop on Mission, as corroborated by the *San Francisco Chronicle* and the *San Francisco Directory*. No one named Blackwine appeared in the directory. Furthermore, the papers later noted that Carrie and Redwine shared a misadventure together while in Oakland, and Mortimer referred to Redwine in a letter he wrote to Police Captain F. B. Tarbett of Oakland.
3. Mortimer, *Life*, 76.
4. *San Francisco Chronicle*, 23 February 1872; *San Francisco Examiner*, 23 February 1872.
5. Mortimer, *Life*, 75.
6. *San Francisco Chronicle*, 23 February 1872.
7. Mortimer, *Life*, 75.
8. Mortimer, *Life*, 75–76.
9. Mortimer, *Life*, 75–76.
10. Joen Madonna, "Viz Valley's Five Mile House: Connection to the Rest of SF," SF Gate, 18 April 2020, https://www.sfgate.com/entertainment/article/Viz-Valley-s-Five-Mile-House-Connection-to-the-3267109.php; Mortimer, *Life*, 77.
11. Mortimer, *Life*, 77.
12. *San Francisco Chronicle*, 2 May 1872.
13. Mortimer, *Life*, 77–78.

CHAPTER 9

1. Anne Decourbez, "Re: Caroline Prenel," message to Matthew Bernstein, 20 July 2020; "Populations Légales 2018," The National Institute of Statistics and Economic Studies, 28 December 2020.
2. *San Francisco Examiner*, 8 June 1872; Mortimer, *Life*, 89; Coroner's Report of Decedents' Property from the 1871 to 1872 San Francisco Municipal Report.

3. *San Francisco Examiner*, 28 May 1872; *San Francisco Examiner*, 3 June 1888.

4. *San Francisco Examiner*, 28 May 1872.

5. Mortimer, *Life*, 81.

6. Mortimer, *Life*, 79–80; *San Francisco Examiner*, 6 December 1869.

7. Mortimer, *Life*, 79–80.

8. Mortimer, *Life*, 81, 84; *San Francisco Examiner*, 28 May 1872.

9. Mortimer, *Life*, 81–82; *Daily Evening Herald* (Stockton), 14 February 1872. Lawrence Selinger, William S. Jones, and Daniel Coffey were well-known San Francisco robbery detectives. In early February the trio had made the papers for catching a particularly bold thief, under the alias "George," who had committed a string of robberies on Stevenson wearing only his stockings and underclothing, so that he could give the excuse if caught that he'd been sleepwalking. "George" had also been driving around in a milk wagon, with stolen watches, gold, silver, and money secured in milk cans.

10. Mortimer, *Life*, 82.

11. *San Francisco Examiner*, 28 May 1872.

12. Mortimer, *Life*, 82.

13. *San Francisco Examiner*, 28 May 1872.

14. Mortimer, *Life*, 82.

15. *San Francisco Examiner*, 25 May 1872.

16. Mortimer, *Life*, 81, 82.

CHAPTER 10

1. *San Francisco Examiner*, 28 May 1872; *San Francisco Examiner*, 3 June 1888.

2. *San Francisco Call*, 11 February 1896.

3. Mortimer, *Life*, 85; *San Francisco Chronicle*, 24 October 1872.

4. Mortimer, *Life*, 85–86.

5. *Sacramento Bee*, 6 June 1872; *San Francisco Examiner*, 7 June 1872.

6. Mortimer, *Life*, 86–87.

7. *San Francisco Examiner*, 3 June 1888.

8. Mortimer, *Life*, 87–88.

9. *Oakland Daily Transcript*, 15 August 1871; *Oakland Daily Transcript*, 8 September 1872.

10. Mortimer, *Life*, 88.

11. Mortimer, *Life*, 88.

CHAPTER 11

1. Mortimer, *Life*, 90.

2. *Sacramento Bee*, 21 September 1872; E. B. Willis, Introduction to *Life of Charles*

Mortimer (Sacramento: Record Steam Book and Job Printing House, 1873), 10; Ron Powers, *Mark Twain: A Life* (New York: Free Press, 2005), 325.

3. Mark Twain, *San Francisco Correspondent*, 110–11.
4. Mortimer, *Life*, 89; Willis, "Introduction," 20.
5. *Sacramento Bee*, 20 September 1872.
6. Mortimer, *Life*, 90.
7. *Sacramento Bee*, 8 July 1872; *Sacramento Bee*, 20 September 1872; *Sacramento Bee*, 21 September 1872.
8. Willis, "Introduction," 18; Mortimer, *Life*, 89–90.
9. Mortimer, *Life*, 89–91.
10. Mortimer, *Life*, 91; Duke, *Celebrated Criminals*, 240–43.
11. Mortimer, *Life*, 92.
12. Willis, "Introduction," 15, 20. Mortimer, *Life*, 92.
13. Mortimer, *Life*, 94.
14. *Sacramento Bee*, 20 September 1872; *San Francisco Chronicle*, 15 March 1873; Mortimer, *Life*, 92; Willis, "Introduction," 10, 15, 20.

CHAPTER 12

1. *Sacramento Bee*, 20 September 1872; *Sacramento Bee*, 21 September 1872; *San Francisco Chronicle*, 14 March 1873.
2. *Sacramento Bee*, 20 September 1872.
3. *Sacramento Bee*, 18 April 1870; *Sacramento Bee*, 6 October 1870; *San Francisco Chronicle*, 13 October 1871; *Sacramento Bee*, 13 March 1872; *Sacramento Bee*, 10 January 1896; *Sacramento Bee*, 10 January 1910; *Sacramento City Directory* (Sacramento: D. S. Cutter & Company), 1859. Chief of Police Matthew Karcher's rise in Sacramento had been apropos. Born in Baden, Germany, around 1833, Karcher had voyaged to Boston at fourteen, learning the trade of a baker. Taking a ship to California by way of Panama in 1851, he opened up a Sacramento bakery on Sixth between I and J, mere feet away from Sacramento County Jail. Officers with a hankering for German pretzels and apple strudel found Karcher, with his expansive family, personable and capable. But Karcher's bakery did not thrive, suffering reverses through fire and flood. As a result, in 1870 he tried his hand as a policeman. Collaring burglars, arsonists, and cattle rustlers became his bread and butter, and in March 1872 Karcher won the position of top policeman in the capital, having the support of the people.
4. Willis, "Introduction," 10.
5. *Sacramento Bee*, 20 September 1872; *Sacramento Bee*, 21 September 1872; John F. Uhlhorn, *Sacramento Directory for the Year January 1873* (Sacramento: H. S. Crocker & Co.), 1873; Willis, "Introduction," 10.

6. *Sacramento Bee*, 20 September 1872; *Sacramento Bee*, 21 September 1872; Uhlhorn, *Sacramento Directory For the Year January 1873*; Willis, "Introduction," 10.
7. Willis, "Introduction," 10; *Sacramento Bee*, 21 September 1872.
8. *Sacramento Bee*, 20 September 1872.
9. *Sacramento Bee*, 21 September 1872; Willis, "Introduction," 21.
10. *Sacramento Bee*, 21 September 1872; Duke, *Celebrated Criminals*.
11. Willis, "Introduction," 11; *Sacramento Bee*, 15 March 1873; *Sacramento Bee*, 21 September 1872.
12. *San Francisco Examiner*, 30 September 1872; Mortimer, *Life*, 97.
13. *Sacramento Bee*, 6 December 1872; *Sacramento Bee*, 5 September 1887.
14. Mortimer, *Life*, 97; *Sacramento Bee*, 15 March 1873.
15. Mortimer, *Life*, 97.
16. *San Francisco Examiner*, 30 September 1872.
17. *Sacramento Bee*, 6 December 1872; *Sacramento Bee*, 5 September 1887.
18. *Sacramento Directory, 1873*, 151; Mortimer, *Life*, 98; *Sacramento Bee*, 11 October 1872. Born in 1828 in the township of Clear Creek, Ohio, in 1850, Mike Bryte had been studying law in Dayton when gold fever struck. In Yolo County, Bryte began working for a German dairyman named Schaadt. Falling in love with Schaadt's eighteen-year-old daughter Elizabeth, they married, and when her father moved to San Francisco, Bryte bought his ranch. He and Elizabeth raised five children to maturity before trading Yolo County for California's capital in 1872. There, despite his lack of experience, Bryte was elected Sacramento County Sheriff.
19. *West Sacramento News-Ledger*, 6 August 2003; Mortimer, *Life*, 98.
20. *Sacramento Bee*, 15 November 1872; *Sacramento Bee*, 15 March 1873; Mortimer, *Life*, 97–98.
21. *San Francisco Chronicle*, 27 October 1872.
22. *San Francisco Examiner*, 3 June 1888.

CHAPTER 13

1. *San Francisco Chronicle*, 24 October 1872; *San Francisco Directory* (San Francisco: Commercial Steam Presses, S.D., Valentine & Sons), 485; Willis, *Life*, 15; *Sacramento Bee*, 15 March 1873.
2. Mortimer, *Life*, 98.
3. *San Francisco Examiner*, 25 October 1872.
4. *San Francisco Chronicle*, 27 October 1872.
5. *Sacramento Bee*, 31 October 1872.
6. *Sacramento Bee*, 15 November 1872.
7. Willis, "Introduction," 16.
8. *Sacramento Bee*, 18 November 1872.

9. *Sacramento Bee*, 18 November 1872.

10. Mortimer, *Life*, 99.

11. Mortimer, *Life*, 99–100.

12. Mortimer, *Life*, 100–101.

13. Willis, "Introduction," 16; *Stanislaus County Weekly News (Modesto)*, 14 April 1876.

14. *Sacramento Bee*, 6 January 1872; *San Francisco Examiner*, 7 January 1873; *San Francisco Chronicle*, 8 January 1872; *The Weekly (Oroville) Mercury*, 2 April 1875; Alfred Doten, *The Journals of Alfred Doten: Book No. 31*, 865.

15. *The Sacramento Bee*, 22 January 1873; Mortimer, *Life*, 101; *The Sacramento Bee*, 27 January 1873.

16. *San Francisco Call*, 29 January 1873; Mortimer, *Life*, 101.

17. *Santa Cruz Weekly Sentinel*, 22 February 1873.

18. Mortimer, *Life*, 83.

19. Mortimer, *Life*, 83, 101–4; *Santa Cruz Weekly Sentinel*, 8 February 1873.

20. *San Francisco Examiner*, 3 June 1888.

21. *Sam Francisco Examiner*, 29 November 1872.

22. Willis, "Introduction," 16–17.

23. *Sacramento Bee*, 11 December 1872.

24. Willis, "Introduction," 16–17.

25. *Sacramento Bee*, 3 January 1873; *Sacramento Bee*, 27 January 1873; *San Francisco Chronicle*, 28 January 1873.

26. Mortimer, *Life*, 83.

27. Mortimer, *Life*, 104–5.

28. *San Francisco Examiner*, 13 February 1873; *Santa Cruz Weekly Sentinel*, 15 February 1873; *Santa Cruz Weekly Sentinel*, 22 March 1873.

CHAPTER 14

1. *Boston Globe*, 27 February 1873.

2. *Sacramento Bee*, 10 February 1873.

3. *Sacramento Bee*, 11 February 1873.

4. Mortimer, *Life*, 105–6; *Sacramento Bee*, 28 February 1873.

5. *Petaluma Evening Argus*, 15 March 1873; Willis, "Introduction," 17–18.

6. *Sacramento Bee*, 13 March 1873; *San Francisco Examiner*, 14 March 1873.

7. *Sacramento Bee*, 13 March 1873; *Sacramento Bee*, 14 March 1873; *San Francisco Examiner*, 14 March 1873; *San Francisco Chronicle*, 14 March 1873.

8. *Sacramento Bee*, 14 March 1873; *San Francisco Chronicle*, 16 March 1873.

9. Willis, "Introduction," 17.

10. *Sacramento Bee*, 14 March 1873; *San Francisco Chronicle*, 15 March 1873.

11. *San Francisco Chronicle*, 15 March 1873.

12. Willis, "Introduction," 17.
13. *San Francisco Chronicle*, 15 March 1873.
14. *San Francisco Chronicle*, 15 March 1873.
15. Willis, "Introduction," 18–23.
16. Willis, "Introduction," 23; *Sacramento Bee*, 17 March 1873.
17. *Sacramento Bee*, 17 March 1873.

CHAPTER 15

1. Willis, "Introduction," 23.
2. Mortimer, *Life*, 29; Pine Grove Cemetery, Lynn, Essex County, Massachusetts. Charley's grandparents Edward and Polly Bates believed fervently in family. Born in Dublin, New Hampshire, in 1774, Edward Bates married Polly Corey despite Polly being four years his senior and having a little one in tow, Marrill Rumrill. After they married, Edward gave the child his last name. In 1799 Polly gave birth to their firstborn, Lucy. Although Lucy lived only a year, Edward and Polly did not give up. Six children followed—Almira (1801), James (1803), Mary (1805), Louisa (1806), Elizabeth (1817), and Lucretia (1820). Each married and sired multiple children. From their home, separated from the street by a roughhewn fence, Edward and Polly presided over their expansive family.
3. Mortimer, *Life*, 12, 29.
4. *Boston Directory* (Boston: Boston, Sampson & Murdock Company, 1835); Mortimer, *Life*, 29.
5. Mortimer, *Life*, 29–30.
6. Mortimer, *Life*, 30–31.
7. Mortimer, *Life*, 31.
8. Mortimer, *Life*, 32.
9. Mortimer, *Life*, 32–34.
10. Mortimer, *Life*, 34–35; Nathan Ames, *Pirate's Glen and Dungeon Rock* (Boston: Redding & Company, 1853), vii. Tales of Pirate Cave were legendary, gaining particular notoriety through Alonzo Lewis's *The History of Lynn, Including Nahant*. According to Lewis, in 1658 four pirates, journeying in a small vessel up the Saugus River, made off with a fortune in silver. Three of the pirates were captured by an English cruiser, and likely executed, but the fourth—Thomas Veal—made it with the treasure to a cave near the Saugus woods. Veal resided there until an earthquake trapped him inside, prompting locals to refer to the cave as Pirate's Cave or Dungeon Rock. Charley learned it somewhat differently. "The traditions of Lynn say that the pirate chieftain Vail (I think that was his name) and his crew at one time made that cave a home," Charley recalled. "During a heavy thunder storm a portion of the rock gave way and closed the entrance to the cave, and it

is thought some of the pirates and a large amount of their treasure was buried in there. I knew there was about enough of the supposed entrance to the cave that was not closed to accommodate me and my crew."

11. Mortimer, *Life*, 35–36.
12. Mortimer, *Life*, 37.
13. Mortimer, *Life*, 37–38.
14. Mortimer, *Life*, 38.
15. Mortimer, *Life*, 38.
16. Mortimer, *Life*, 39.
17. Mortimer, *Life*, 39.
18. George Adams, *Salem Directory* (Salem: Henry Whipple & Son Publishers, 1857); Mortimer, *Life*, 39.
19. *New England Farmer* (Boston), 17 October 1857; *New York Tribune*, 15 October 1857; Mortimer, *Life*, 39.
20. Mortimer, *Life*, 39–40. Prison might have worked out better for Jerry Aiken. On October 9, 1857, at about 9 p.m., Jerry was arrested in Downtown Boston for disturbing the peace, having gotten into trouble with John Mead, a respected Boston citizen. When John Mead refused to press charges, Jerry was released. At about 10 p.m. Jerry was drinking at a saloon on Court and Stoddard, where he asked John Mead's brother, Thomas, to take a drink with him. "I don't drink with a thief," Thomas Mead reportedly replied. Jerry then grabbed Thomas by the throat. Thomas responded by pulling his pistol and shooting Jerry in the chest. To the sympathy of very few, Jerry bled out and died.
21. Mortimer, *Life*, 39–40.
22. Mortimer, *Life*, 40–41. Uncle James would be laid to rest in Gilsum, New Hampshire, nine miles north of Keene, just across the Ashuelot River. James had married Sarah Whittemore, from Worcester, Massachusetts, their union providing Charley with eight cousins: Ellen Maria Bates Church (1820), Almira Bates Sears (1823), George Washington Bates (1827), Jotham Alexander Bates (1829), Harvey Leonard Bates (1835), Sarah Bates Howe (1837), Martin Van Buren Bates (1839), and Clement Uriah Bates (1843).
23. Mortimer, *Life*, 41. Criminal genealogist Gwen Kubberness uncovered that Charley's grandfather Edward Bates, buried in the Old Landgrove Cemetery, had died in 1844 when Charley was about ten. Grandma Polly wouldn't pass until March 24, 1850, when Charley would have been around sixteen, placing his age at about fifteen when he visited the Landgrove house. Technically, the home no longer belonged to Polly but to her daughter Mary's husband, George Valentine, a member of the lucrative Valentine Brothers Builders. With his trade in construction, by the time Charley arrived Valentine had added to the house its "Noah's

Ark," or high-posted cape, that gave the house its distinctive look. Charley hadn't stayed long before a feeling of homesickness overtook him.

24. Mortimer, *Life*, 41.

25. Nathaniel Hawthorne, *Passages From the American Note-Books*, Vol. 9 (Boston and New York: Houghton Mifflin Company, 1914), 181; Ralph Waldo Emerson, *The Journals and Miscellaneous Notebooks of Ralph Waldo Emerson*, Vol. 16: *1866–1882*, ed. Ronald A. Bosco and Glen M. Johnson (Cambridge: The Belknap Press of Harvard University Press, 1982), 17; Mortimer, *Life*, 42.

26. Mortimer, *Life*, 42–43.

27. Mortimer, *Life*, 43–44.

28. *Brattleboro' Eagle*, 10 March 1851; *Brattleboro' Eagle*, 9 June 1851; *Brattleboro' Eagle*, 31 March 1854; Mortimer, *Life*, 44.

29. Mortimer, *Life*, 44–45.

30. Mortimer, *Life*, 46–47.

31. Mortimer, *Life*, 47–48.

CHAPTER 16

1. Mortimer, *Life*, 49; Gordon Morris Bakken, *Practicing Law in Frontier California* (Lincoln: University of Nebraska Press, 1991), 103. A letter composed by Henry Haight and sent to Samuel Haight provides the reason for the San Francisco Vigilance Committee's creation: "The insufficiency of the courts, the imperfection of the laws, and the corruption of public officers have heretofore rendered the punishment of crime very uncertain, sin frequent, and hence the organization of this committee to administer summary judgement . . . It will dissolve . . . after the worst criminals have been hung or imprisoned or fled."

2. Nancy Taniguchi, *Dirty Deeds: Land, Violence, and the 1856 San Francisco Vigilance Committee* (Norman: University of Oklahoma Press, 2016), 56–62; Bakken, *Practicing Law*, 104–6.

3. Mortimer, *Life*, 49.

4. Mortimer, *Life*, 50.

5. Mortimer, *Life*, 50.

6. Matthew Bernstein, *George Hearst: Silver King of the Gilded Age* (Norman: University of Oklahoma Press, 2021), 55; Mortimer, *Life*, 50.

7. Mortimer, *Life*, 50.

8. Mortimer, *Life*, 50.

9. *San Francisco Chronicle*, 31 August 1883; Mortimer, *Life*, 50–51.

10. Mortimer, *Life*, 50–51; *Sacramento Directory, 1857–1858* (Sacramento: R. H. McDonald & Co), 72.

11. Mortimer, *Life*, 51.

12. *San Francisco Examiner*, 8 May 1873; Mortimer, *Life*, 51.
13. Chuck Lyons, "The Great Western Flood," *Wild West* 28, no. 6 (April 2016), 37.
14. Lyons, "Flood," 39. For the small towns, encampments, and shantytowns filled with Chinese laborers in the Central Valley, many were completely obliterated by the Great Western Flood. Large brown lakes formed throughout the Golden State, some even covering stretches of the Mojave Desert. The *Sacramento Daily Union* estimated that one-third of all taxable value in the state was lost. To many people, all of their belongings, everything they had squirreled away over the years, had washed away.
15. Mortimer, *Life*, 51. The Stanford House is not to be confused with the Stanford Building, built at the behest of the ambitious mercantile man Leland Stanford in 1851, a mile to the west of the Stanford House. Flinn had a long memory for powerful men and never mentioned the railroad millionaire in his memoirs.
16. De Wolk, 128; Mortimer, *Life*, 51.
17. *San Francisco Chronicle*, 13 October 1870; Mortimer, *Life*, 51.
18. *San Francisco Examiner*, 3 April 1894; Mortimer, *Life*, 52. The *San Francisco Examiner* described Officer Ben Bohen as "a wiry, muscular man" and that, because of "his ability to take care of himself in an emergency, he was detailed to a beat that took in part of Dupont street . . . when that section of the city was the resort of the toughest characters that remained stranded in the West after the gold boom days."
19. Mortimer, *Life*, 52; *San Francisco Chronicle*, 13 October 1870.
20. *San Francisco Chronicle*, 13 October 1870.
21. Mortimer, *Life*, 52.
22. *San Francisco Call*, 6 May 1900.
23. Mortimer, *Life*, 52; *San Francisco Examiner*, 24 October 1872; *San Francisco Daily Morning Call*, 11 September 1864.
24. William B. Secrest, *Behind San Quentin's Walls: The History of California's Legendary Prison and Its Inmates, 1851—1900* (Fresno: Craven Street Books, 2015), 108.

CHAPTER 17

1. Willis, "Introduction," 23; *Sacramento Bee*, 16 May 1873.
2. *Alameda Gazette*, 24 May 1873.
3. Mortimer, *Life*, 107–8.
4. Willis, "Introduction," 23.
5. Mortimer, *Life*, 108.
6. Willis, "Introduction," 23.
7. Mortimer, *Life*, 108.
8. *San Francisco Examiner*, 8 May 1873.

9. *Sacramento Bee*, 7 April 1873; *Sacramento Bee*, 18 April 1873.
10. *Sacramento Bee*, 16 April 1873; Willis, "Introduction," 25.
11. *Sacramento Bee*, 16 April 1873; *United Opinion* (Bradford, VT), 30 May 1873.
12. Willis, "Introduction," 24; *Sacramento Bee*, 16 April 1873.
13. Willis, "Introduction," 25.
14. *Sacramento Bee*, 16 April 1873; Willis, "Introduction," 25.
15. Willis, "Introduction," 25.
16. *Sacramento Bee*, 16 April 1873.
17. *Sacramento Bee*, 16 April 1873; Willis, "Introduction," 25.
18. *Sacramento Bee*, 16 April 1873; Willis, "Introduction," 26; Frank M. Flinn, *Campaigning with Banks in Louisiana '63 and '64 And with Sheridan in the Shenandoah Valley '64 and 65* (Boston: W. B. Clarke & Co., 1889), 1–2, 15, 54.
19. *Sacramento Bee*, 16 April 1873.
20. Willis, "Introduction," 24.
21. *Sacramento Bee*, 16 April 1873; Willis, "Introduction," 25.
22. *Sacramento Bee*, 16 April 1873; Mortimer, "Introduction," 109.
23. Willis, "Introduction," 25.
24. *Sacramento Bee*, 16 April 1873; Willis, "Introduction," 25.
25. *Sacramento Bee*, 17 April 1873.
26. Willis, "Introduction," 26; Mortimer, *Life*, 109.
27. *Sacramento Bee*, 18 April 1873; *San Francisco Examiner*, 18 April 1873.
28. *San Francisco Examiner*, 18 April 1873; *Sacramento Bee*, 18 April 1873.
29. Mortimer, *Life*, iv, 108, 110; *San Francisco Call*, 6 May 1900. In 1900 Ben Bohen echoed Mortimer's sentiment that crime didn't pay, stating, "In forty years' experience with criminals I've never met or heard of one who didn't sooner or later reap what he has sown. A criminal is a fool. If he put the same amount of industry, energy and daring into anything else he'd have a long bank account."
30. *San Francisco Examiner*, 22 April 1873; *Oakland Daily Transcript*, 23 April 1873; *Sacramento Bee*, 12 April 1873.
31. *San Francisco Chronicle*, 28 April 1873.
32. *Sacramento Bee*, 23 April 1873; *Boston Globe*, 17 November 1873; Willis, "Introduction," 27; *Sacramento Bee*, 24 April 1873.
33. Willis, "Introduction," 26–27.
34. *Sacramento Bee*, 12 May 1873.

CHAPTER 18

1. *Sacramento Bee*, 8 May 1873; Willis, "Introduction," 27–28; *Daily Evening* (Stockton) *Herald*, 4 May 1874.
2. *Sacramento Bee*, 12 May 1873; *San Francisco Chronicle*, 16 May 1873.

3. *San Francisco Chronicle*, 16 May 1873; *Boston Globe*, 8 December 1890; www. FamilySearch.org, https://www.familysearch.org/tree/pedigree/landscape/L441–74H.

4. *San Francisco Chronicle*, 16 May 1873; Flinn, *Campaigning*, 1–2, 7, 55, 78; George Whitefield Powers, *The Story of the Thirty Eighth Regiment of Massachusetts Volunteers* (Cambridge: Cambridge Press, 1866), 28–29.

5. *Sacramento Bee*, 12 May 1873; *Oakland Daily Tribune*, 13 May 1873; *San Francisco Chronicle*, 16 May 1873; George Augustus Shurtleff, *Autobiography and Reminiscence of Dr. George Augustus Shurtleff, Stockton, 1901.* Although today's medical community would determine G. A. Shurtleff a quack, the doctor was respected in his time. Born in 1819 in Carver, Massachusetts, about forty miles south of Boston, G. A. Shurtleff had begun studying medicine in 1842, and in 1845 received a Medical Degree from the Vermont Medical College. Afflicted with gold fever, Shurtleff served as surgeon aboard the *Mount Vernon*, landing in San Francisco in October of 1849. Shurtleff tried his hand at mining, but by 1856 he found reason to give it up, appointed the director of the State Insane Asylum in Stockton. From there his career took an upward trajectory. In 1873 his opinion resulted in Mortimer taking a downward one.

6. G. A. Shurtleff, "Address Delivered Before the Medical Society of the State of California at Its Annual Session," April 1873, 5.

7. Shurtleff, "Address," 8–9.

8. *Sacramento Bee*, 12 May 1873; *San Francisco Chronicle*, 12 October 1873; *San Francisco Examiner*, 28 November 1873; *San Francisco Examiner*, 13 May 1873.

9. *San Francisco Examiner*, 15 May 1873; *San Francisco Chronicle*, 16 May 1873.

10. *Sacramento Bee*, 13 May 1873.

11. *San Francisco Examiner*, 15 May 1873; Bernstein, "The Shadow."

12. *San Francisco Chronicle*, 16 May 1873.

13. *San Francisco Chronicle*, 16 May 1873; *Sacramento Bee*, 26 April 1873.

14. Willis, "Introduction," 112.

15. *San Francisco Chronicle*, 16 May 1873; John Boessenecker, "The Human Wildcat," *Wild West* 30, no. 1 (June 2017), 46–51.

16. *Sacramento Daily Record*, 16 May 1873; *San Francisco Chronicle*, 16 May 1873.

17. *San Francisco Chronicle*, 16 May 1873.

EPILOGUE

1. *Sacramento Bee*, 16 May 1873; *San Francisco Chronicle*, 16 May 1873.

2. *San Francisco Chronicle*, 16 May 1873.

3. *Sacramento Bee*, 16 May 1873.

4. *Sacramento Bee*, 5 May 1873; *San Francisco Examiner*, 8 May 1873; *Petaluma Weekly Argus*, 30 May 1873; *Sacramento Bee*, 5 June 1873; *San Francisco Chronicle*, 23 June 1873; *Pioche Record*, 16 September 1873; *San Francisco Chronicle*, 19 September 1874.

5. *Los Angeles Herald*, 28 January 1876; *Los Angeles Herald*, 29 January 1876; *San Francisco Chronicle*, 28 January 1876.

6. *Santa Cruz Weekly Sentinel*, 14 March 1874.

7. *Sacramento Bee*, 20 April 1875; *Sacramento Bee*, 29 March 1875.

8. *Deseret News*, 1 November 1876.

9. Willem H. J. Martens, "The Hidden Suffering of the Psychopath," *Psychiatric Times* 31, no. 10; Kent A. Kiehl and Morris B. Hoffman, "The Criminal Psychopath: History, Neuroscience, Treatment, and Economics," *Jurimetrics* (Summer 2011); *Stockton Daily Evening Herald*, 11 October 1870; *Sacramento Bee*, 17 June 1870; David Dary, *Red Blood and Black Ink: Journalism in the Old West* (New York: Alfred A. Knopf 1998), 227. Writing in a similar style exhibited by frontier newspapermen, Mortimer's oftentimes adopted a playful tongue-in-cheek style in his memoir, pretending his thefts were mere accidents, just as witty penpushers reported criminals were made "guests" in San Quentin.

10. Mortimer, *Life*, iv.

11. Duke, *Celebrated Criminals*.

12. *Boston Globe*, 8 December 1890.

13. Frank Flinn, *Campaigning*, iii–iv.

14. *Boston Globe*, 8 December 1890; *Boston Globe*, 10 December 1890.

Bibliography

WORKS CONCERNING CHARLES JAMES "MORTIMER" FLINN

Bernstein, Matthew. "The Shadow." *Wild West* 32, no. 6 (April 2020), 62–67.

Duke, Thomas S. *Celebrated Criminal Cases of America*. San Francisco: The James H. Barry Company, 1910.

Mortimer, Charles J. *Life of Charles Mortimer*. Sacramento: Record Steam Book and Job Printing House, 1873.

Hoods, Holly. "Local Girl Makes Bad: Carrie Spencer and the Charles Mortimer (Flynn) Murder Trial." *Russian River Recorder* (Winter 2007), 9–12.

Kubberness, Gwen. "Charles F Flinn Aka Charles J Mortimer: Murder." *Criminal Genealogy* 21 (Aug. 2020). https://criminalgenealogy.blogspot.com/2020/08/charles-f-flinn-aka-charles-j-mortimer.html.

Willis, E. B. "Introduction." *Life of Charles Mortimer*. Sacramento: Record Steam Book and Job Printing House, 1873.

REFERENCES

Adams, George. *Salem Directory*. Salem: Henry Whipple & Son Publishers, 1857.

Ames, Nathan. *Pirate's Glen and Dungeon Rock*. Boston: Redding & Company, 1853.

Bakken, Gordon Morris. *Practicing Law in Frontier California*. Lincoln: University of Nebraska Press, 1991.

The Bay of San Francisco, Vol. 1, Chicago: Lewis Publishing Co., 1892, 543–44.

Bernstein, Matthew. *George Hearst: Silver King of the Gilded Age*. Norman: University of Oklahoma Press, 2021.

Boessenecker, John. *Badge and Buckshot: Lawlessness in Old California*. Norman: University of Oklahoma Press, 1988.

Boston Directory. Boston: Boston, Sampson & Murdock Company: 1835.

Campbell, Mike. "Belmont History." *San Mateo County Times*, 2021.

Chase, John Leighton. *The Sidewalk Companion to Santa Cruz, Third Edition*, edited by Judith Steen. Santa Cruz: The Museum of Art & History, 2005.

Dary, David. *Red Blood and Black Ink: Journalism in the Old West*. New York: Alfred A. Knopf, 1998.

De Wolk, Roland. *American Disruptor: The Scandalous Life of Leland Stanford*. Oakland: University of California Press, 2019.

Doten, Alfred. *The Journals of Alfred Doten: Book 15*. Reno: University of Nevada.

Emerson, Ralph Waldo. *The Journals and Miscellaneous Notebooks of Ralph Waldo Emerson, Vol. 16: 1866–1882*, edited by Ronald A. Bosco and Glen M. Johnson. Cambridge: The Belknap Press of Harvard University Press, 1982.

Flinn, Frank M. *Campaigning with Banks in Louisiana '63 and '64 And with Sheridan in the Shenandoah Valley '64 and '65*. Boston: W. B. Clarke & Co., 1889.

Hall, Frederic. *The History of San José and Surroundings: with Biographical Sketches of Early Settlers*. San Francisco: A. L. Bancroft and Co., 1871.

Hawthorne, Nathaniel. *Passages From the American Note-Books*, Vol. 9. Boston and New York: Houghton Mifflin Company, 1914.

History of Siskiyou County. Oakland: D. J. Stewart and Co., 1881.

Howells, William Dean. *My Mark Twain: Reminiscence and Criticisms*. New York: Harper & Brothers Publishers, 1910.

Hume, James B., and John N. Thacker. *Wells, Fargo & Co.: Stagecoach and Train Robberies, 1870—1884, The Corporate Report of 1885 with Additional Facts about the Crimes and Their Perpetrators*, edited by R. Michael Wilson. London: McFarland and Company, 2007.

Kiehl, Kent A., and Morris B. Hoffman. "The Criminal Psychopath: History, Neuroscience, Treatment, and Economics." *Jurimetrics* (Summer 2011).

Langley, Henry G. *The San Francisco Directory for the Year 1861*. San Francisco: Commercial Steam Presses, 1861.

———. *The San Francisco Directory for the Year 1862*. San Francisco: Commercial Steam Presses, 1862.

———. *The San Francisco Directory for the Year 1863*. San Francisco: Commercial Steam Presses, 1863.

———. *The San Francisco Directory for the Year 1864*. San Francisco: Commercial Steam Presses, 1864.

———. *The San Francisco Directory for the Year 1865*. San Francisco: Commercial Steam Presses, 1865.

Lloyd, Benjamin E. *Lights and Shades in San Francisco*. San Francisco: A. L. Bancroft, 1876.

Lyons, Chuck. "The Great Western Flood." *Wild West* 28, no. 6 (April 2016). 36–41.

Martens, Willem H. J. "The Hidden Suffering of the Psychopath." *Psychiatric Times* 31, no. 10.

McKenney, L. M. *McKenney's Sacramento Directory for the Year 1870*. Sacramento: Russell & Winterburn, Steam Book and Job Printers, 1870.

Mears, Leonard. *Mears' Sacramento Directory for the Years 1863–1864*. Sacramento: A Badlam, 1863.

Newhall, James R. *History of Lynn*, Vol. 2. Lynn, MA: Israel Augustus Newhall and Howard Mudge Newhall, 1897.

Powers, George Whitefield. *The Story of the Thirty Eighth Regiment of Massachusetts Volunteers*. Cambridge: Cambridge Press, 1866.

Powers, Ron. *Mark Twain: A Life*. New York: Free Press, 2005.

Sacramento City Directory. Sacramento: D. S. Cutter & Company, 1859.

Sacramento Directory, 1857–1858. Sacramento: R. H. McDonald & Co.

Secrest, William B. *Behind San Quentin's Walls: The History of California's Legendary Prison and Its Inmates, 1851–1900*. Fresno: Craven Street Books, 2015.

———. *California Desperadoes: Stories of Early California Outlaws in Their Own Words*. Clovis: Word Dancer Press, 2000.

———. *Dark and Tangled Threads of Crime: San Francisco's Famous Police Detective, Isaiah W. Lees*. Sanger, CA: Quill Driver Books/Word Dancer Press, Inc., 2004.

———. *Lawmen & Desperadoes: A Compendium of Noted, Early California Peace Officers, Badmen and Outlaws, 1850–1900*. Spokane: The Arthur H. Clark Company, 1994.

Shakespeare, William. *Henry VI, Part I. The Complete Works of Shakespeare*. New York: Longman, 1997.

Taniguchi, Nancy. *Dirty Deeds: Land, Violence, and the 1856 San Francisco Vigilance Committee*. Norman: University of Oklahoma Press, 2016.

Twain, Mark. *Complete Letters of Mark Twain*. Boston: IndyPublish.com, 2002.

———. *Roughing It*. New York: Penguin Putnam Inc., 1962.

———. *Mark Twain: San Francisco Correspondent: Selections From His Letters To The Territorial Enterprise: 1865–1866*. San Francisco: The Book Club of California, 1957.

Uhlhorn, John F. *Sacramento Directory For the Year January 1873*. Sacramento: H. S. Crocker & Co., 1873.

NEWSPAPERS

Alameda Gazette

Boston Globe

Brattleboro Eagle

Buffalo Daily Republic

Buffalo Morning Express

Daily Alta California (San Francisco)

Daily National Democrat (Marysville, CA)

Deseret News (Salt Lake City)

El Paso Times

Francisco Daily
Gold Hill Daily News
New England Farmer (Boston)
Oakland Daily Transcript
Petaluma Weekly Argus
Placer Herald (Rocklin)
Russian River Flag
Sacramento Bee
Sacramento Daily Record
San Francisco Call
San Francisco Chronicle
San Francisco Examiner
Santa Cruz Weekly Sentinel
Stockton Daily Evening Herald
Virginia City Evening Bulletin
Weekly Butte Democrat
Weekly (Oroville) Mercury
Weekly (Portland) Oregonian
West Sacramento News-Ledger

Index